Published Annually

LLEWELLYN'S

MOON SIGN BOOK

Plan Your Life by the Cycles of the Moon

Llewellyn's 2021 Moon Sign Book®

ISBN 978-0-7387-5484-0

Cover design by Kevin R. Brown
Editing by Hanna Grimson
Stock photography models used for illustrative purposes only and may not endorse or represent the book's subject.
Interior photographs: Getty Images
Typography owned by Llewellyn Worldwide Ltd.

Weekly tips by Penny Kelly, Mireille Blacke, and Shelby Deering.

Any Internet references contained in this work are current at publication time, but the publisher cannot guarantee that a specific location will continue to be maintained.

Astrological data compiled and programmed by Rique Pottenger. Based on the earlier work of Neil F. Michelsen.

You can order Llewellyn annuals and books from *New Worlds*, Llewellyn's catalog. To request a free copy of the catalog, call toll-free 1-877-NEW-WRLD, or visit our website at www.llewellyn.com.

Llewellyn Publications
A Division of Llewellyn Worldwide Ltd.
2143 Wooddale Drive
Woodbury, MN 55125-2989
www.llewellyn.com

Printed in the United States of America

Table of Contents

The Methods of the
Moon Sign Book

Whether we live in simple, primitive times or a time of high technology and mass communication, we need our connection to Mother Nature and an understanding of how all of her systems work together—soil, sun, wind, water, plants, animals, people, and planets.

The connections among elements of nature become especially relevant when we recognize that many energies—both subtle and obvious—flow through our world and affect all things. Ancient civilizations knew about these changing energies and were much more attuned to the subtle effects that they had on us.

In the world of unseen energies, it has long been accepted in many quarters that the position of the planets makes a difference in the energy flowing around planet Earth. Those who question these energy flows are often sadly divorced from nature.

Imagine placing a large rock in the waters of a flowing stream or creek. Immediately you would notice numerous changes in the flow of the water moving over, around, and past the rock.

It is no different with our solar system. We live on a planet that floats in a solar sea of energies and frequency waves. As the planets move around the sun, the currents of energy flowing through the solar sea change in the same way that flowing water changes around the rock placed in a creek or stream…and we are affected by those changes at every level—physically, mentally, emotionally, and spiritually.

The ability to detect these changes and their effect on us has long been organized into knowledge systems, and the *Moon Sign Book* has always been a stable anchor in maintaining this knowledge and recognizing its importance. We call these organized methods of gaining knowledge *astrology*, and ancient cultures around the globe used this as their science. It was how they found and maintained a sense of prediction, control, and security, something we are still striving for even today as we try to anticipate the cycles and events of our daily lives.

Although there are several ways of organizing and assessing these energy flows based on planetary positions, the *Moon Sign Book* uses the tropical system, which says that spring officially begins when the Sun is directly over the equator at noon, something that occurs around March 20 to 21 every year. Once that moment has been determined, the rest of the zodiac calendar is laid out at thirty-degree intervals. This allows us to be precise, but also flex with the changing nature of all things, including our solar system. We support a knowledge base that upholds the ancient wisdom and teaches it to all who are interested. We invite you to read what we have written here and to celebrate the interactions of these energies with the plants, animals, earth, and stars that share this time and space with us.

Weekly Almanac

Your Guide to
Lunar Gardening
& Good Timing for Activities

♉ January

December 27–January 2

*Dwell on the beauty of life. Watch the stars, and see yourself
running with them.*   ⁓MARCUS AURELIUS, *MEDITATIONS*

Date	Qtr.	Sign	Activity
Dec. 29, 5:28 am– Dec. 29, 10:28 pm	2nd	Cancer	Plant grains, leafy annuals. Fertilize (chemical). Graft or bud plants. Irrigate. Trim to increase growth.
Dec. 29, 10:28 pm– Dec. 31, 1:58 pm	3rd	Cancer	Plant biennials, perennials, bulbs and roots. Prune. Irrigate. Fertilize (organic).

As another year begins, survey your world and make a list of all the ways that your life could change for the better. Without making any commitments, put this list somewhere you will see it from time to time. At the end of the year, look at the list and put a check mark by those things that did change, noticing how often changes were natural and effortless.

_____

_____

_____

_____

○
December 29
10:28 pm EST

JANUARY

S	M	T	W	T	F	S
					1	2
3	4	5	6	7	8	9
10	11	12	13	14	15	16
17	18	19	20	21	22	23
24	25	26	27	28	29	30
31						

January 3–9

Life is a series of baby steps.

~HODA KOTB

Date	Qtr.	Sign	Activity
Jan. 7, 3:53 am– Jan. 9, 6:15 am	4th	Scorpio	Plant biennials, perennials, bulbs and roots. Prune. Irrigate. Fertilize (organic).
Jan. 9, 6:15 am– Jan. 11, 8:30 am	4th	Sagittarius	Cultivate. Destroy weeds and pests. Harvest fruits and root crops for food. Trim to retard growth.

Come up with a personal affirmation or mantra that you can recall when the going gets tough. It could be a favorite quote you often turn to for comfort, or you can create a personal phrase that resonates with you. You could even jot down several affirmations in a small notebook to refer to in particularly low or challenging moments.

January 6
4:37 am EST

JANUARY

S	M	T	W	T	F	S
					1	2
3	4	5	6	7	8	9
10	11	12	13	14	15	16
17	18	19	20	21	22	23
24	25	26	27	28	29	30
31						

January 10–16

Our doubts are traitors and make us lose the good we oft might win, by fearing to attempt. ~SHAKESPEARE

Date	Qtr.	Sign	Activity
Jan. 11, 8:30 am– Jan. 13, 12:00 am	4th	Capricorn	Plant potatoes and tubers. Trim to retard growth.
Jan. 13, 12:00 am– Jan. 13, 11:44 am	1st	Capricorn	Graft or bud plants. Trim to increase growth.
Jan. 15, 5:17 pm– Jan. 18, 2:07 am	1st	Pisces	Plant grains, leafy annuals. Fertilize (chemical). Graft or bud plants. Irrigate. Trim to increase growth.

Make this the year to get yourself off the financial grid by writing out an honest portrayal of your expenses and how you use money. Look at each expense and answer the question, "Why do I spend money on this?" Choose three areas to reduce your spending, and work on one at a time, getting each under control before taking on the next thing.

_____

_____

_____

_____

January 13
12:00 am EST

JANUARY

S	M	T	W	T	F	S
					1	2
3	4	5	6	7	8	9
10	11	12	13	14	15	16
17	18	19	20	21	22	23
24	25	26	27	28	29	30
31						

January 17–23

One day or day one. It's your decision.

~UNKNOWN

Date	Qtr.	Sign	Activity
Jan. 20, 1:56 pm– Jan. 20, 4:02 pm	1st	Taurus	Plant annuals for hardiness. Trim to increase growth.
Jan. 20, 4:02 pm– Jan. 23, 2:43 am	2nd	Taurus	Plant annuals for hardiness. Trim to increase growth.

Simply conserving electricity can go a long way: replace traditional light bulbs with high-quality, energy-efficient LEDs, plug holes in baseboards to preserve heat, switch showerheads to low-flow, and add weather strips to doors (even closets matter!). Implementing simple measures like these will lower your carbon footprint while also saving you money on utilities.

_____

_____

_____

_____

January 20
4:02 pm EST

JANUARY

S	M	T	W	T	F	S
					1	2
3	4	5	6	7	8	9
10	11	12	13	14	15	16
17	18	19	20	21	22	23
24	25	26	27	28	29	30
31						

~~~ January 24–January 30

What and how much had I lost by trying to do only what was
expected of me instead of what I myself had wished to do?

~RALPH ELLISON, *INVISIBLE MAN*

Date	Qtr.	Sign	Activity
Jan. 25, 1:52 pm– Jan. 27, 9:54 pm	2nd	Cancer	Plant grains, leafy annuals. Fertilize (chemical). Graft or bud plants. Irrigate. Trim to increase growth.
Jan. 28, 2:16 pm– Jan. 30, 3:02 am	3rd	Leo	Cultivate. Destroy weeds and pests. Harvest fruits and root crops for food. Trim to retard growth.
Jan. 30, 3:02 am– Feb. 1, 6:25 am	3rd	Virgo	Cultivate, especially medicinal plants. Destroy weeds and pests. Trim to retard growth.

Buy a new photo album for each of your children and organize your photos into a small record of each of their lives. Give them the photo album for Christmas or Valentine's Day.

_____

_____

_____

_____

O
January 28
2:16 pm EST

JANUARYY

S	M	T	W	T	F	S
					1	2
3	4	5	6	7	8	9
10	11	12	13	14	15	16
17	18	19	20	21	22	23
24	25	26	27	28	29	30
31						

February ≈

January 31–February 6

If everything was perfect, you would never learn and you would never grow.

~BEYONCÉ

Date	Qtr.	Sign	Activity
Feb. 3, 9:15 am– Feb. 4, 12:37 pm	3rd	Scorpio	Plant biennials, perennials, bulbs and roots. Prune. Irrigate. Fertilize (organic).
Feb. 4, 12:37 pm– Feb. 5, 12:16 pm	4th	Scorpio	Plant biennials, perennials, bulbs and roots. Prune. Irrigate. Fertilize (organic).
Feb. 5, 12:16 pm– Feb. 7, 3:52 pm	4th	Sagittarius	Cultivate. Destroy weeds and pests. Harvest fruits and root crops for food. Trim to retard growth.

Here's a way to gently scent your laundry with your favorite essential oils. Select lavender, lemongrass, rose, jasmine, or any oil you please, and trickle two to three drops onto your dryer ball. Allow it to dry before adding it to your laundry. The scent will freshen your linens and clothes and new drops can be added every five or so loads.

February 4
12:37 pm EST

FEBRUARY

S	M	T	W	T	F	S
	1	2	3	4	5	6
7	8	9	10	11	12	13
14	15	16	17	18	19	20
21	22	23	24	25	26	27
28						

〰 February 7–13

Our favorite people and our favorite stories become so not by any inherent virtue, but because they illustrate something deep in the grain, something unadmitted.   ～JOAN DIDION

Date	Qtr.	Sign	Activity
Feb. 7, 3:52 pm– Feb. 9, 8:20 pm	4th	Capricorn	Plant potatoes and tubers. Trim to retard growth.
Feb. 9, 8:20 pm– Feb. 11, 2:06 pm	4th	Aquarius	Cultivate. Destroy weeds and pests. Harvest fruits and root crops for food. Trim to retard growth.
Feb. 12, 2:23 am– Feb. 14, 10:54 am	1st	Pisces	Plant grains, leafy annuals. Fertilize (chemical). Graft or bud plants. Irrigate. Trim to increase growth.

Buy a quart or two of vinegar, either apple cider or white. Make sure it has 5 percent acidity. Divide it in half and put a few stalks of fresh rosemary and garlic in one, and a few stems of oregano and thyme in the other. Close tightly and let sit for at least four to six weeks. Use your gourmet vinegar to make a homemade Italian dressing. Delicious!

February 11
2:06 pm EST

FEBRUARY

S	M	T	W	T	F	S
	1	2	3	4	5	6
7	8	9	10	11	12	13
14	15	16	17	18	19	20
21	22	23	24	25	26	27
28						

February 14–20 〰️

*There are far, far better things ahead than any we leave
behind.*   ~C. S. Lewis

Date	Qtr.	Sign	Activity
Feb. 16, 10:12 pm– Feb. 19, 11:04 am	1st	Taurus	Plant annuals for hardiness. Trim to increase growth.

Focus on food for healthy eyes! Plant-based, antioxidant-rich
food sources high in two specific nutrients, lutein and zeaxanthin, can help reduce the risk of vision loss from cataracts and
macular degeneration. Cooked, dark green, leafy vegetables (kale,
spinach, collard greens) provide the highest amount of lutein and
zeaxanthin, but "eat the rainbow" of colorful fruits and vegetables
daily to increase your intake of eye-protecting carotenoids, flavo-
noids, and vitamin C.

◑

*February 19
1:47 pm EST*

February

S	M	T	W	T	F	S
	1	2	3	4	5	6
7	8	9	10	11	12	13
14	15	16	17	18	19	20
21	22	23	24	25	26	27
28						

February 21–27

I've failed over and over and over again in my life. And that is why I succeed.   ~MICHAEL JORDAN

Date	Qtr.	Sign	Activity
Feb. 21, 10:53 pm– Feb. 24, 7:23 am	2nd	Cancer	Plant grains, leafy annuals. Fertilize (chemical). Graft or bud plants. Irrigate. Trim to increase growth.
Feb. 27, 3:17 am– Feb. 28, 2:17 pm	3rd	Virgo	Cultivate, especially medicinal plants. Destroy weeds and pests. Trim to retard growth.

Feeling anxious? There are several pressure points throughout the body that, when pressed, release tension, along with feel-good chemicals. During a tense moment, apply soft pressure to the space between your eyebrows, the webbing between your thumb and index finger, or the tips of your ears. Massage the spot for a few seconds and breathe in and out as your worries melt away.

_____

_____

_____

_____

○
February 27
3:17 am EST

FEBRUARY

S	M	T	W	T	F	S
	1	2	3	4	5	6
7	8	9	10	11	12	13
14	15	16	17	18	19	20
21	22	23	24	25	26	27
28

March ♓

February 28–March 6

We ran as if to meet the moon.

~ROBERT FROST, "GOING FOR WATER"

Date	Qtr.	Sign	Activity
Mar. 2, 3:38 pm–Mar. 4, 5:43 pm	3rd	Scorpio	Plant biennials, perennials, bulbs and roots. Prune. Irrigate. Fertilize (organic).
Mar. 4, 5:43 pm–Mar. 5, 8:30 pm	3rd	Sagittarius	Cultivate. Destroy weeds and pests. Harvest fruits and root crops for food. Trim to retard growth.
Mar. 5, 8:30 pm–Mar. 6, 9:20 pm	4th	Sagittarius	Cultivate. Destroy weeds and pests. Harvest fruits and root crops for food. Trim to retard growth.
Mar. 6, 9:20 pm–Mar. 9, 2:41 am	4th	Capricorn	Plant potatoes and tubers. Trim to retard growth.

Expand your understanding of history and the world by reading at least one nonfiction book this year that delves into an area you haven't explored before. It could be a look at another country, at international relations, a biography of a famous person, or describe how a historical issue developed or was resolved.

_____

_____

_____

March 5
8:30 pm EST

MARCH

S	M	T	W	T	F	S
	1	2	3	4	5	6
7	8	9	10	11	12	13
14	15	16	17	18	19	20
21	22	23	24	25	26	27
28	29	30	31			

March 7–13

If you don't have any shadows you're not standing in the light.
                                                    ~LADY GAGA

Date	Qtr.	Sign	Activity
Mar. 9, 2:41 am– Mar. 11, 9:44 am	4th	Aquarius	Cultivate. Destroy weeds and pests. Harvest fruits and root crops for food. Trim to retard growth.
Mar. 11, 9:44 am– Mar. 13, 5:21 am	4th	Pisces	Plant biennials, perennials, bulbs and roots. Prune. Irrigate. Fertilize (organic).
Mar. 13, 5:21 am– Mar. 13, 6:44 pm	1st	Pisces	Plant grains, leafy annuals. Fertilize (chemical). Graft or bud plants. Irrigate. Trim to increase growth.

Canned produce can help to reduce food waste around the world, due to a longer shelf life and no need for refrigeration (until opened). Stock up on your seasonal favorites, including tomatoes, peaches, cherries, and pears for off-season eating. Look for cans with no added sugars or salt. Don't forget to include canned water chestnuts, bamboo shoots, jackfruit, artichokes, and chipotle peppers in your pantry!

_____

_____

_____

_____

March 13
5:21 am EST

MARCH

S	M	T	W	T	F	S
		1	2	3	4	5	6
7	8	9	10	11	12	13
14	15	16	17	18	19	20
21	22	23	24	25	26	27
28	29	30	31			

March 14–20

Education is the most powerful weapon which you can use to change the world.   ~NELSON MANDELA

Date	Qtr.	Sign	Activity
Mar. 16, 6:56 am– Mar. 18, 7:47 pm	1st	Taurus	Plant annuals for hardiness. Trim to increase growth.

Bentonite clay is helpful for a wide variety of health woes. Composed of volcanic ash, it can be purchased online or at health food stores, and it's been scientifically proven to be a powerful detoxifier. Pour a cup into your bath to calm rashes and inflammatory skin conditions. Make a paste and use it as an acne-fighting face mask. Apply it to sunburns and insect bites to pacify the skin.

_____

_____

_____

_____

Daylight Saving Time begins March 14, 2:00 am

MARCH

S	M	T	W	T	F	S
	1	2	3	4	5	6
7	8	9	10	11	12	13
14	15	16	17	18	19	20
21	22	23	24	25	26	27
28	29	30	31			

♈ March 21–27

Don't be satisfied with stories, how things have gone with others. Unfold your own myth.   ~RUMI

Date	Qtr.	Sign	Activity
Mar. 21, 8:18 am– Mar. 21, 10:40 am	1st	Cancer	Plant grains, leafy annuals. Fertilize (chemical). Graft or bud plants. Irrigate. Trim to increase growth.
Mar. 21, 10:40 am– Mar. 23, 5:56 pm	2nd	Cancer	Plant grains, leafy annuals. Fertilize (chemical). Graft or bud plants. Irrigate. Trim to increase growth.

Mold matters! Kill mold on hard surfaces naturally with soap and water. Natural antimicrobials such as plain white vinegar and baking soda are also powerful cleansers. Tea tree oil is a natural, antibacterial, and antiseptic fungicide that will kill black mold on impermeable surfaces. Remediation of extensive mold growth on drywall and other permeable building materials, however, is best left to professionals to arrest its spread and prevent toxic spores from becoming airborne.

March 21
10:40 am EDT

MARCH

S	M	T	W	T	F	S
	1	2	3	4	5	6
7	8	9	10	11	12	13
14	15	16	17	18	19	20
21	22	23	24	25	26	27
28	29	30	31			

April ♈

March 28–April 3

First we eat, then we do everything else.

~M. F. K. Fisher

Date	Qtr.	Sign	Activity
Mar. 28, 1:22 am– Mar. 28, 2:48 pm	2nd	Libra	Plant annuals for fragrance and beauty. Trim to increase growth.
Mar. 30, 1:33 am– Apr. 1, 1:59 am	3rd	Scorpio	Plant biennials, perennials, bulbs and roots. Prune. Irrigate. Fertilize (organic).
Apr. 1, 1:59 am– Apr. 3, 4:13 am	3rd	Sagittarius	Cultivate. Destroy weeds and pests. Harvest fruits and root crops for food. Trim to retard growth.
Apr. 3, 4:13 am– Apr. 4, 6:02 am	3rd	Capricorn	Plant potatoes and tubers. Trim to retard growth.

Keep your entire body hydrated and feeling fresh by putting one drop of peppermint oil and ten to fifteen drops of concentrated trace minerals in a quart of water. Drink over the course of a day.

○
March 28
2:48 pm EDT

April

S	M	T	W	T	F	S
				1	2	3
4	5	6	7	8	9	10
11	12	13	14	15	16	17
18	19	20	21	22	23	24
25	26	27	28	29	30	

♈ April 4–10

Joy is strength.   ~MOTHER TERESA

Date	Qtr.	Sign	Activity
Apr. 4, 6:02 am– Apr. 5, 9:04 am	4th	Capricorn	Plant potatoes and tubers. Trim to retard growth.
Apr. 5, 9:04 am– Apr. 7, 4:30 pm	4th	Aquarius	Cultivate. Destroy weeds and pests. Harvest fruits and root crops for food. Trim to retard growth.
Apr. 7, 4:30 pm– Apr. 10, 2:11 am	4th	Pisces	Plant biennials, perennials, bulbs and roots. Prune. Irrigate. Fertilize (organic).
Apr. 10, 2:11 am– Apr. 11, 10:31 pm	4th	Aries	Cultivate. Destroy weeds and pests. Harvest fruits and root crops for food. Trim to retard growth.

When spring rolls around, take down curtains and put away clutter, including those "homey" touches. The house will feel cool and calm over the summer. When fall comes, put the curtains back up and get out those homey touches again. The house will feel warm and inviting over the winter.

_____

_____

_____

_____

April 4
6:02 am EDT

APRIL

S	M	T	W	T	F	S
				1	2	3
4	5	6	7	8	9	10
11	12	13	14	15	16	17
18	19	20	21	22	23	24
25	26	27	28	29	30	

April 11–17 ♈

We do not grow absolutely, chronologically.   ~ANAÏS NIN

Date	Qtr.	Sign	Activity
Apr. 12, 1:44 pm– Apr. 15, 2:35 am	1st	Taurus	Plant annuals for hardiness. Trim to increase growth.
Apr. 17, 3:25 pm– Apr. 20, 2:11 am	1st	Cancer	Plant grains, leafy annuals. Fertilize (chemical). Graft or bud plants. Irrigate. Trim to increase growth.

Did you know that getting your hands dirty and gardening every day has the same effect as an antidepressant? Studies have shown that the bacteria and microbes in soil can lower stress. For a happier and healthier mind, plant some bulbs, weed your flower beds, nurture a houseplant, and breathe in the wet, earthy scent.

_____

_____

_____

_____

●

April 11
10:31 pm EDT

APRIL

S	M	T	W	T	F	S
				1	2	3
4	5	6	7	8	9	10
11	12	13	14	15	16	17
18	19	20	21	22	23	24
25	26	27	28	29	30	

 April 18–24

You can have it all. Just not all at once.   ∽OPRAH WINFREY

Date	Qtr.	Sign	Activity
Apr. 24, 12:06 pm– Apr. 26, 12:18 pm	2nd	Libra	Plant annuals for fragrance and beauty. Trim to increase growth.

Discover new places to donate old or unused items. If there's a cause that's close to your heart, such as helping a local animal shelter, see if they have a thrift shop that's in need of donations. Go online to find coat or book drives in your area so you can give away specific items. Or track down a nearby food pantry—bring nonperishable items and, if you can, donate your time too.

_____

_____

_____

_____

April 20
2:59 am EDT

APRIL

S	M	T	W	T	F	S
				1	2	3
4	5	6	7	8	9	10
11	12	13	14	15	16	17
18	19	20	21	22	23	24
25	26	27	28	29	30	

May ♉

April 25–May 1

Always do what is right. It will gratify half of mankind and astound the other.
                                                    ～MARK TWAIN

Date	Qtr.	Sign	Activity
Apr. 26, 12:18 pm– Apr. 26, 11:32 pm	2nd	Scorpio	Plant grains, leafy annuals. Fertilize (chemical). Graft or bud plants. Irrigate. Trim to increase growth.
Apr. 26, 11:32 pm– Apr. 28, 11:42 am	3rd	Scorpio	Plant biennials, perennials, bulbs and roots. Prune. Irrigate. Fertilize (organic).
Apr. 28, 11:42 am– Apr. 30, 12:16 pm	3rd	Sagittarius	Cultivate. Destroy weeds and pests. Harvest fruits and root crops for food. Trim to retard growth.
Apr. 30, 12:16 pm– May 2, 3:31 pm	3rd	Capricorn	Plant potatoes and tubers. Trim to retard growth.

Take a blanket outside on a warm day and lay down on it. Close your eyes. Listen, smell, and feel. How many things can you hear or smell that you never noticed before? What are you feeling when you're in the lap of nature?

_____

_____

_____

_____

○
April 26
11:32 pm EDT

MAY

S	M	T	W	T	F	S
						1
2	3	4	5	6	7	8
9	10	11	12	13	14	15
16	17	18	19	20	21	22
23	24	25	26	27	28	29
30	31					

May 2–8

Love does not begin and end the way we seem to think it does.
Love is a battle, love is a war; love is a growing up.

~JAMES BALDWIN

Date	Qtr.	Sign	Activity
May 2, 3:31 pm– May 3, 3:50 pm	3rd	Aquarius	Cultivate. Destroy weeds and pests. Harvest fruits and root crops for food. Trim to retard growth.
May 3, 3:50 pm– May 4, 10:09 pm	4th	Aquarius	Cultivate. Destroy weeds and pests. Harvest fruits and root crops for food. Trim to retard growth.
May 4, 10:09 pm– May 7, 7:52 am	4th	Pisces	Plant biennials, perennials, bulbs and roots. Prune. Irrigate. Fertilize (organic).
May 7, 7:52 am– May 9, 7:46 pm	4th	Aries	Cultivate. Destroy weeds and pests. Harvest fruits and root crops for food. Trim to retard growth.

Learn to preserve food by drying, canning, pickling, or freezing. Try your hand at making jams, jellies, sauerkraut, wine, beer, breads, and interesting herbal combinations to use in salads, meat dishes, casseroles, or in barbecuing.

_____

_____

_____

_____

May 3
3:50 pm EDT

MAY

S	M	T	W	T	F	S
						1
2	3	4	5	6	7	8
9	10	11	12	13	14	15
16	17	18	19	20	21	22
23	24	25	26	27	28	29
30	31					

May 9–15

A life spent making mistakes is not only more honorable, but more useful than a life spent doing nothing.

~George Bernard Shaw

Date	Qtr.	Sign	Activity
May 9, 7:46 pm– May 11, 3:00 pm	4th	Taurus	Plant potatoes and tubers. Trim to retard growth.
May 11, 3:00 pm– May 12, 8:43 am	1st	Taurus	Plant annuals for hardiness. Trim to increase growth.
May 14, 9:30 pm– May 17, 8:44 am	1st	Cancer	Plant grains, leafy annuals. Fertilize (chemical). Graft or bud plants. Irrigate. Trim to increase growth.

If your mind tends to wander when you sit down to meditate, try a movement-focused form of meditation instead. Walking meditation is a lovely and effective way to practice mindfulness every day. You can simply walk around your neighborhood and match one deep inhale to two or three of your footsteps, then breathe out. Keep a slow pace. And immerse yourself in your surroundings.

May 11
3:00 pm EDT

MAY

S	M	T	W	T	F	S
						1
2	3	4	5	6	7	8
9	10	11	12	13	14	15
16	17	18	19	20	21	22
23	24	25	26	27	28	29
30	31					

May 16–22

Talent hits a target no one else can hit. Genius hits a target no one else can see.   ~ARTHUR SCHOPENHAUER

Date	Qtr.	Sign	Activity
May 21, 9:35 pm– May 23, 11:00 pm	2nd	Libra	Plant annuals for fragrance and beauty. Trim to increase growth.

Till up a small area of ground about five by nine feet. Put one inch of compost on top (available at a local hardware shop). Plant a tiny garden and train everything to go *up*. You will be amazed at how much food you get out of such a small space. At the end of the season, put another inch of compost on top and cover with hay or straw until the next growing season…then repeat.

_____

_____

_____

_____

May 19
3:13 pm EDT

MAY

S	M	T	W	T	F	S
						1
2	3	4	5	6	7	8
9	10	11	12	13	14	15
16	17	18	19	20	21	22
23	24	25	26	27	28	29
30	31					

May 23–May 29

Beware; for I am fearless, and therefore powerful.
~MARY SHELLEY, *FRANKENSTEIN*

Date	Qtr.	Sign	Activity
May 23, 11:00 pm– May 25, 10:39 pm	2nd	Scorpio	Plant grains, leafy annuals. Fertilize (chemical). Graft or bud plants. Irrigate. Trim to increase growth.
May 26, 7:14 am– May 27, 10:23 pm	3rd	Sagittarius	Cultivate. Destroy weeds and pests. Harvest fruits and root crops for food. Trim to retard growth.
May 27, 10:23 pm– May 30, 12:04 am	3rd	Capricorn	Plant potatoes and tubers. Trim to retard growth.

If you're searching for some truly unique garden décor, look no further than a flea market. There you can uncover whimsical pieces to place amid your flowers, such as well-loved trellises, children's toys, wheels, milk cans, or even a rusted bicycle. Search for items that can double as creative pots, like a wagon or an old sink. Even a chippy chair can act as a charming planter.

○
May 26
7:14 am EDT

MAY

S	M	T	W	T	F	S
						1
2	3	4	5	6	7	8
9	10	11	12	13	14	15
16	17	18	19	20	21	22
23	24	25	26	27	28	29
30	31					

♊ June

May 30–June 5

You can't use up creativity. The more you use, the more you have.   ~MAYA ANGELOU

Date	Qtr.	Sign	Activity
May 30, 12:04 am–Jun. 1, 5:07 am	3rd	Aquarius	Cultivate. Destroy weeds and pests. Harvest fruits and root crops for food. Trim to retard growth.
Jun. 1, 5:07 am–Jun. 2, 3:24 am	3rd	Pisces	Plant biennials, perennials, bulbs and roots. Prune. Irrigate. Fertilize (organic).
Jun. 2, 3:24 am–Jun. 3, 1:59 pm	4th	Pisces	Plant biennials, perennials, bulbs and roots. Prune. Irrigate. Fertilize (organic).
Jun. 3, 1:59 pm–Jun. 6, 1:46 am	4th	Aries	Cultivate. Destroy weeds and pests. Harvest fruits and root crops for food. Trim to retard growth.

Buy a couple of three- to six-pound weights and get creative with them for thirty seconds each morning and evening. Research has shown that it takes as few as six curls to maintain strength and shapeliness in your upper body!

◑
June 2
3:24 am EDT

	JUNE					
S	M	T	W	T	F	S
		1	2	3	4	5
6	7	8	9	10	11	12
13	14	15	16	17	18	19
20	21	22	23	24	25	26
27	28	29	30			

June 6–12

There is something infinitely healing in the repeated refrains of nature—the assurance that dawn comes after night, and spring after winter.   ~RACHEL CARSON

Date	Qtr.	Sign	Activity
Jun. 6, 1:46 am– Jun. 8, 2:47 pm	4th	Taurus	Plant potatoes and tubers. Trim to retard growth.
Jun. 8, 2:47 pm– Jun. 10, 6:53 am	4th	Gemini	Cultivate. Destroy weeds and pests. Harvest fruits and root crops for food. Trim to retard growth.
Jun. 11, 3:23 am– Jun. 13, 2:22 pm	1st	Cancer	Plant grains, leafy annuals. Fertilize (chemical). Graft or bud plants. Irrigate. Trim to increase growth.

You likely keep a garden so you can harvest fresh vegetables and beautiful blossoms, but what about harvesting some good luck? Legends and folklore say that some plants promote good fortune and prosperity. Plant bamboo, peace lilies, orchids, shamrocks, or even a money tree or two and see if you experience a bit of extra luck in your life.

_____

_____

_____

_____

June 10
6:53 am EDT

JUNE

S	M	T	W	T	F	S
			1	2	3	4	5
6	7	8	9	10	11	12
13	14	15	16	17	18	19
20	21	22	23	24	25	26
27	28	29	30			

June 13–19

Never be afraid to sit a while and think.

~LORRAINE HANSBERRY, *A RAISIN IN THE SUN*

Date	Qtr.	Sign	Activity
Jun. 18, 4:54 am– Jun. 20, 7:58 am	2nd	Libra	Plant annuals for fragrance and beauty. Trim to increase growth.

An Epsom salt bath is a relaxing and potent way to detox the body and soothe achy muscles. Make the most of your Epsom salt soak by dropping in at least two cups of salts (you can purchase them at grocery stores and drugstores) and sitting in the warm water for twelve to twenty minutes. You can also add half a cup of baking soda for increased detoxifying benefits.

_____

_____

_____

June 17
11:54 pm EST

JUNE

S	M	T	W	T	F	S
		1	2	3	4	5
6	7	8	9	10	11	12
13	14	15	16	17	18	19
20	21	22	23	24	25	26
27	28	29	30			

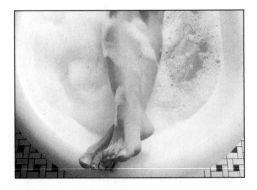

June 20–26

Books have to be heavy because the whole world's inside them.
                              ~CORNELIA FUNKE, *INKHEART*

Date	Qtr.	Sign	Activity
Jun. 20, 7:58 am– Jun. 22, 8:55 am	2nd	Scorpio	Plant grains, leafy annuals. Fertilize (chemical). Graft or bud plants. Irrigate. Trim to increase growth.
Jun. 24, 9:05 am– Jun. 24, 2:40 pm	2nd	Capricorn	Graft or bud plants. Trim to increase growth.
Jun. 24, 2:40 pm– Jun. 26, 10:09 am	3rd	Capricorn	Plant potatoes and tubers. Trim to retard growth.
Jun. 26, 10:09 am– Jun. 28, 1:51 pm	3rd	Aquarius	Cultivate. Destroy weeds and pests. Harvest fruits and root crops for food. Trim to retard growth.

If you are plagued by ants, put a small saucer with one tablespoon of honey on your porch and ask the ants to stay outside. You'll be surprised at the drop in the ant population inside the house, or the tent if you're camping.

○
June 24
2:40 pm EDT

JUNE

S	M	T	W	T	F	S
		1	2	3	4	5
6	7	8	9	10	11	12
13	14	15	16	17	18	19
20	21	22	23	24	25	26
27	28	29	30			

♋ July

June 27–July 3

I can't go back to yesterday—because I was a different person then.

~LEWIS CARROLL, *ALICE'S ADVENTURES IN WONDERLAND*

Date	Qtr.	Sign	Activity
Jun. 28, 1:51 pm– Jun. 30, 9:21 pm	3rd	Pisces	Plant biennials, perennials, bulbs and roots. Prune. Irrigate. Fertilize (organic).
Jun. 30, 9:21 pm– Jul. 1, 5:11 pm	3rd	Aries	Cultivate. Destroy weeds and pests. Harvest fruits and root crops for food. Trim to retard growth.
Jul. 1, 5:11 pm– Jul. 3, 8:28 am	4th	Aries	Cultivate. Destroy weeds and pests. Harvest fruits and root crops for food. Trim to retard growth.
Jul. 3, 8:28 am– Jul. 5, 9:24 pm	4th	Taurus	Plant potatoes and tubers. Trim to retard growth.

There are few things that help you sort out life better than writing. Get a small journal. Give it an interesting title. Write out anything that feels overwhelming, is inspiring, or expresses your dreams and hopes for your life.

_____

_____

_____

◑
July 1
5:11 pm EDT

JULY

S	M	T	W	T	F	S
				1	2	3
4	5	6	7	8	9	10
11	12	13	14	15	16	17
18	19	20	21	22	23	24
25	26	27	28	29	30	31

July 4–10 ♋

Over every mountain there is a path, although it may not be seen from the valley.   ~THEODORE ROETHKE

Date	Qtr.	Sign	Activity
Jul. 5, 9:24 pm– Jul. 8, 9:51 am	4th	Gemini	Cultivate. Destroy weeds and pests. Harvest fruits and root crops for food. Trim to retard growth.
Jul. 8, 9:51 am– Jul. 9, 9:17 pm	4th	Cancer	Plant biennials, perennials, bulbs and roots. Prune. Irrigate. Fertilize (organic).
Jul. 9, 9:17 pm– Jul. 10, 8:21 pm	1st	Cancer	Plant grains, leafy annuals. Fertilize (chemical). Graft or bud plants. Irrigate. Trim to increase growth.

No matter where you live, you can grow tropical plants right in your own backyard. Just be sure to look at a USDA Hardiness Zone Map before you purchase any plants. Even in a northern climate, you can plant resilient tropical varieties like hibiscus plants designed for cold regions, windmill palms, elephant ears, and yucca plants.

July 9
9:17 pm EDT

JULY

S	M	T	W	T	F	S
				1	2	3
4	5	6	7	8	9	10
11	12	13	14	15	16	17
18	19	20	21	22	23	24
25	26	27	28	29	30	31

 **July 11–17**

Everything you can imagine is real.

~ PABLO PICASSO

Date	Qtr.	Sign	Activity
Jul. 15, 10:32 am–Jul. 17, 6:11 am	1st	Libra	Plant annuals for fragrance and beauty. Trim to increase growth.
Jul. 17, 6:11 am–Jul. 17, 2:38 pm	2nd	Libra	Plant annuals for fragrance and beauty. Trim to increase growth.
Jul. 17, 2:38 pm–Jul. 19, 5:08 pm	2nd	Scorpio	Plant grains, leafy annuals. Fertilize (chemical). Graft or bud plants. Irrigate. Trim to increase growth.

Make life comfortable for the honeybees who visit your yard. Bees are an increasingly threatened species, so you can do your part by providing a bee house where they can rest and care for their young, growing a pollinator-friendly garden, or keeping them hydrated by putting down a plate or shallow bowl of water and marbles so they'll have plenty of spots to land and quench their thirst.

_____

_____

_____

◑
July 17
6:11 am EDT

JULY

S	M	T	W	T	F	S
				1	2	3
4	5	6	7	8	9	10
11	12	13	14	15	16	17
18	19	20	21	22	23	24
25	26	27	28	29	30	31

July 18–24

There are some things you learn best in calm, and some in storm.

~WILLA CATHER, *THE SONG OF THE LARK*

Date	Qtr.	Sign	Activity
Jul. 21, 6:36 pm– Jul. 23, 8:12 pm	2nd	Capricorn	Graft or bud plants. Trim to increase growth.
Jul. 23, 10:37 pm– Jul. 25, 11:30 pm	3rd	Aquarius	Cultivate. Destroy weeds and pests. Harvest fruits and root crops for food. Trim to retard growth.

Are neighborhood cats digging up your garden? According to alleycat.org, certain fragrances act as natural deterrents for felines who are instinctively drawn to dig in loose soil or mulch: wet coffee grounds, fresh orange or lemon peels, or vinegar (left in a pan) are good options. For an additional digger-deterrent (and trendy decorative element), consider covering exposed grounds of flower beds with river rocks.

O
July 23
10:37 pm EDT

JULY

S	M	T	W	T	F	S
				1	2	3
4	5	6	7	8	9	10
11	12	13	14	15	16	17
18	19	20	21	22	23	24
25	26	27	28	29	30	31

♌ July 25–July 31

In a time of destruction, create something.

~MAXINE HONG KINGSTON

Date	Qtr.	Sign	Activity
Jul. 25, 11:30 pm– Jul. 28, 5:58 am	3rd	Pisces	Plant biennials, perennials, bulbs and roots. Prune. Irrigate. Fertilize (organic).
Jul. 28, 5:58 am– Jul. 30, 4:08 pm	3rd	Aries	Cultivate. Destroy weeds and pests. Harvest fruits and root crops for food. Trim to retard growth.
Jul. 30, 4:08 pm– Jul. 31, 9:16 am	3rd	Taurus	Plant potatoes and tubers. Trim to retard growth.
Jul. 31, 9:16 am– Aug. 2, 4:46 am	4th	Taurus	Plant potatoes and tubers. Trim to retard growth.

Create an interesting change of pace for a summer meal by setting up a *mezza*, the Middle Eastern term for a variety of salads, dips, and finger foods. It's both refreshing and light, leaving you satisfied but not feeling heavy.

July 31
9:16 am EDT

AUGUST

S	M	T	W	T	F	S
	1	2	3	4	5	6	7
8	9	10	11	12	13	14
15	16	17	18	19	20	21
22	23	24	25	26	27	28
29	30	31

August ♌

August 1–7

You're smart, brave, and strong enough.

~KATARA, *AVATAR: THE LAST AIRBENDER*

Date	Qtr.	Sign	Activity
Aug. 2, 4:46 am– Aug. 4, 5:17 pm	4th	Gemini	Cultivate. Destroy weeds and pests. Harvest fruits and root crops for food. Trim to retard growth.
Aug. 4, 5:17 pm– Aug. 7, 3:31 am	4th	Cancer	Plant biennials, perennials, bulbs and roots. Prune. Irrigate. Fertilize (organic).
Aug. 7, 3:31 am– Aug. 8, 9:50 am	4th	Leo	Cultivate. Destroy weeds and pests. Harvest fruits and root crops for food. Trim to retard growth.

Try this sensory meditation with your eyes open. Name five things you can see, four things you can feel, three things you can hear, two things you can smell, and one thing you can taste. It's a grounding technique that's often used in the mental health world, and it's very helpful if you're having an anxious moment or just need to bring yourself back to the present.

AUGUST

S	M	T	W	T	F	S
1	2	3	4	5	6	7
8	9	10	11	12	13	14
15	16	17	18	19	20	21
22	23	24	25	26	27	28
29	30	31				

♌ August 8–14

Furthermore, we have not even to risk the adventure alone;
for the heroes of all time have gone before us...
~JOSEPH CAMPBELL, *THE HERO WITH A THOUSAND FACES*

Date	Qtr.	Sign	Activity
Aug. 11, 4:08 pm– Aug. 13, 8:01 pm	1st	Libra	Plant annuals for fragrance and beauty. Trim to increase growth.
Aug. 13, 8:01 pm– Aug. 15, 11:20 am	1st	Scorpio	Plant grains, leafy annuals. Fertilize (chemical). Graft or bud plants. Irrigate. Trim to increase growth.

Nurture your hair and yourself by bending at the waist and brushing your hair one-hundred strokes every night with a boar bristle brush. In the morning when you awaken, use your fingertips to gently massage your scalp while breathing in deeply. Drink a full glass of water upon arising to keep hair follicles hydrated.

August 8
9:50 am EDT

AUGUST

S	M	T	W	T	F	S
1	2	3	4	5	6	7
8	9	10	11	12	13	14
15	16	17	18	19	20	21
22	23	24	25	26	27	28
29	30	31				

August 15–21

And I say to any man or woman, Let your soul stand cool and composed before a million universes.

~WALT WHITMAN, "SONG OF MYSELF"

Date	Qtr.	Sign	Activity
Aug. 15, 11:20 am– Aug. 15, 11:12 pm	2nd	Scorpio	Plant grains, leafy annuals. Fertilize (chemical). Graft or bud plants. Irrigate. Trim to increase growth.
Aug. 18, 1:58 am– Aug. 20, 4:49 am	2nd	Capricorn	Graft or bud plants. Trim to increase growth.

Anxious? Increasing consumption of certain nutrients may help! (1) Complex carbs: brown rice and dark chocolate; (2) Folate and B vitamins: beef, pork, chicken, leafy greens, legumes, citrus fruits, nuts, and eggs; (3) Zinc: oysters, cashews, liver, beef, and egg yolks; (4) Probiotics: pickles, kefir, and kimchi; (5) Protein: Greek yogurt, fish, nuts, beans, soy, and lentils. Eat small meals combining protein and carbs throughout the day to maximize nutritional support for anxiety relief.

August 15
11:20 am EDT

AUGUST

S	M	T	W	T	F	S
1	2	3	4	5	6	7
8	9	10	11	12	13	14
15	16	17	18	19	20	21
22	23	24	25	26	27	28
29	30	31				

♍ August 22–28

Just remember, every time you look up at the moon I, too, will be looking at a moon. Not the same moon, obviously. That's impossible.   ~ANDY DWYER, PARKS AND RECREATION

Date	Qtr.	Sign	Activity
Aug. 22, 8:02 am–Aug. 22, 8:43 am	3rd	Aquarius	Cultivate. Destroy weeds and pests. Harvest fruits and root crops for food. Trim to retard growth.
Aug. 22, 8:43 am–Aug. 24, 2:57 pm	3rd	Pisces	Plant biennials, perennials, bulbs and roots. Prune. Irrigate. Fertilize (organic).
Aug. 24, 2:57 pm–Aug. 27, 12:27 am	3rd	Aries	Cultivate. Destroy weeds and pests. Harvest fruits and root crops for food. Trim to retard growth.
Aug. 27, 12:27 am–Aug. 29, 12:42 pm	3rd	Taurus	Plant potatoes and tubers. Trim to retard growth.

If you have a collection of natural objects, such as seashells or rocks, simply sitting in a box or vase, consider dropping them into your garden. You'll bring back fond memories of when you found your treasures every time you work in the garden, and you can arrange them in patterns or swirls for even more prettiness.

○
August 22
8:02 am EDT

AUGUST

S	M	T	W	T	F	S
	1	2	3	4	5	6	7
8	9	10	11	12	13	14
15	16	17	18	19	20	21
22	23	24	25	26	27	28
29	30	31				

September ♍

August 29–September 4

Life's not short; it's long.   ~Lin-Manuel Miranda

Date	Qtr.	Sign	Activity
Aug. 29, 12:42 pm– Aug. 30, 3:13 am	3rd	Gemini	Cultivate. Destroy weeds and pests. Harvest fruits and root crops for food. Trim to retard growth.
Aug. 30, 3:13 am– Sep. 1, 1:26 am	4th	Gemini	Cultivate. Destroy weeds and pests. Harvest fruits and root crops for food. Trim to retard growth.
Sep. 1, 1:26 am– Sep. 3, 11:58 am	4th	Cancer	Plant biennials, perennials, bulbs and roots. Prune. Irrigate. Fertilize (organic).
Sep. 3, 11:58 am– Sep. 5, 7:06 pm	4th	Leo	Cultivate. Destroy weeds and pests. Harvest fruits and root crops for food. Trim to retard growth.

Be a tourist in your hometown. If a far-flung vacation isn't currently in the cards, you can act as an intrepid traveler in your own backyard. Visit a nearby ethnic restaurant you've never tried. Set out on a new-to-you trail for a day of hiking. Stop by your local historical society and discover things you never knew about your town.

August 30
3:13 am EDT

September

S	M	T	W	T	F	S
				1	2	3	4
5	6	7	8	9	10	11
12	13	14	15	16	17	18
19	20	21	22	23	24	25
26	27	28	29	30		

♍ September 5–11

*Yes, I thought, now I see the earth as it really is; never again
will I see things as I saw them yesterday or the day before.*
~N. Scott Momaday, *The Way to Rainy Mountain*

Date	Qtr.	Sign	Activity
Sep. 5, 7:06 pm– Sep. 6, 8:52 pm	4th	Virgo	Cultivate, especially medicinal plants. Destroy weeds and pests. Trim to retard growth.
Sep. 7, 11:20 pm– Sep. 10, 2:05 am	1st	Libra	Plant annuals for fragrance and beauty. Trim to increase growth.
Sep. 10, 2:05 am– Sep. 12, 4:34 am	1st	Scorpio	Plant grains, leafy annuals. Fertilize (chemical). Graft or bud plants. Irrigate. Trim to increase growth.

Even if you're not in school, it's always a good time to learn
something new. With near-endless classes available online
or through your local community college, now is the time to
embrace a new hobby or skill. Pick up that ukulele that's been
gathering dust and learn how to play it. Try out a new language.
Brush up on biology. Or take a class in a topic that interests you,
like fashion or architecture.

*September 6
8:52 pm EDT*

SEPTEMBER

S	M	T	W	T	F	S
			1	2	3	4
5	6	7	8	9	10	11
12	13	14	15	16	17	18
19	20	21	22	23	24	25
26	27	28	29	30		

September 12–18 ♍

Stumbling is not falling.   ~MALCOLM X

Date	Qtr.	Sign	Activity
Sep. 14, 7:34 am– Sep. 16, 11:23 am	2nd	Capricorn	Graft or bud plants. Trim to increase growth.
Sep. 18, 4:22 pm– Sep. 20, 7:55 pm	2nd	Pisces	Plant grains, leafy annuals. Fertilize (chemical). Graft or bud plants. Irrigate. Trim to increase growth.

Want to create an impressive cheese board? First, choose cheeses you love; playfully combine soft, hard, earthy, nutty, or salty selections. Select nuts, fresh berries or grapes, dried fruit, olives, or sprigs of herbs (thyme or basil) as accompaniments. Opt for a neutral cracker and a sliced baguette. A black slate or dark cherry board will help the cheeses and colorful companions "pop"!

◗

September 13
4:39 pm EDT

SEPTEMBER

S	M	T	W	T	F	S
			1	2	3	4
5	6	7	8	9	10	11
12	13	14	15	16	17	18
19	20	21	22	23	24	25
26	27	28	29	30		

♍ September 19–25

Success isn't overnight. It's when every day you get a little bit better than the day before.

~Dwayne "The Rock" Johnson

Date	Qtr.	Sign	Activity
Sep. 20, 7:55 pm– Sep. 20, 11:13 pm	3rd	Pisces	Plant biennials, perennials, bulbs and roots. Prune. Irrigate. Fertilize (organic).
Sep. 20, 11:13 pm– Sep. 23, 8:38 am	3rd	Aries	Cultivate. Destroy weeds and pests. Harvest fruits and root crops for food. Trim to retard growth.
Sep. 23, 8:38 am– Sep. 25, 8:36 pm	3rd	Taurus	Plant potatoes and tubers. Trim to retard growth.
Sep. 25, 8:36 pm– Sep. 28, 9:34 am	3rd	Gemini	Cultivate. Destroy weeds and pests. Harvest fruits and root crops for food. Trim to retard growth.

Get back in touch with Mother Nature and the natural world. Take time to really see trees, flowers, insects, and birds. Try to feel a sense of gratitude for their presence in your life and take a moment to imagine each of them surrounded in golden light.

○
September 20
7:55 pm EDT

SEPTEMBER

S	M	T	W	T	F	S
			1	2	3	4
5	6	7	8	9	10	11
12	13	14	15	16	17	18
19	20	21	22	23	24	25
26	27	28	29	30		

October ♎

September 26–October 2

Only a fool is not afraid.

~MADELEINE L'ENGLE, *A WRINKLE IN TIME*

Date	Qtr.	Sign	Activity
Sep. 28, 9:34 am– Sep. 28, 9:57 pm	3rd	Cancer	Plant biennials, perennials, bulbs and roots. Prune. Irrigate. Fertilize (organic).
Sep. 28, 9:57 pm– Sep. 30, 8:53 pm	4th	Cancer	Plant biennials, perennials, bulbs and roots. Prune. Irrigate. Fertilize (organic).
Sep. 30, 8:53 pm– Oct. 3, 4:38 am	4th	Leo	Cultivate. Destroy weeds and pests. Harvest fruits and root crops for food. Trim to retard growth.

Plan a Halloween party with a "futuristic" theme. Ask those who are invited to dress as if they are living in the future. Take photos and share on social media along with their comments on what their costume represents.

September 28
9:57 pm EDT

OCTOBER

S	M	T	W	T	F	S
					1	2
3	4	5	6	7	8	9
10	11	12	13	14	15	16
17	18	19	20	21	22	23
24	25	26	27	28	29	30
31						

♎ October 3–9

When will you have a little pity for every soft thing that walks through the world, yourself included? ∼MARY OLIVER

Date	Qtr.	Sign	Activity
Oct. 3, 4:38 am– Oct. 5, 8:41 am	4th	Virgo	Cultivate, especially medicinal plants. Destroy weeds and pests. Trim to retard growth.
Oct. 6, 7:05 am– Oct. 7, 10:22 am	1st	Libra	Plant annuals for fragrance and beauty. Trim to increase growth.
Oct. 7, 10:22 am– Oct. 9, 11:24 am	1st	Scorpio	Plant grains, leafy annuals. Fertilize (chemical). Graft or bud plants. Irrigate. Trim to increase growth.

Renew your kitchen skills by taking a class in a foreign cuisine or asking a friend from another culture to share her kitchen secrets. Expand your creativity by creating a small collection of recipes, and you will experience a renewal of interest in feeding yourself as well as a better understanding of food.

October 6
7:05 am EDT

OCTOBER

S	M	T	W	T	F	S
					1	2
3	4	5	6	7	8	9
10	11	12	13	14	15	16
17	18	19	20	21	22	23
24	25	26	27	28	29	30
31						

October 10–16 ♎

It is better to fail in originality than to succeed in imitation.

~HERMAN MELVILLE

Date	Qtr.	Sign	Activity
Oct. 11, 1:15 pm– Oct. 12, 11:25 pm	1st	Capricorn	Graft or bud plants. Trim to increase growth.
Oct. 12, 11:25 pm– Oct. 13, 4:47 pm	2nd	Capricorn	Graft or bud plants. Trim to increase growth.
Oct. 15, 10:22 pm– Oct. 18, 6:04 am	2nd	Pisces	Plant grains, leafy annuals. Fertilize (chemical). Graft or bud plants. Irrigate. Trim to increase growth.

Create a small compost pile in a corner of your yard or a plastic tub in the corner of your deck. Put leaves and other organic materials in it, add a bit of water to moisten it from time to time, and stir now and then. Watch it become soil over the year, then plant flowers or a couple of vegetables in it. You'll be amazed at how healthy the plants will be and how tasty the veggies are.

October 12
11:25 pm EDT

OCTOBER

S	M	T	W	T	F	S
					1	2
3	4	5	6	7	8	9
10	11	12	13	14	15	16
17	18	19	20	21	22	23
24	25	26	27	28	29	30
31						

October 17–23

> *My view is that if your philosophy is not unsettled daily then you are blind to all the universe has to offer.*
>
> ~Neil deGrasse Tyson

Date	Qtr.	Sign	Activity
Oct. 20, 3:59 pm– Oct. 23, 3:57 am	3rd	Taurus	Plant potatoes and tubers. Trim to retard growth.
Oct. 23, 3:57 am– Oct. 25, 5:00 pm	3rd	Gemini	Cultivate. Destroy weeds and pests. Harvest fruits and root crops for food. Trim to retard growth.

Turn your bedroom into a soothing sanctuary. Paint the walls in calming colors; incorporate a connection to the outdoors, such as a miniature fountain or driftwood headboard; bring in a plant or two; and include a diffuser so you can breathe in aromatherapeutic scents. Also, make sure to keep your electronic devices and phone in another room so you can focus on your peaceful surroundings.

_____

_____

_____

_____

○
October 20
10:57 am EDT

OCTOBER

S	M	T	W	T	F	S
					1	2
3	4	5	6	7	8	9
10	11	12	13	14	15	16
17	18	19	20	21	22	23
24	25	26	27	28	29	30
31						

October 24–30 ♏

And the secret garden bloomed and bloomed and every
morning revealed new miracles.

~FRANCES HODGSON BURNETT, *THE SECRET GARDEN*

Date	Qtr.	Sign	Activity
Oct. 25, 5:00 pm– Oct. 28, 5:07 am	3rd	Cancer	Plant biennials, perennials, bulbs and roots. Prune. Irrigate. Fertilize (organic).
Oct. 28, 5:07 am– Oct. 28, 4:05 pm	3rd	Leo	Cultivate. Destroy weeds and pests. Harvest fruits and root crops for food. Trim to retard growth.
Oct. 28, 4:05 pm– Oct. 30, 2:09 pm	4th	Leo	Cultivate. Destroy weeds and pests. Harvest fruits and root crops for food. Trim to retard growth.
Oct. 30, 2:09 pm– Nov. 1, 7:11 pm	4th	Virgo	Cultivate, especially medicinal plants. Destroy weeds and pests. Trim to retard growth.

Do a little research online to see if there are haunted houses near you; then plan a vacation that will take you to visit one of them. Before the visit, read a book or two on ghosts and haunted houses to heighten the experience!

◑

October 28
4:05 pm EDT

OCTOBER

S	M	T	W	T	F	S
					1	2
3	4	5	6	7	8	9
10	11	12	13	14	15	16
17	18	19	20	21	22	23
24	25	26	27	28	29	30
31						

♏ November
October 31–November 6

Try again. Fail again. Fail better.
~Samuel Beckett, *Worstward Ho*

Date	Qtr.	Sign	Activity
Nov. 3, 8:52 pm– Nov. 4, 5:15 pm	4th	Scorpio	Plant biennials, perennials, bulbs and roots. Prune. Irrigate. Fertilize (organic).
Nov. 4, 5:15 pm– Nov. 5, 8:52 pm	1st	Scorpio	Plant grains, leafy annuals. Fertilize (chemical). Graft or bud plants. Irrigate. Trim to increase growth.

Restaurant portions are larger than we need and contribute to expanding waistlines! To combat portion distortion, try the following: Once your plate is in front of you, divide the serving in half and ask your server to wrap up the other half for you to take home. Consider ordering from the appetizer menu to ensure a smaller size, or request that the bread basket not approach the vicinity of your table!

November 4
5:15 pm EST

NOVEMBER

S	M	T	W	T	F	S
	1	2	3	4	5	6
7	8	9	10	11	12	13
14	15	16	17	18	19	20
21	22	23	24	25	26	27
28	29	30				

November 7–13 ♏

*There is a stubbornness about me that never can bear to be
frightened at the will of others. My courage always rises at
every attempt to intimidate me.*

~JANE AUSTEN, PRIDE AND PREJUDICE

Date	Qtr.	Sign	Activity
Nov. 7, 8:03 pm– Nov. 9, 10:03 pm	1st	Capricorn	Graft or bud plants. Trim to increase growth.
Nov. 12, 2:54 am– Nov. 14, 10:48 am	2nd	Pisces	Plant grains, leafy annuals. Fertilize (chemical). Graft or bud plants. Irrigate. Trim to increase growth.

An inspiration board is a wonderful way to get creative juices flowing. Choose an area of your home where you work, create, or practice a hobby, and hang a corkboard or several cork pieces to make a larger board. Collect magazine cutouts, sweet notes from friends, childhood artwork, family photos, bits of string and ribbon, vintage ephemera—anything that makes your heart soar. Then tack it all up and arrange the pieces however you like.

*Daylight Saving Time
begins November 7, 2:00 am*

*November 11
7:46 am EDT*

NOVEMBER

S	M	T	W	T	F	S
	1	2	3	4	5	6
7	8	9	10	11	12	13
14	15	16	17	18	19	20
21	22	23	24	25	26	27
28	29	30				

♏ November 14–20

Learn to value yourself, which means: fight for your happiness.
                                              ~Ayn Rand

Date	Qtr.	Sign	Activity
Nov. 16, 9:18 pm– Nov. 19, 3:57 am	2nd	Taurus	Plant annuals for hardiness. Trim to increase growth.
Nov. 19, 3:57 am– Nov. 19, 9:33 am	3rd	Taurus	Plant potatoes and tubers. Trim to retard growth.
Nov. 19, 9:33 am– Nov. 21, 10:33 pm	3rd	Gemini	Cultivate. Destroy weeds and pests. Harvest fruits and root crops for food. Trim to retard growth.

Brush your teeth to protect your heart! Poor oral hygiene, including untreated cavities, bleeding or infected gums, and periodontal disease, may lead to heart disease (atherosclerosis and endocarditis). To improve oral hygiene, brush twice a day (using a fluoride toothpaste), floss or use an interdental cleaner daily, and attend regular dentist checkups.

○
November 19
3:57 am EST

November

S	M	T	W	T	F	S
	1	2	3	4	5	6
7	8	9	10	11	12	13
14	15	16	17	18	19	20
21	22	23	24	25	26	27
28	29	30				

November 21–27

I knew I would never again see anything so splendid as the
round red sun coming up over the earth.
~Jean Craighead George, *My Side of the Mountain*

Date	Qtr.	Sign	Activity
Nov. 21, 10:33 pm– Nov. 24, 10:59 am	3rd	Cancer	Plant biennials, perennials, bulbs and roots. Prune. Irrigate. Fertilize (organic).
Nov. 24, 10:59 am– Nov. 26, 9:12 pm	3rd	Leo	Cultivate. Destroy weeds and pests. Harvest fruits and root crops for food. Trim to retard growth.
Nov. 26, 9:12 pm– Nov. 27, 7:28 am	3rd	Virgo	Cultivate, especially medicinal plants. Destroy weeds and pests. Trim to retard growth.
Nov. 27, 7:28 am– Nov. 29, 3:55 am	4th	Virgo	Cultivate, especially medicinal plants. Destroy weeds and pests. Trim to retard growth.

Teach yourself to crochet, which is quite simple, and make several eight-by-eight-inch dishcloths out of colorful cotton yarn. Tuck one into each Christmas gift you give to friends and family. They are amazingly durable, just the right size for one-handed wringing out, and a pleasure to use.

◗

November 27
7:28 am EST

November

S	M	T	W	T	F	S
	1	2	3	4	5	6
7	8	9	10	11	12	13
14	15	16	17	18	19	20
21	22	23	24	25	26	27
28	29	30				

December
November 28–December 4

May you live every day of your life.

~JONATHON SWIFT

Date	Qtr.	Sign	Activity
Dec. 1, 6:55 am– Dec. 3, 7:13 am	4th	Scorpio	Plant biennials, perennials, bulbs and roots. Prune. Irrigate. Fertilize (organic).
Dec. 3, 7:13 am– Dec. 4, 2:43 am	4th	Sagittarius	Cultivate. Destroy weeds and pests. Harvest fruits and root crops for food. Trim to retard growth.

Place air-purifying plants all around your home for a happier respiratory system. Plants can absorb bothersome chemicals, pollutants, and gases from the air, which can make your home a healthier place to live. Some air-purifying plants you can grow in your living spaces include spider plants, bamboo palms, Boston ferns, and snake plants.

December 4
2:43 am EST

DECEMBER

S	M	T	W	T	F	S
			1	2	3	4
5	6	7	8	9	10	11
12	13	14	15	16	17	18
19	20	21	22	23	24	25
26	27	28	29	30	31	

December 5–11

Go forth on your path, as it exists only through your walking.
                                                    ∼St. Augustine

Date	Qtr.	Sign	Activity
Dec. 5, 6:31 am– Dec. 7, 6:49 am	1st	Capricorn	Graft or bud plants. Trim to increase growth.
Dec. 9, 9:53 am– Dec. 10, 8:36 pm	1st	Pisces	Plant grains, leafy annuals. Fertilize (chemical). Graft or bud plants. Irrigate. Trim to increase growth.
Dec. 10, 8:36 pm– Dec. 11, 4:46 pm	2nd	Pisces	Plant grains, leafy annuals. Fertilize (chemical). Graft or bud plants. Irrigate. Trim to increase growth.

If your hands look old and worn, decide that you will spend one year taking extra good care of them. Start with a professional manicure without the heavy layers of nail polish. Maintain their good condition by soaking them in spearmint tea for twenty minutes twice a month. Rub them with vitamin E oil. Take before and after photos. You'll be amazed!

◑

December 10
8:36 pm EST

DECEMBER

S	M	T	W	T	F	S
			1	2	3	4
5	6	7	8	9	10	11
12	13	14	15	16	17	18
19	20	21	22	23	24	25
26	27	28	29	30	31	

December 12–18

Keep your eyes on the stars, and your feet on the ground.
~THEODORE ROOSEVELT

Date	Qtr.	Sign	Activity
Dec. 14, 3:11 am– Dec. 16, 3:43 pm	2nd	Taurus	Plant annuals for hardiness. Trim to increase growth.
Dec. 18, 11:36 pm– Dec. 19, 4:42 am	3rd	Gemini	Cultivate. Destroy weeds and pests. Harvest fruits and root crops for food. Trim to retard growth.

Are food and mood related? Several studies linked some forms of depression with inflammation in the body. Foods that work as anti-inflammatories are beets, black beans, blueberries, broccoli, chia seeds, dark chocolate, garlic, ginger, green tea, oysters, pineapple, raw oats, spinach, tomatoes, turmeric, and wild salmon. Nutrition support for depression includes eating more vegetables, whole grains, legumes, cold-water fish, raw nuts, and seeds. Avoid caffeine, nicotine, alcohol, sugar, and artificial sweeteners.

_____

_____

_____

_____

○
December 18
11:36 pm EST

DECEMBER

S	M	T	W	T	F	S
			1	2	3	4
5	6	7	8	9	10	11
12	13	14	15	16	17	18
19	20	21	22	23	24	25
26	27	28	29	30	31	

December 19–25

My point is, while you're spending all this time on your own, building computers or practicing your cello, what you're really doing is becoming interesting.

~LEONARD HOFSTADTER, *THE BIG BANG THEORY*

Date	Qtr.	Sign	Activity
Dec. 19, 4:42 am– Dec. 21, 4:54 pm	3rd	Cancer	Plant biennials, perennials, bulbs and roots. Prune. Irrigate. Fertilize (organic).
Dec. 21, 4:54 pm– Dec. 24, 3:24 am	3rd	Leo	Cultivate. Destroy weeds and pests. Harvest fruits and root crops for food. Trim to retard growth.
Dec. 24, 3:24 am– Dec. 26, 11:24 am	3rd	Virgo	Cultivate, especially medicinal plants. Destroy weeds and pests. Trim to retard growth.

When world chaos becomes overwhelming, retreat to your bathtub and soak yourself in lavender scented water and Epsom salts. Listen to quiet music while in the tub, and go to bed early to get not seven, not eight, but nine and a half hours of sleep! Your perspective will be much different the next day.

DECEMBER

S	M	T	W	T	F	S
				1	2	3	4
5	6	7	8	9	10	11
12	13	14	15	16	17	18
19	20	21	22	23	24	25
26	27	28	29	30	31	

December 26–January 1, 2022

Nobody in life gets exactly what they thought they were going to get. But if you work really hard and you're kind, amazing things will happen.   ~CONAN O'BRIEN

Date	Qtr.	Sign	Activity
Dec. 28, 4:16 pm– Dec. 30, 6:08 pm	4th	Scorpio	Plant biennials, perennials, bulbs and roots. Prune. Irrigate. Fertilize (organic).

Don't throw away those tea bags quite yet. In the spirit of upcycling, you can utilize used tea bags in your natural beauty routine. Drop lavender or jasmine tea bags into your bath to literally soak up the antioxidant benefits (and enjoy the scent), put chilled tea bags on your eyes to de-puff bags and tired skin, or tear open a bag and mix the loose tea with honey for an exfoliating facial treatment.

_____

_____

_____

_____

December 26
9:24 pm EST

DECEMBER

S	M	T	W	T	F	S
			1	2	3	4
5	6	7	8	9	10	11
12	13	14	15	16	17	18
19	20	21	22	23	24	25
26	27	28	29	30	31	

Gardening by the Moon

Welcome to the world of gardening by the Moon! Unlike most gardening advice, this article is not about how to garden, it's about when to garden. Timing is everything; if you know how to use the Moon, you'll not only be in sync with nature but you can sit back and watch your garden grow beyond your wildest dreams.

Gardening by the Moon is nothing new. It's been around since ancient times when people used both the Sun and the Moon to predict the tides, as well as fertility and growth cycles for plants and animals.

Lunar gardening is simple and the results are immediate. It doesn't matter whether you're a beginner gardener with a single pot or an old hand with years of master gardening experience— your garden will grow bigger and better if you follow the cycles of the Moon and match up the right time with the right garden activity. When the temperature has dropped and the sun is low on the horizon you can apply what you've learned to your indoor plants as well.

The sky is a celestial clock, with the Sun and the Moon as the "hands" that tell the time. The Sun tells the season, and the light and location of the Moon tell the best times for birth, growth, and death in the garden. The Moon doesn't generate any light by itself, but as it circles the Earth it reflects the light of the Sun, which makes the Moon look like it's getting bigger and smaller. The cyclical increases and decreases in the light of the Moon are phases and tell times of growth.

Moon Phases

The theory behind gardening by the Moon is "as the Moon goes, so goes the garden." The Earth circles around the Sun once a year but the Moon has a much shorter "life span" of twenty-eight to thirty days. Every month, as the light of the Moon increases and decreases, it mirrors the cycle of birth, growth, and death in the garden. After adjusting your garden activities to the light of the Moon you'll be amazed to see how well your garden grows.

The **waxing phase** is the growth cycle in the garden. It begins with the New Moon and lasts for two weeks. Each month the Moon is "born" at the New Moon (day one) and grows bigger and brighter until it reaches maturity at the Full Moon (day fourteen). When the light of the Moon is increasing it's the best time of the month to sow seeds, plant leafy annuals, and cut back or prune plants to encourage bigger growth.

The **waning phase** is the declining cycle in the garden. It begins with the Full Moon (day fourteen) and lasts for two weeks. The Moon grows older after the Full Moon as the light begins to decrease, until it disappears or "dies" at day twenty-eight. The decreasing light of the Moon is the time to plant bulbs, root vegetables, and perennials that store their energy underground. The waning Moon phase is also a good time for garden maintenance, including weeding, raking, deadheading, mowing, working the soil, destroying insects, and burning brush.

How can you tell if the Moon is waxing or waning?

Cup your right hand into a C shape and look up into the sky. If the crescent Moon fits into the closed part of your right hand, it's a waxing Moon.

Cup your left hand into a C shape and look up into the sky. If the crescent Moon fits into the closed part of your left hand, it's a waning Moon.

New Moon and Full Moon

Every month, the Moon takes one day off. This time-out between waning and waxing is called the New Moon. The time-out between waxing and waning is called the Full Moon. When the Moon reaches either of these stopping points, it's time for you to follow its example and take a one-day break from the garden.

Moon Signs

Once you know the Moon phases, the next step is to locate where the Moon is in the zodiac. The Moon hangs out in each of the zodiac signs for two to three days per month.

There's no such thing as a "bad" time in the garden, but there are Moon signs that are better for growth and others that are better for digging and weeding. Growth times alternate every two to three days with maintenance times. The trick is knowing which one is which.

The grow signs are Taurus, Cancer, Libra, Scorpio, Capricorn, and Pisces. When the Moon is in these signs it's time to seed and plant.

The no-grow/maintenance signs are Aries, Gemini, Leo, Virgo, Sagittarius, and Aquarius. When the Moon is in these signs it's time for digging, weeding, mowing, and pruning.

Remember: It's always a good time to garden something!

Putting It All Together

In order to get started, you'll need three tools: a calendar with New and Full Moons, the Moon tables (pg. 136), and the Moon phases and signs below.

Then follow these simple steps:

1. Mark your calendar with your time frame for gardening.

2. Figure out when the Moon is waxing (1st and 2nd quarters) and waning (3rd and 4th quarters). Use the tables in the Weekly Almanac section.

3. Locate the Moon by zodiac sign.

4. Check out the gardening advice below, which takes into account the Moon's phase and sign.

Moon Phases and Signs

Note: Can be applied to any calendar year.

Waxing Aries Moon (October–April)

Aries is one of the three fire signs that is hot and barren. Seeds planted under a waxing Aries Moon tend to be bitter or bolt quickly, but if you're feeling lucky you could try your hand at hot and spicy peppers or herbs that thrive in dry heat.

Waning Aries Moon (April–October)

The decreasing light of the waning Aries Moon makes these two to three days a good time to focus on harvesting, cutting back, mowing the lawn, and getting rid of pests.

Waxing Taurus Moon (November–May)

Taurus is one of the three semi-fruitful earth signs. These days are perfect ones to establish your garden by planting or fertilizing annuals. Annuals with outside seeds like lettuces, cabbage, corn, and broccoli grow faster when planted under a waxing Taurus Moon that is one to seven days old. Vegetables with inside seeds like cucumbers, melons, squash, tomatoes, and beans should be planted when the Moon is seven to twelve days old. Annual flowers can be planted any time during this two-week phase.

Waning Taurus Moon (May–November)

The decreasing light of this semi-fruitful waning Taurus Moon gives you a perfect two- or three-day window for planting perennials or digging in root vegetables and flower bulbs.

Waxing Gemini Moon (December–June)

Gemini is one of the three dry and barren signs. But with the light of the Moon increasing you can use these two to three days to prune or cut back plants you want to flourish and grow bigger.

Waning Gemini Moon (June–December)

Gemini can be all over the place, so use these couple of dry and barren days when the light is decreasing to weed invasive plants that are out of control.

Waxing Cancer Moon (January–July)

Cancer is one of the three wet and fruitful signs, so when the Moon is waxing in Cancer it's the perfect time to plant seeds or set out seedlings and annual flowers that live for only one season. Annuals with outside seeds grow faster when planted under a Moon that is one to seven days old. Vegetables with inside seeds should be planted when the Moon is seven to twelve days old. Annual flowers can be planted any time during these two weeks.

Waning Cancer Moon (July–January)

Plant perennials, root vegetables, and bulbs to your heart's content under the decreasing light of this fruitful Moon.

Waxing Leo Moon (February–August)

The light of the Moon is increasing, but Leo is one of the three hot and barren fire signs. Use the two or three days of this waxing Leo Moon to cut and prune the plants and shrubs you want to be the king or queen of your garden.

Waning Leo Moon (August–February)

With the light of the Moon decreasing, this Leo Moon is a good period to dig the soil, destroy pests and insects, and burn brush.

Waxing Virgo Moon (March–September)

Virgo is a semi-barren sign, which is good for fertilizing (Virgo is a "greenie" type that loves organics) and for planting woody vines and hardy herbs.

Waning Virgo Moon (September–March)

With the light of this semi-barren Moon decreasing for a couple of days, plan to hoe those rows and get rid of your weeds. Harvest Moon in September.

Waxing Libra Moon (October–April)

Libra is a semi-fruitful sign focused on beauty. Because the Moon is growing brighter in Libra, these two to three days are a great time to give your flower garden some heavy-duty TLC.

Waning Libra Moon (April–October)

If you want to encourage re-blooming, try deadheading your vegetables and flowers under the light of this decreasing Libra Moon. Harvest your flowers.

Waxing Scorpio Moon (November–May)

Scorpio is one of the three wet and fruitful signs. When the Moon is waxing in Scorpio it's the perfect time for planting annuals that have a bite, like arugula and hot peppers. Annuals with outside seeds grow faster when planted under a Moon that is one to seven days old. Vegetables with inside seeds should be planted when the Moon is seven to twelve days old. Annual flowers can be planted anytime during this two-week phase.

Waning Scorpio Moon (May–November)

With the light of the Moon decreasing in Scorpio, a sign that likes strong and intense flavors, this is the perfect period to plant hardy perennials, garlic bulbs, and onion sets.

Waxing Sagittarius Moon (June–December)

Sagittarius is one of the three hot and barren signs. Because Sagittarius prefers roaming to staying still, this waxing Moon is not good time for planting. But you can encourage growth during the two or three days when the light is increasing by cutting back, mowing, and pruning.

Waning Sagittarius Moon (December–June)

It's time to discourage growth during the days when the light of the Moon is decreasing in Sagittarius. Cut back, mow the lawn, prune, and destroy pests and insects you never want to darken your garden again.

Waxing Capricorn Moon (July–January)

Capricorn is a semi-fruitful earth sign. The couple of days when the light of the Moon is increasing in Capricorn are good for getting the garden into shape, setting out plants and transplants, and fertilizing.

Waning Capricorn Moon (January–July)

The decreasing light of this fruitful Capricorn Moon is the perfect window for digging and dividing bulbs and pinching back suckers to encourage bigger blooms on your flowers and vegetables.

Waxing Aquarius Moon (August–February)

Aquarius is a dry and barren sign. However, the increasing light of the Aquarian Moon makes this a good opportunity to experiment by pruning or cutting back plants you want to flourish.

Waning Aquarius Moon (February–August)

The light of the Moon is decreasing. Use this time to harvest or to weed, cut back, and prune the shrubs and plants that you want to banish forever from your garden. Harvest vegetables.

Waxing Pisces Moon (September–March)

When the Moon is increasing in fruitful Pisces, it's a perfect period for planting seeds and annuals. Annuals with outside seeds grow faster when planted under a Moon that is one to seven days old. Vegetables with inside seeds should be planted when the Moon is seven to twelve days old. Annual flowers can be planted any time during these two weeks.

Waning Pisces Moon (March–September)

With the light of the Moon decreasing it's time to plant all perennials, bulbs, and root vegetables except potatoes. Garden lore has it that potatoes planted under a Pisces Moon tend to grow bumps or "toes," because Pisces is associated with the feet.

Here's hoping that this has inspired you to give gardening by the Moon a try. Not only is it the secret ingredient that will make your garden more abundant, but you can use it as long as the Sun is in the sky and the Moon circles the Earth!

A Guide to Planting

Plant	Quarter	Sign
Annuals	1st or 2nd	
Apple tree	2nd or 3rd	Cancer, Pisces, Virgo
Artichoke	1st	Cancer, Pisces
Asparagus	1st	Cancer, Scorpio, Pisces
Aster	1st or 2nd	Virgo, Libra
Barley	1st or 2nd	Cancer, Pisces, Libra, Capricorn, Virgo
Beans (bush & pole)	2nd	Cancer, Taurus, Pisces, Libra
Beans (kidney, white & navy)	1st or 2nd	Cancer, Pisces
Beech tree	2nd or 3rd	Virgo, Taurus
Beets	3rd	Cancer, Capricorn, Pisces, Libra
Biennials	3rd or 4th	
Broccoli	1st	Cancer, Scorpio, Pisces, Libra
Brussels sprouts	1st	Cancer, Scorpio, Pisces, Libra
Buckwheat	1st or 2nd	Capricorn
Bulbs	3rd	Cancer, Scorpio, Pisces
Bulbs for seed	2nd or 3rd	
Cabbage	1st	Cancer, Scorpio, Pisces, Taurus, Libra
Canes (raspberry, blackberry & gooseberry)	2nd	Cancer, Scorpio, Pisces
Cantaloupe	1st or 2nd	Cancer, Scorpio, Pisces, Taurus, Libra
Carrots	3rd	Cancer, Scorpio, Pisces, Taurus, Libra
Cauliflower	1st	Cancer, Scorpio, Pisces, Libra
Celeriac	3rd	Cancer, Scorpio, Pisces
Celery	1st	Cancer, Scorpio, Pisces
Cereals	1st or 2nd	Cancer, Scorpio, Pisces, Libra
Chard	1st or 2nd	Cancer, Scorpio, Pisces
Chicory	2nd or 3rd	Cancer, Scorpio, Pisces
Chrysanthemum	1st or 2nd	Virgo
Clover	1st or 2nd	Cancer, Scorpio, Pisces

Plant	Quarter	Sign
Coreopsis	2nd or 3rd	Libra
Corn	1st	Cancer, Scorpio, Pisces
Corn for fodder	1st or 2nd	Libra
Cosmos	2nd or 3rd	Libra
Cress	1st	Cancer, Scorpio, Pisces
Crocus	1st or 2nd	Virgo
Cucumber	1st	Cancer, Scorpio, Pisces
Daffodil	1st or 2nd	Libra, Virgo
Dahlia	1st or 2nd	Libra, Virgo
Deciduous trees	2nd or 3rd	Cancer, Scorpio, Pisces, Virgo, Libra
Eggplant	2nd	Cancer, Scorpio, Pisces, Libra
Endive	1st	Cancer, Scorpio, Pisces, Libra
Flowers	1st	Cancer, Scorpio, Pisces, Libra, Taurus, Virgo
Garlic	3rd	Libra, Taurus, Pisces
Gladiola	1st or 2nd	Libra, Virgo
Gourds	1st or 2nd	Cancer, Scorpio, Pisces, Libra
Grapes	2nd or 3rd	Cancer, Scorpio, Pisces, Virgo
Hay	1st or 2nd	Cancer, Scorpio, Pisces, Libra, Taurus
Herbs	1st or 2nd	Cancer, Scorpio, Pisces
Honeysuckle	1st or 2nd	Scorpio, Virgo
Hops	1st or 2nd	Scorpio, Libra
Horseradish	1st or 2nd	Cancer, Scorpio, Pisces
Houseplants	1st	Cancer, Scorpio, Pisces, Libra
Hyacinth	3rd	Cancer, Scorpio, Pisces
Iris	1st or 2nd	Cancer, Virgo
Kohlrabi	1st or 2nd	Cancer, Scorpio, Pisces, Libra
Leek	2nd or 3rd	Sagittarius
Lettuce	1st	Cancer, Scorpio, Pisces, Libra, Taurus
Lily	1st or 2nd	Cancer, Scorpio, Pisces
Maple tree	2nd or 3rd	Taurus, Virgo, Cancer, Pisces
Melon	2nd	Cancer, Scorpio, Pisces
Moon vine	1st or 2nd	Virgo

Plant	Quarter	Sign
Morning glory	1st or 2nd	Cancer, Scorpio, Pisces, Virgo
Oak tree	2nd or 3rd	Taurus, Virgo, Cancer, Pisces
Oats	1st or 2nd	Cancer, Scorpio, Pisces, Libra
Okra	1st or 2nd	Cancer, Scorpio, Pisces, Libra
Onion seed	2nd	Cancer, Scorpio, Sagittarius
Onion set	3rd or 4th	Cancer, Pisces, Taurus, Libra
Pansies	1st or 2nd	Cancer, Scorpio, Pisces
Parsley	1st	Cancer, Scorpio, Pisces, Libra
Parsnip	3rd	Cancer, Scorpio, Taurus, Capricorn
Peach tree	2nd or 3rd	Cancer, Taurus, Virgo, Libra
Peanuts	3rd	Cancer, Scorpio, Pisces
Pear tree	2nd or 3rd	Cancer, Scorpio, Pisces, Libra
Peas	2nd	Cancer, Scorpio, Pisces, Libra
Peony	1st or 2nd	Virgo
Peppers	2nd	Cancer, Scorpio, Pisces
Perennials	3rd	
Petunia	1st or 2nd	Libra, Virgo
Plum tree	2nd or 3rd	Cancer, Pisces, Taurus, Virgo
Poppies	1st or 2nd	Virgo
Portulaca	1st or 2nd	Virgo
Potatoes	3rd	Cancer, Scorpio, Libra, Taurus, Capricorn
Privet	1st or 2nd	Taurus, Libra
Pumpkin	2nd	Cancer, Scorpio, Pisces, Libra
Quince	1st or 2nd	Capricorn
Radishes	3rd	Cancer, Scorpio, Pisces, Libra, Capricorn
Rhubarb	3rd	Cancer, Pisces
Rice	1st or 2nd	Scorpio
Roses	1st or 2nd	Cancer, Virgo
Rutabaga	3rd	Cancer, Scorpio, Pisces, Taurus
Saffron	1st or 2nd	Cancer, Scorpio, Pisces
Sage	3rd	Cancer, Scorpio, Pisces

Plant	Quarter	Sign
Salsify	1st	Cancer, Scorpio, Pisces
Shallot	2nd	Scorpio
Spinach	1st	Cancer, Scorpio, Pisces
Squash	2nd	Cancer, Scorpio, Pisces, Libra
Strawberries	3rd	Cancer, Scorpio, Pisces
String beans	1st or 2nd	Taurus
Sunflowers	1st or 2nd	Libra, Cancer
Sweet peas	1st or 2nd	Any
Tomatoes	2nd	Cancer, Scorpio, Pisces, Capricorn
Trees, shade	3rd	Taurus, Capricorn
Trees, ornamental	2nd	Libra, Taurus
Trumpet vine	1st or 2nd	Cancer, Scorpio, Pisces
Tubers for seed	3rd	Cancer, Scorpio, Pisces, Libra
Tulips	1st or 2nd	Libra, Virgo
Turnips	3rd	Cancer, Scorpio, Pisces, Taurus, Capricorn, Libra
Valerian	1st or 2nd	Virgo, Gemini
Watermelon	1st or 2nd	Cancer, Scorpio, Pisces, Libra
Wheat	1st or 2nd	Cancer, Scorpio, Pisces, Libra

Companion Planting Guide

Plant	Companions	Hindered by
Asparagus	Tomatoes, parsley, basil	None known
Beans	Tomatoes, carrots, cucumbers, garlic, cabbage, beets, corn	Onions, gladiolas
Beets	Onions, cabbage, lettuce, mint, catnip	Pole beans
Broccoli	Beans, celery, potatoes, onions	Tomatoes
Cabbage	Peppermint, sage, thyme, tomatoes	Strawberries, grapes
Carrots	Peas, lettuce, chives, radishes, leeks, onions, sage	Dill, anise
Citrus trees	Guava, live oak, rubber trees, peppers	None known
Corn	Potatoes, beans, peas, melon, squash, pumpkin, sunflowers, soybeans	Quack grass, wheat, straw, mulch
Cucumbers	Beans, cabbage, radishes, sunflowers, lettuce, broccoli, squash	Aromatic herbs
Eggplant	Green beans, lettuce, kale	None known
Grapes	Peas, beans, blackberries	Cabbage, radishes
Melons	Corn, peas	Potatoes, gourds
Onions, leeks	Beets, chamomile, carrots, lettuce	Peas, beans, sage
Parsnip	Peas	None known
Peas	Radishes, carrots, corn, cucumbers, beans, tomatoes, spinach, turnips	Onion, garlic
Potatoes	Beans, corn, peas, cabbage, hemp, cucumbers, eggplant, catnip	Raspberries, pumpkins, tomatoes, sunflowers
Radishes	Peas, lettuce, nasturtiums, cucumbers	Hyssop
Spinach	Strawberries	None known
Squash/Pumpkin	Nasturtiums, corn, mint, catnip	Potatoes
Tomatoes	Asparagus, parsley, chives, onions, carrots, marigolds, nasturtiums, dill	Black walnut roots, fennel, potatoes
Turnips	Peas, beans, brussels sprouts	Potatoes

Plant	Companions	Uses
Anise	Coriander	Flavor candy, pastry, cheeses, cookies
Basil	Tomatoes	Dislikes rue; repels flies and mosquitoes
Borage	Tomatoes, squash	Use in teas
Buttercup	Clover	Hinders delphinium, peonies, monkshood, columbine
Catnip		Repels flea beetles
Chamomile	Peppermint, wheat, onions, cabbage	Roman chamomile may control damping-off disease; use in herbal sprays
Chervil	Radishes	Good in soups and other dishes
Chives	Carrots	Use in spray to deter black spot on roses
Coriander	Plant anywhere	Hinders seed formation in fennel
Cosmos		Repels corn earworms
Dill	Cabbage	Hinders carrots and tomatoes
Fennel	Plant in borders	Disliked by all garden plants
Horseradish		Repels potato bugs
Horsetail		Makes fungicide spray
Hyssop		Attracts cabbage flies; harmful to radishes
Lavender	Plant anywhere	Use in spray to control insects on cotton, repels clothes moths
Lovage		Lures horn worms away from tomatoes
Marigolds		Pest repellent; use against Mexican bean beetles and nematodes
Mint	Cabbage, tomatoes	Repels ants, flea beetles, cabbage worm butterflies
Morning glory	Corn	Helps melon germination
Nasturtium	Cabbage, cucumbers	Deters aphids, squash bugs, pumpkin beetles
Okra	Eggplant	Attracts leafhopper (lure insects from other plants)
Parsley	Tomatoes, asparagus	Freeze chopped-up leaves to flavor foods
Purslane		Good ground cover
Rosemary		Repels cabbage moths, bean beetles, carrot flies
Savory		Plant with onions for added sweetness
Tansy		Deters Japanese beetles, striped cucumber beetles, squash bugs
Thyme		Repels cabbage worms
Yarrow		Increases essential oils of neighbors

Moon Void-of-Course

by Kim Rogers-Gallagher

The Moon circles the Earth in about twenty-eight days, moving through each zodiac sign in two and a half days. As she passes through the thirty degrees of each sign, she "visits" with the planets in numerical order, forming aspects with them. Because she moves one degree in just two to two and a half hours, her influence on each planet lasts only a few hours. She eventually reaches the planet that's in the highest degree of any sign and forms what will be her final aspect before leaving the sign. From this point until she enters the next sign, she is referred to as void-of-course.

Think of it this way: the Moon is the emotional "tone" of the day, carrying feelings with her particular to the sign she's "wearing" at the moment. After she has contacted each of the planets, she symbolically "rests" before changing her costume, so her instinct is temporarily on hold. It's during this time that many people feel "fuzzy" or "vague." Plans or decisions made now often do not pan out. Without the instinctual "knowing" the Moon provides as she touches each planet, we tend to be unrealistic or exercise poor judgment. The traditional definition of the void Moon is that "nothing will come of this." Actions initiated under a void Moon are often wasted, irrelevant, or incorrect—usually because information is hidden, missing, or has been overlooked.

Although it's not a good time to initiate plans, routine tasks seem to go along just fine. This period is ideal for reflection. On the lighter side, remember there are good uses for the void Moon. It is the period when the universe seems to be most open to loopholes. It's a great time to make plans you don't want to fulfill or schedule things you don't want to do. See the tables on pages 76–81 for a schedule of the Moon's void-of-course times.

Last Aspect   Moon Enters New Sign

January				
2	5:00 pm	2	Virgo	8:13 pm
4	4:34 pm	5	Libra	12:42 am
7	12:55 am	7	Scorpio	3:53 am
8	8:59 pm	9	Sagittarius	6:15 am
10	1:29 pm	11	Capricorn	8:30 am
13	2:22 am	13	Aquarius	11:44 am
14	4:28 am	15	Pisces	5:17 pm
17	10:44 pm	18	Aries	2:07 am
20	3:29 am	20	Taurus	1:56 pm
22	4:28 pm	23	Gemini	2:43 am
25	2:17 am	25	Cancer	1:52 pm
27	12:55 pm	27	Leo	9:54 pm
29	8:53 pm	30	Virgo	3:02 am
February				
1	6:10 am	1	Libra	6:25 am
3	1:15 am	3	Scorpio	9:15 am
5	4:20 am	5	Sagittarius	12:16 pm
7	1:16 am	7	Capricorn	3:52 pm
9	12:22 pm	9	Aquarius	8:20 pm
11	2:06 pm	12	Pisces	2:23 am
14	2:29 am	14	Aries	10:54 am
16	7:17 pm	16	Taurus	10:12 pm
19	2:28 am	19	Gemini	11:04 am
21	1:39 pm	21	Cancer	10:53 pm
23	11:54 pm	24	Leo	7:23 am
26	6:32 am	26	Virgo	12:07 pm
28	10:58 am	28	Libra	2:17 pm

Last Aspect   Moon Enters New Sign

		March			
2	9:09 am	2	Scorpio	3:38 pm
4	11:10 am	4	Sagittarius	5:43 pm
6	4:44 am	6	Capricorn	9:20 pm
8	7:52 pm	9	Aquarius	2:41 am
10	10:32 pm	11	Pisces	9:44 am
13	11:38 am	13	Aries	6:44 pm
15	11:40 pm	16	Taurus	6:56 am
18	4:40 pm	18	Gemini	7:47 pm
21	8:04 am	21	Cancer	8:18 am
23	11:26 am	23	Leo	5:56 pm
25	9:27 am	25	Virgo	11:25 pm
27	7:48 pm	28	Libra	1:22 am
29	8:08 pm	30	Scorpio	1:33 am
31	8:29 pm	1	Sagittarius	1:59 am
		April			
3	1:24 am	3	Capricorn	4:13 am
5	3:05 am	5	Aquarius	9:04 am
7	6:05 am	7	Pisces	4:30 pm
9	7:48 pm	10	Aries	2:11 am
12	8:06 am	12	Taurus	1:44 pm
14	8:00 pm	15	Gemini	2:35 am
17	11:03 am	17	Cancer	3:25 pm
19	8:03 pm	20	Leo	2:11 am
22	8:05 am	22	Virgo	9:08 am
24	6:50 am	24	Libra	12:06 pm
26	8:40 am	26	Scorpio	12:18 pm
28	8:31 am	28	Sagittarius	11:42 am
30	9:27 am	30	Capricorn	12:16 pm

Last Aspect   **Moon Enters New Sign**

		May			
2	10:38 am	2	Aquarius	3:31 pm	
4	8:05 pm	4	Pisces	10:09 pm	
7	3:36 am	7	Aries	7:52 am	
9	6:50 pm	9	Taurus	7:46 pm	
12	8:23 am	12	Gemini	8:43 am	
14	6:51 am	14	Cancer	9:30 pm	
17	2:23 am	17	Leo	8:44 am	
19	3:13 pm	19	Virgo	4:59 pm	
21	3:56 pm	21	Libra	9:35 pm	
23	5:36 pm	23	Scorpio	11:00 pm	
25	5:20 pm	25	Sagittarius	10:39 pm	
27	1:35 pm	27	Capricorn	10:23 pm	
29	6:15 pm	30	Aquarius	12:04 am	
		June			
1	2:14 am	1	Pisces	5:07 am	
3	7:10 am	3	Aries	1:59 pm	
5	6:47 pm	6	Taurus	1:46 am	
8	11:07 am	8	Gemini	2:47 pm	
10	1:38 pm	11	Cancer	3:23 am	
13	7:16 am	13	Leo	2:22 pm	
15	1:27 pm	15	Virgo	11:02 pm	
17	11:54 pm	18	Libra	4:54 am	
20	6:52 am	20	Scorpio	7:58 am	
22	2:43 am	22	Sagittarius	8:55 am	
23	10:09 pm	24	Capricorn	9:05 am	
26	8:49 am	26	Aquarius	10:09 am	
27	3:08 pm	28	Pisces	1:51 pm	
30	1:40 pm	30	Aries	9:21 pm	

Last Aspect   Moon Enters New Sign

		July			
3	12:15 am	3		Taurus	8:28 am
5	12:57 pm	5		Gemini	9:24 pm
8	12:20 am	8		Cancer	9:51 am
10	12:10 pm	10		Leo	8:21 pm
12	8:29 am	13		Virgo	4:30 am
15	2:46 am	15		Libra	10:32 am
17	7:03 am	17		Scorpio	2:38 pm
19	12:30 pm	19		Sagittarius	5:08 pm
21	6:26 pm	21		Capricorn	6:36 pm
23	12:34 pm	23		Aquarius	8:12 pm
25	7:14 pm	25		Pisces	11:30 pm
27	9:13 pm	28		Aries	5:58 am
30	3:38 pm	30		Taurus	4:08 pm
		August			
2	3:41 am	2		Gemini	4:46 am
4	3:38 pm	4		Cancer	5:17 pm
6	6:12 pm	7		Leo	3:31 am
9	8:23 am	9		Virgo	10:56 am
11	7:22 am	11		Libra	4:08 pm
13	4:39 pm	13		Scorpio	8:01 pm
15	11:05 pm	15		Sagittarius	11:12 pm
17	9:43 pm	18		Capricorn	1:58 am
19	7:59 pm	20		Aquarius	4:49 am
22	8:02 am	22		Pisces	8:43 am
24	5:12 am	24		Aries	2:57 pm
26	5:14 pm	27		Taurus	12:27 am
29	10:59 am	29		Gemini	12:42 pm
31	4:48 pm	1		Cancer	1:26 am

Last Aspect   Moon Enters New Sign

		September			
3	1:37 am	3	Leo	11:58 am	
5	10:22 am	5	Virgo	7:06 pm	
7	3:24 pm	7	Libra	11:20 pm	
10	12:48 am	10	Scorpio	2:05 am	
12	1:33 am	12	Sagittarius	4:34 am	
14	6:57 am	14	Capricorn	7:34 am	
16	1:40 am	16	Aquarius	11:23 am	
18	5:14 am	18	Pisces	4:22 pm	
20	7:55 pm	20	Aries	11:13 pm	
22	10:05 pm	23	Taurus	8:38 am	
25	9:09 am	25	Gemini	8:36 pm	
28	12:18 am	28	Cancer	9:34 am	
30	10:49 am	30	Leo	8:53 pm	
		October			
2	7:43 pm	3	Virgo	4:38 am	
5	4:46 am	5	Libra	8:41 am	
7	1:03 am	7	Scorpio	10:22 am	
9	2:05 am	9	Sagittarius	11:24 am	
11	12:30 am	11	Capricorn	1:15 pm	
13	6:53 am	13	Aquarius	4:47 pm	
15	8:33 am	15	Pisces	10:22 pm	
17	7:24 pm	18	Aries	6:04 am	
20	10:57 am	20	Taurus	3:59 pm	
22	4:35 pm	23	Gemini	3:57 am	
25	10:11 am	25	Cancer	5:00 pm	
28	2:02 am	28	Leo	5:07 am	
30	3:05 am	30	Virgo	2:09 pm	

Last Aspect   Moon Enters New Sign

		November		
1	1:00 pm	1	Libra	7:11 pm
3	6:32 pm	3	Scorpio	8:52 pm
5	12:10 pm	5	Sagittarius	8:52 pm
7	8:44 am	7	Capricorn	8:03 pm
9	12:51 pm	9	Aquarius	10:03 pm
11	2:52 pm	12	Pisces	2:54 am
14	12:40 am	14	Aries	10:48 am
16	10:51 am	16	Taurus	9:18 pm
19	3:57 am	19	Gemini	9:33 am
21	10:52 am	21	Cancer	10:33 pm
24	12:46 am	24	Leo	10:59 am
26	11:24 am	26	Virgo	9:12 pm
28	7:02 pm	29	Libra	3:55 am
30	11:20 pm	1	Scorpio	6:55 am
		December		
3	12:22 am	3	Sagittarius	7:13 am
5	12:08 am	5	Capricorn	6:31 am
6	11:42 pm	7	Aquarius	6:49 am
9	5:00 am	9	Pisces	9:53 am
11	2:40 pm	11	Aries	4:46 pm
13	9:52 pm	14	Taurus	3:11 am
16	11:08 am	16	Gemini	3:43 pm
19	1:02 am	19	Cancer	4:42 am
21	9:44 am	21	Leo	4:54 pm
24	1:39 am	24	Virgo	3:24 am
26	3:39 am	26	Libra	11:24 am
28	4:11 pm	28	Scorpio	4:16 pm
30	12:10 pm	30	Sagittarius	6:08 pm

The Moon's Rhythm

The Moon journeys around Earth in an elliptical orbit that takes about 27.33 days, which is known as a sidereal month (period of revolution of one body about another). She can move up to 15 degrees or as few as 11 degrees in a day, with the fastest motion occurring when the Moon is at perigee (closest approach to Earth). The Moon is never retrograde, but when her motion is slow, the effect is similar to a retrograde period.

Astrologers have observed that people born on a day when the Moon is fast will process information differently from those who are born when the Moon is slow in motion. People born when the Moon is fast process information quickly and tend to react quickly, while those born during a slow Moon will be more deliberate.

The time from New Moon to New Moon is called the synodic month (involving a conjunction), and the average time span between this Sun-Moon alignment is 29.53 days. Since 29.53 won't divide into 365 evenly, we can have a month with two Full Moons or two New Moons.

Moon Aspects

The aspects the Moon will make during the times you are considering are also important. A trine or sextile, and sometimes a conjunction, are considered favorable aspects. A trine or sextile between the Sun and Moon is an excellent foundation for success. Whether or not a conjunction is considered favorable depends upon the planet the Moon is making a conjunction to. If it's joining the Sun, Venus, Mercury, Jupiter, or even Saturn, the aspect is favorable. If the Moon joins Pluto or Mars, however, that would not be considered favorable. There may be exceptions, but it would depend on what you are electing to do. For example, a trine to Pluto might hasten the end of a relationship you want to be free of.

It is important to avoid times when the Moon makes an aspect to or is conjoining any retrograde planet, unless, of course, you want the thing started to end in failure.

After the Moon has completed an aspect to a planet, that planetary energy has passed. For example, if the Moon squares Saturn at 10:00 am, you can disregard Saturn's influence on your activity if it will occur after that time. You should always look ahead at aspects the Moon will make on the day in question, though, because if the Moon opposes Mars at 11:30 pm on that day, you can expect events that stretch into the evening to be affected by the Moon-Mars aspect. A testy conversation might lead to an argument, or more.

Moon Signs

Much agricultural work is ruled by earth signs—Virgo, Capricorn, and Taurus. The air signs—Gemini, Aquarius, and Libra—rule flying and intellectual pursuits.

Each planet has one or two signs in which its characteristics are enhanced or "dignified," and the planet is said to "rule" that sign. The Sun rules Leo and the Moon rules Cancer, for example. The ruling planet for each sign is listed below. These should not be considered complete lists. We recommend that you purchase a book of planetary rulerships for more complete information.

Aries Moon

The energy of an Aries Moon is masculine, dry, barren, and fiery. Aries provides great start-up energy, but things started at this time may be the result of impulsive action that lacks research or necessary support. Aries lacks staying power.

Use this assertive, outgoing Moon sign to initiate change, but have a plan in place for someone to pick up the reins when you're impatient to move on to the next thing. Work that requires skillful but not necessarily patient use of tools—cutting down trees, hammering, etc.—is appropriate in Aries. Expect things to occur rapidly but to also quickly pass. If you are prone to injury or accidents, exercise caution and good judgment in Aries-related activities.

RULER: Mars

IMPULSE: Action

RULES: Head and face

Taurus Moon

A Taurus Moon's energy is feminine, semi-fruitful, and earthy. The Moon is exalted—very strong—in Taurus. Taurus is known as the farmer's sign because of its associations with farmland and precipitation that is the typical day-long "soaker" variety. Taurus energy is good to incorporate into your plans when patience, practicality, and perseverance are needed. Be aware, though, that you may also experience stubbornness in this sign.

Things started in Taurus tend to be long lasting and to increase in value. This can be very supportive energy in a marriage election. On the downside, the fixed energy of this sign resists change or the letting go of even the most difficult situations. A divorce following a marriage that occurred during a Taurus Moon may be difficult and costly to end. Things begun now tend to become habitual and hard to alter. If you want to make changes in something you started, it would be better to wait for Gemini. This is a good time to get a loan, but expect the people in charge of money to be cautious and slow to make decisions.

RULER: Venus

IMPULSE: Stability

RULES: Neck, throat, and voice

Gemini Moon

A Gemini Moon's energy is masculine, dry, barren, and airy. People are more changeable than usual and may prefer to follow intellectual pursuits and play mental games rather than apply themselves to practical concerns.

This sign is not favored for agricultural matters, but it is an excellent time to prepare for activities, to run errands, and write letters. Plan to use a Gemini Moon to exchange ideas, meet people, go on vacations that include walking or biking, or be in situations that require versatility and quick thinking on your feet.

RULER: Mercury

IMPULSE: Versatility

RULES: Shoulders, hands, arms, lungs, and nervous system

Cancer Moon

A Cancer Moon's energy is feminine, fruitful, moist, and very strong. Use this sign when you want to grow things—flowers, fruits, vegetables, commodities, stocks, or collections—for example. This sensitive sign stimulates rapport between people. Considered the most fertile of the signs, it is often associated with mothering. You can use this moontime to build personal friendships that support mutual growth.

Cancer is associated with emotions and feelings. Prominent Cancer energy promotes growth, but it can also turn people pouty and prone to withdrawing into their shells.

RULER: The Moon

IMPULSE: Tenacity

RULES: Chest area, breasts, and stomach

Leo Moon

A Leo Moon's energy is masculine, hot, dry, fiery, and barren. Use it whenever you need to put on a show, make a presentation, or entertain colleagues or guests. This is a proud yet playful energy that exudes self-confidence and is often associated with romance.

This is an excellent time for fundraisers and ceremonies or to be straightforward, frank, and honest about something. It is advisable not to put yourself in a position of needing public approval or where you might have to cope with underhandedness, as trouble in these areas can bring out the worst Leo traits. There is a tendency in this sign to become arrogant or self-centered.

RULER: The Sun

IMPULSE: I am

RULES: Heart and upper back

Virgo Moon

A Virgo Moon is feminine, dry, barren, earthy energy. It is favorable for anything that needs painstaking attention—especially those things where exactness rather than innovation is preferred.

Use this sign for activities when you must analyze information or when you must determine the value of something. Virgo is the sign of bargain hunting. It's friendly toward agricultural matters with an emphasis on animals and harvesting vegetables. It is an excellent time to care for animals, especially training them and veterinary work.

This sign is most beneficial when decisions have already been made and now need to be carried out. The inclination here is to see details rather than the bigger picture.

There is a tendency in this sign to overdo. Precautions should be taken to avoid becoming too dull from all work and no play. Build a little relaxation and pleasure into your routine from the beginning.

RULER: Mercury

IMPULSE: Discriminating

RULES: Abdomen and intestines

Libra Moon

A Libra Moon's energy is masculine, semi-fruitful, and airy. This energy will benefit any attempt to bring beauty to a place or thing. Libra is considered good energy for starting things of an intellectual nature. Libra is the sign of partnership and unions, which makes it an excellent time to form partnerships of any kind, to make agreements, and to negotiate. Even though this sign is good for initiating things, it is crucial to work with a partner who will provide incentive and encouragement, however. A Libra Moon accentuates teamwork (particularly teams of two) and artistic work (especially work that involves color). Make use of this sign when you are decorating your home or shopping for better-quality clothing.

RULER: Venus

IMPULSE: Balance

RULES: Lower back, kidneys, and buttocks

Scorpio Moon

The Scorpio Moon is feminine, fruitful, cold, and moist. It is useful when intensity (that sometimes borders on obsession) is needed. Scorpio is considered a very psychic sign. Use this Moon sign when you must back up something you strongly believe in, such as union or employer relations. There is strong group loyalty here, but a Scorpio Moon is also a good time to end connections thoroughly. This is also a good time to conduct research.

The desire nature is so strong here that there is a tendency to manipulate situations to get what one wants or to not see one's responsibility in an act.

RULER: Pluto, Mars (traditional)

IMPULSE: Transformation

RULES: Reproductive organs, genitals, groin, and pelvis

Sagittarius Moon

The Moon's energy is masculine, dry, barren, and fiery in Sagittarius, encouraging flights of imagination and confidence in the flow of life. Sagittarius is the most philosophical sign. Candor and honesty are enhanced when the Moon is here. This is an excellent time to "get things off your chest" and to deal with institutions of higher learning, publishing companies, and the law. It's also a good time for sport and adventure.

Sagittarians are the crusaders of this world. This is a good time to tackle things that need improvement, but don't try to be the diplomat while influenced by this energy. Opinions can run strong, and the tendency to proselytize is increased.

RULER: Jupiter

IMPULSE: Expansion

RULES: Thighs and hips

Capricorn Moon

In Capricorn the Moon's energy is feminine, semi-fruitful, and earthy. Because Cancer and Capricorn are polar opposites, the Moon's energy is thought to be weakened here. This energy encourages the need for structure, discipline, and organization. This is a good time to set goals and plan for the future, tend to family business, and to take care of details requiring patience or a businesslike manner. Institutional activities are favored. This sign should be avoided if you're seeking favors, as those in authority can be insensitive under this influence.

RULER: Saturn

IMPULSE: Ambitious

RULES: Bones, skin, and knees

Aquarius Moon

An Aquarius Moon's energy is masculine, barren, dry, and airy. Activities that are unique, individualistic, concerned with humanitarian issues, society as a whole, and making improvements are favored under this Moon. It is this quality of making improvements that has caused this sign to be associated with inventors and new inventions.

An Aquarius Moon promotes the gathering of social groups for friendly exchanges. People tend to react and speak from an intellectual rather than emotional viewpoint when the Moon is in this sign.

RULER: Uranus and Saturn

IMPULSE: Reformer

RULES: Calves and ankles

Pisces Moon

A Pisces Moon is feminine, fruitful, cool, and moist. This is an excellent time to retreat, meditate, sleep, pray, or make that dreamed-of escape into a fantasy vacation. However, things are not always what they seem to be with the Moon in Pisces. Personal boundaries tend to be fuzzy, and you may not be seeing things clearly. People tend to be idealistic under this sign, which can prevent them from seeing reality.

There is a live-and-let-live philosophy attached to this sign, which in the idealistic world may work well enough, but chaos is frequently the result. That's why this sign is also associated with alcohol and drug abuse, drug trafficking, and counterfeiting. On the lighter side, many musicians and artists are ruled by Pisces. It's only when they move too far away from reality that the dark side of substance abuse, suicide, or crime takes away life.

RULER: Jupiter and Neptune

IMPULSE: Empathetic

RULES: Feet

More About Zodiac Signs

Element (Triplicity)

Each of the zodiac signs is classified as belonging to an element; these are the four basic elements:

Fire Signs

Aries, Sagittarius, and Leo are action-oriented, outgoing, energetic, and spontaneous.

Earth Signs

Taurus, Capricorn, and Virgo are stable, conservative, practical, and oriented to the physical and material realm.

Air Signs

Gemini, Aquarius, and Libra are sociable and critical, and they tend to represent intellectual responses rather than feelings.

Water Signs

Cancer, Scorpio, and Pisces are emotional, receptive, intuitive, and can be very sensitive.

Quality (Quadruplicity)

Each zodiac sign is further classified as being cardinal, mutable, or fixed. There are four signs in each quadruplicity, one sign from each element.

Cardinal Signs

Aries, Cancer, Libra, and Capricorn represent beginnings and newly initiated action. They initiate each new season in the cycle of the year.

Fixed Signs

Taurus, Leo, Scorpio, and Aquarius want to maintain the status quo through stubbornness and persistence; they represent that "between" time. For example, Leo is the month when summer really feels like summer.

Mutable Signs

Pisces, Gemini, Virgo, and Sagittarius adapt to change and tolerate situations. They represent the last month of each season, when things are changing in preparation for the coming season.

Nature and Fertility

In addition to a sign's element and quality, each sign is further classified as either fruitful, semi-fruitful, or barren. This classification is the most important for readers who use the gardening information in the **Moon Sign Book** because the timing of most events depends on the fertility of the sign occupied by the Moon. The water signs of Cancer, Scorpio, and Pisces are the most fruitful. The semi-fruitful signs are the earth signs Taurus and Capricorn, and the air sign Libra. The barren signs correspond to fire-signs Aries, Leo, and Sagittarius; air-signs Gemini and Aquarius; and earth-sign Virgo.

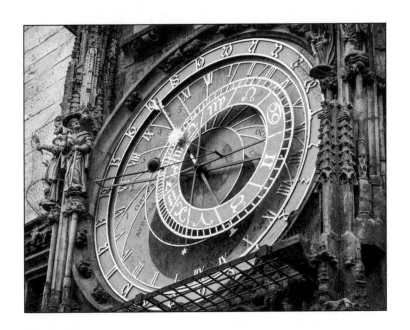

Good Timing

by Sharon Leah

Electional astrology is the art of electing times to begin any undertaking. Say, for example, you want to start a business. That business will experience ups and downs, as well as reach its potential, according to the promise held in the universe at the time the business was started—its birth time. The horoscope (birth chart) set for the date, time, and place that a business starts would indicate the outcome—its potential to succeed.

So, you might ask yourself the question: If the horoscope for a business start can show success or failure, why not begin at a time that is more favorable to the venture? Well, you can.

While no time is perfect, there are better times and better days to undertake specific activities. There are thousands of examples that prove electional astrology is not only practical, but that it can make a difference in our lives. There are rules for electing times to begin various activities—even shopping. You'll find detailed instructions about how to make elections beginning on page 107.

Personalizing Elections

The election rules in this almanac are based upon the planetary positions at the time for which the election is made. They do not depend on any type of birth chart. However, a birth chart based upon the time, date, and birthplace of an event has advantages. No election is effective for every person. For example, you may leave home to begin a trip at the same time as a friend, but each of you will have a different experience according to whether or not your birth chart favors the trip.

Not all elections require a birth chart, but the timing of very important events—business starts, marriages, etc.—would benefit from the additional accuracy a birth chart provides. To order a birth chart for yourself or a planned event, visit our website at www.llewellyn.com.

Some Things to Consider

You've probably experienced good timing in your life. Maybe you were at the right place at the right time to meet a friend whom you hadn't seen in years. Frequently, when something like that happens, it is the result of following an intuitive impulse—that "gut instinct." Consider for a moment that you were actually responding to planetary energies. Electional astrology is a tool that can help you to align with energies, present and future, that are available to us through planetary placements.

Significators

Decide upon the important significators (planet, sign, and house ruling the matter) for which the election is being made. The Moon is the most important significator in any election, so the Moon should always be fortified (strong by sign and making favorable aspects to other planets). The Moon's aspects to other planets are more important than the sign the Moon is in.

Other important considerations are the significators of the Ascendant and Midheaven—the house ruling the election matter and the ruler of the sign on that house cusp. Finally, any planet or sign that has a general rulership over the matter in question should be taken into consideration.

Nature and Fertility

Determine the general nature of the sign that is appropriate for your election. For example, much agricultural work is ruled by the earth signs of Virgo, Capricorn, and Taurus; while the air signs—Gemini, Aquarius, and Libra—rule intellectual pursuits.

One Final Comment

Use common sense. If you must do something, like plant your garden or take an airplane trip on a day that doesn't have the best aspects, proceed anyway, but try to minimize problems. For example, leave early for the airport to avoid being left behind due to delays in the security lanes. When you have no other choice, do the best that you can under the circumstances at the time.

If you want to personalize your elections, please turn to page 107 for more information. If you want a quick and easy answer, you can refer to Llewellyn's Astro Almanac on the following pages.

Llewellyn's Astro Almanac

The Astro Almanac tables, beginning on the next page, can help you find the dates best suited to particular activities. The dates provided are determined from the Moon's sign, phase, and aspects to other planets. Please note that the Astro Almanac does not take personal factors, such as your Sun and Moon sign, into account. The dates are general, and they will apply for everyone. Some activities will not have ideal dates during a particular month.

Activity	January
Animals (Neuter or spay)	9–12
Animals (Sell or buy)	16, 18, 22, 23
Automobile (Buy)	3, 4, 11, 23, 25, 30
Brewing	7, 8
Build (Start foundation)	13
Business (Conducting for self and others)	3, 8, 17, 23
Business (Start new)	21
Can Fruits and Vegetables	7, 8
Can Preserves	7, 8
Concrete (Pour)	1, 2, 29
Construction (Begin new)	3, 5, 9, 18, 23
Consultants (Begin work with)	4, 5, 9, 13, 14, 18, 19, 23, 25
Contracts (Bid on)	14, 18, 19, 23, 25
Cultivate	no ideal dates
Decorating	13, 14, 23–25
Demolition	1, 9, 10, 28, 29
Electronics (Buy)	14, 25
Entertain Guests	2, 22
Floor Covering (Laying new)	1–7, 29–31
Habits (Break)	11
Hair (Cut to increase growth)	16, 17, 20–24, 27
Hair (Cut to decrease growth)	9–12
Harvest (Grain for storage)	1, 2, 29
Harvest (Root crops)	1, 2, 9, 10, 28, 29
Investments (New)	3, 23
Loan (Ask for)	20–22, 27, 28
Massage (Relaxing)	2, 7, 22
Mow Lawn (Decrease growth)	1–11, 29–31
Mow Lawn (Increase growth)	14, 16–27
Mushrooms (Pick)	27–29
Negotiate (Business for the elderly)	9, 18, 23
Prune for Better Fruit	7–10
Prune to Promote Healing	11, 12
Wean Children	9–14
Wood Floors (Installing)	11, 12
Write Letters or Contracts	3, 11, 14, 16, 26, 30

Activity	February
Animals (Neuter or spay)	6–9
Animals (Sell or buy)	15, 20, 21
Automobile (Buy)	8, 20, 27
Brewing	4, 5
Build (Start foundation)	no ideal dates
Business (Conducting for self and others)	2, 6, 16, 22
Business (Start new)	18
Can Fruits and Vegetables	4
Can Preserves	4
Concrete (Pour)	10
Construction (Begin new)	1, 2, 6, 15, 16, 20, 22
Consultants (Begin work with)	1, 3, 6, 7, 10, 11, 15, 20
Contracts (Bid on)	14, 15, 20
Cultivate	10, 11
Decorating	11, 19–21
Demolition	5, 6
Electronics (Buy)	3, 11, 20
Entertain Guests	1, 21
Floor Covering (Laying new)	1–3, 10, 11, 28
Habits (Break)	7–10
Hair (Cut to increase growth)	12, 13, 16–20, 24
Hair (Cut to decrease growth)	5–8
Harvest (Grain for storage)	no ideal dates
Harvest (Root crops)	5–7, 10
Investments (New)	2, 22
Loan (Ask for)	16–19, 24–26
Massage (Relaxing)	10
Mow Lawn (Decrease growth)	1–10, 28
Mow Lawn (Increase growth)	12–26
Mushrooms (Pick)	26–28
Negotiate (Business for the elderly)	1, 5
Prune for Better Fruit	3–6
Prune to Promote Healing	8, 9
Wean Children	6–11
Wood Floors (Installing)	7–9
Write Letters or Contracts	8, 11, 12, 22, 27

Activity	March
Animals (Neuter or spay)	5–8, 12, 13
Animals (Sell or buy)	15, 18, 20
Automobile (Buy)	7, 19, 26
Brewing	3, 4, 12, 30
Build (Start foundation)	no ideal dates
Business (Conducting for self and others)	3, 8, 18, 24
Business (Start new)	18
Can Fruits and Vegetables	3, 4, 12, 13, 30
Can Preserves	3, 4, 30
Concrete (Pour)	9, 10
Construction (Begin new)	1, 6, 8, 15, 18, 20, 24, 29
Consultants (Begin work with)	1, 6, 10, 15, 16, 20, 22, 29, 31
Contracts (Bid on)	15, 16, 20, 22
Cultivate	5, 9, 10
Decorating	19, 20, 21, 28
Demolition	4, 5
Electronics (Buy)	1, 10
Entertain Guests	18, 23
Floor Covering (Laying new)	1, 2, 9, 10, 29
Habits (Break)	7–10
Hair (Cut to increase growth)	16–20, 23
Hair (Cut to decrease growth)	4–8, 12
Harvest (Grain for storage)	4, 5
Harvest (Root crops)	4–6, 9, 10
Investments (New)	3, 24
Loan (Ask for)	16–18, 23–25
Massage (Relaxing)	18, 23
Mow Lawn (Decrease growth)	1–12, 29–31
Mow Lawn (Increase growth)	14–27
Mushrooms (Pick)	27–29
Negotiate (Business for the elderly)	5, 14, 19, 28
Prune for Better Fruit	2–5, 30, 31
Prune to Promote Healing	7, 8
Wean Children	5– 10
Wood Floors (Installing)	7, 8
Write Letters or Contracts	7, 10, 12, 22, 26

Activity	April
Animals (Neuter or spay)	4, 8
Animals (Sell or buy)	12, 17, 23
Automobile (Buy)	3, 16, 17, 22, 23
Brewing	8, 27
Build (Start foundation)	no ideal dates
Business (Conducting for self and others)	1, 6, 17, 22
Business (Start new)	14
Can Fruits and Vegetables	8, 27
Can Preserves	27
Concrete (Pour)	6, 7
Construction (Begin new)	1, 2, 6, 12, 17, 22, 26, 30
Consultants (Begin work with)	2, 5, 7, 11, 12, 17, 22, 26, 30
Contracts (Bid on)	12, 17, 22, 26
Cultivate	1, 2, 6, 7, 10, 11, 29, 30
Decorating	15–17, 24–26
Demolition	1, 2, 10, 11, 28, 29
Electronics (Buy)	5, 17
Entertain Guests	17
Floor Covering (Laying new)	5–7
Habits (Break)	5–7, 10
Hair (Cut to increase growth)	12–16
Hair (Cut to decrease growth)	1–4, 8, 9, 28–30
Harvest (Grain for storage)	1–3, 28–30
Harvest (Root crops)	1, 2, 5–7, 10, 28–30
Investments (New)	1, 22
Loan (Ask for)	13, 14, 20–22
Massage (Relaxing)	6, 17
Mow Lawn (Decrease growth)	1–10, 27–30
Mow Lawn (Increase growth)	12–25
Mushrooms (Pick)	25–27
Negotiate (Business for the elderly)	1, 25, 29
Prune for Better Fruit	1, 2, 26–29
Prune to Promote Healing	3–5, 30
Wean Children	1–7, 29, 30
Wood Floors (Installing)	3–5, 30
Write Letters or Contracts	8, 11, 18, 23

Activity	May
Animals (Neuter or spay)	5, 6, 7
Animals (Sell or buy)	14, 18, 24
Automobile (Buy)	1, 2, 13, 20, 28
Brewing	5, 6
Build (Start foundation)	no ideal dates
Business (Conducting for self and others)	1, 6, 17, 21, 30
Business (Start new)	12, 19
Can Fruits and Vegetables	5, 6
Can Preserves	10
Concrete (Pour)	3, 4, 10, 30, 31
Construction (Begin new)	1, 9, 14, 17, 21, 28, 30
Consultants (Begin work with)	2, 4, 7, 9, 13, 14, 18, 23, 24, 28, 31
Contracts (Bid on)	13, 14, 18, 23, 24
Cultivate	4, 8, 9, 26, 27
Decorating	12–14, 21–23
Demolition	7, 8, 26
Electronics (Buy)	13, 23, 31
Entertain Guests	12, 18, 23
Floor Covering (Laying new)	3, 4, 10, 30, 31
Habits (Break)	4, 7–9
Hair (Cut to increase growth)	12, 13, 17
Hair (Cut to decrease growth)	1, 5, 6, 9–11, 27–29
Harvest (Grain for storage)	2, 3, 27, 30, 31
Harvest (Root crops)	3, 4, 7–9, 26, 27, 30, 31
Investments (New)	1, 21, 30
Loan (Ask for)	12, 17–19
Massage (Relaxing)	18, 23
Mow Lawn (Decrease growth)	1–10, 27–31
Mow Lawn (Increase growth)	12–25
Mushrooms (Pick)	25–27
Negotiate (Business for the elderly)	8, 13, 22, 26
Prune for Better Fruit	26, 27
Prune to Promote Healing	1, 2, 28, 29
Wean Children	1–4, 26–31
Wood Floors (Installing)	1, 2, 28, 29
Write Letters or Contracts	1, 13, 15, 20, 28

Activity	June
Animals (Neuter or spay)	2, 3
Animals (Sell or buy)	11, 21
Automobile (Buy)	9, 10, 16, 25
Brewing	2, 3, 29, 30
Build (Start foundation)	no ideal dates
Business (Conducting for self and others)	4, 15, 20, 29
Business (Start new)	16, 24
Can Fruits and Vegetables	2, 29, 30
Can Preserves	6, 7
Concrete (Pour)	6, 7, 27
Construction (Begin new)	4, 6, 11, 15, 20, 24
Consultants (Begin work with)	1, 5, 6, 10, 11, 15, 19, 20, 24, 27, 28
Contracts (Bid on)	11, 15, 19, 20, 24
Cultivate	4, 5, 9
Decorating	10, 18–20
Demolition	3–5
Electronics (Buy)	10, 19, 27
Entertain Guests	6, 12
Floor Covering (Laying new)	6–9, 26–28
Habits (Break)	3, 4, 9
Hair (Cut to increase growth)	10, 13, 22–24
Hair (Cut to decrease growth)	2, 6–9, 25, 29
Harvest (Grain for storage)	26, 27, 30
Harvest (Root crops)	3–5, 8, 9, 26, 27
Investments (New)	20, 29
Loan (Ask for)	13–15
Massage (Relaxing)	1, 6, 12
Mow Lawn (Decrease growth)	1–9, 25–30
Mow Lawn (Increase growth)	11–23
Mushrooms (Pick)	23–25
Negotiate (Business for the elderly)	4, 9
Prune for Better Fruit	no ideal dates
Prune to Promote Healing	24–26
Wean Children	1, 23–27
Wood Floors (Installing)	24–26
Write Letters or Contracts	2, 10, 12, 16, 25

Activity	July
Animals (Neuter or spay)	no ideal dates
Animals (Sell or buy)	21
Automobile (Buy)	6, 8, 13, 14, 22
Brewing	26, 27
Build (Start foundation)	no ideal dates
Business (Conducting for self and others)	4, 14, 19, 28
Business (Start new)	13, 21
Can Fruits and Vegetables	9, 26, 27
Can Preserves	4, 5, 9, 31
Concrete (Pour)	4, 5, 24, 25, 31
Construction (Begin new)	3, 4, 8, 14, 21, 28, 30
Consultants (Begin work with)	2, 3, 8, 13, 17, 18, 21, 25, 28, 30
Contracts (Bid on)	12, 13, 17, 18, 21
Cultivate	2, 6, 7
Decorating	15–17
Demolition	1, 2, 28, 29
Electronics (Buy)	8
Entertain Guests	12, 17, 31
Floor Covering (Laying new)	3–7, 24, 25, 31
Habits (Break)	2, 3, 7, 8
Hair (Cut to increase growth)	10, 19, 20–22
Hair (Cut to decrease growth)	3–7, 26, 27, 30, 31
Harvest (Grain for storage)	1, 24, 25, 28–30
Harvest (Root crops)	1, 2, 6, 7, 24, 25, 28–30
Investments (New)	19, 28
Loan (Ask for)	10–13
Massage (Relaxing)	12, 17, 37
Mow Lawn (Decrease growth)	1–8, 24–31
Mow Lawn (Increase growth)	12–22
Mushrooms (Pick)	22–24
Negotiate (Business for the elderly)	1, 6, 20
Prune for Better Fruit	no ideal dates
Prune to Promote Healing	no ideal dates
Wean Children	20–25
Wood Floors (Installing)	no ideal dates
Write Letters or Contracts	8, 9, 14, 22, 27

Activity	August
Animals (Neuter or spay)	no ideal dates
Animals (Sell or buy)	13, 17, 20
Automobile (Buy)	3, 10, 18, 19, 30
Brewing	5, 6, 23, 24
Build (Start foundation)	no ideal dates
Business (Conducting for self and others)	3, 13, 17, 27
Business (Start new)	no ideal dates
Can Fruits and Vegetables	5, 6, 23
Can Preserves	1, 5, 6, 27, 28
Concrete (Pour)	1, 7, 27, 28
Construction (Begin new)	3, 4, 13, 17, 26, 27, 31
Consultants (Begin work with)	3, 4, 9, 13, 14, 17, 18, 22, 26, 29, 31
Contracts (Bid on)	9, 13, 14, 17, 18, 22
Cultivate	2–4, 7, 30, 31
Decorating	11–13, 20–22
Demolition	7, 8, 24–26
Electronics (Buy)	3
Entertain Guests	6, 31
Floor Covering (Laying new)	1–8, 27, 28–31
Habits (Break)	3, 4, 7
Hair (Cut to increase growth)	16–19
Hair (Cut to decrease growth)	1–3, 7, 23, 27–31
Harvest (Grain for storage)	24, 25, 29
Harvest (Root crops)	2–4, 7, 24–26, 29–31
Investments (New)	17, 27
Loan (Ask for)	8, 9
Massage (Relaxing)	6, 20
Mow Lawn (Decrease growth)	1–7, 23–31
Mow Lawn (Increase growth)	9–21
Mushrooms (Pick)	21–23
Negotiate (Business for the elderly)	12, 16
Prune for Better Fruit	no ideal dates
Prune to Promote Healing	no ideal dates
Wean Children	16–22
Wood Floors (Installing)	no ideal dates
Write Letters or Contracts	5, 9, 10, 19, 23

Activity	September
Animals (Neuter or spay)	no ideal dates
Animals (Sell or buy)	9, 19
Automobile (Buy)	6, 15, 26, 28
Brewing	1, 2, 29, 30
Build (Start foundation)	no ideal dates
Business (Conducting for self and others)	1, 11, 16, 26
Business (Start new)	no ideal dates
Can Fruits and Vegetables	1, 2, 29, 30
Can Preserves	1, 2, 24, 25, 29, 30
Concrete (Pour)	4, 5, 24, 25
Construction (Begin new)	1, 9, 13, 16, 22, 26, 27
Consultants (Begin work with)	4, 8, 9, 13, 18, 22, 27, 28
Contracts (Bid on)	8, 9, 13, 18, 20
Cultivate	4, 5
Decorating	8–10, 16–18
Demolition	4, 21, 22
Electronics (Buy)	8, 18, 28
Entertain Guests	5, 9, 30
Floor Covering (Laying new)	3–6, 23–27
Habits (Break)	4
Hair (Cut to increase growth)	12–15, 19
Hair (Cut to decrease growth)	3. 23–27.30
Harvest (Grain for storage)	21, 22, 25–27
Harvest (Root crops)	4, 5, 21, 22, 26, 27
Investments (New)	16, 26
Loan (Ask for)	no ideal dates
Massage (Relaxing)	5, 10, 30
Mow Lawn (Decrease growth)	1–5, 21–30
Mow Lawn (Increase growth)	7–19
Mushrooms (Pick)	19–21
Negotiate (Business for the elderly)	8, 12, 21, 26
Prune for Better Fruit	no ideal dates
Prune to Promote Healing	no ideal dates
Wean Children	12–18
Wood Floors (Installing)	no ideal dates
Write Letters or Contracts	2, 6, 8, 19, 29

Activity	October
Animals (Neuter or spay)	no ideal dates
Animals (Sell or buy)	11, 14
Automobile (Buy)	4, 12, 23, 24, 31
Brewing	26, 27
Build (Start foundation)	no ideal dates
Business (Conducting for self and others)	1, 10, 15, 25, 31
Business (Start new)	no ideal dates
Can Fruits and Vegetables	26, 27
Can Preserves	21, 22, 26, 27
Concrete (Pour)	1, 2, 21, 22, 29
Construction (Begin new)	1, 6, 10, 11, 15, 20, 25, 31
Consultants (Begin work with)	2, 6, 10, 11, 14, 15, 20, 24, 25, 29
Contracts (Bid on)	10, 11, 14, 15
Cultivate	1, 2, 28-30
Decorating	6, 7, 14, 15
Demolition	1, 2, 28, 29
Electronics (Buy)	6, 14, 24
Entertain Guests	5, 30
Floor Covering (Laying new)	1–6, 21–25, 28–31
Habits (Break)	1, 29
Hair (Cut to increase growth)	9–12, 16, 17
Hair (Cut to decrease growth)	21–24 ,28
Harvest (Grain for storage)	23–25, 28
Harvest (Root crops)	1, 2, 20, 23–25, 28–30
Investments (New)	15, 25
Loan (Ask for)	no ideal dates
Massage (Relaxing)	14, 30
Mow Lawn (Decrease growth)	1–5, 21–31
Mow Lawn (Increase growth)	7–19
Mushrooms (Pick)	19–21
Negotiate (Business for the elderly)	5, 9, 18, 23
Prune for Better Fruit	no ideal dates
Prune to Promote Healing	no ideal dates
Wean Children	10–15
Wood Floors (Installing)	no ideal dates
Write Letters or Contracts	4, 6, 16, 26, 31

Activity	November
Animals (Neuter or spay)	no ideal dates
Animals (Sell or buy)	12, 16
Automobile (Buy)	8, 20, 27
Brewing	22, 23
Build (Start foundation)	10
Business (Conducting for self and others)	9, 13, 24, 29
Business (Start new)	18
Can Fruits and Vegetables	4, 22, 23
Can Preserves	4, 22, 23
Concrete (Pour)	25, 26
Construction (Begin new)	3, 7, 9, 16, 21, 24, 29, 30
Consultants (Begin work with)	3, 7, 8, 11, 13, 16, 21, 24, 29, 30
Contracts (Bid on)	7, 8, 11, 13, 16
Cultivate	no ideal dates
Decorating	10, 11
Demolition	24, 25
Electronics (Buy)	3, 29
Entertain Guests	3
Floor Covering (Laying new)	1–3, 20, 21, 24–30
Habits (Break)	no ideal dates
Hair (Cut to increase growth)	6–8, 13, 16–18
Hair (Cut to decrease growth)	20, 24
Harvest (Grain for storage)	20, 21, 24–26
Harvest (Root crops)	19–21, 24–26
Investments (New)	13, 24
Loan (Ask for)	16–18
Massage (Relaxing)	3, 17
Mow Lawn (Decrease growth)	1–3, 20–30
Mow Lawn (Increase growth)	5, 6, 8–18
Mushrooms (Pick)	18–20
Negotiate (Business for the elderly)	6, 29
Prune for Better Fruit	4
Prune to Promote Healing	no ideal dates
Wean Children	6–11
Wood Floors (Installing)	no ideal dates
Write Letters or Contracts	3, 8, 13, 22

Activity	December
Animals (Neuter or spay)	31
Animals (Sell or buy)	5, 11, 13
Automobile (Buy)	6, 17, 25
Brewing	2, 20, 21, 29, 30
Build (Start foundation)	7
Business (Conducting for self and others)	8, 13, 24, 29
Business (Start new)	16
Can Fruits and Vegetables	2, 20, 21, 29, 30
Can Preserves	2, 20, 21, 29, 30
Concrete (Pour)	22, 23
Construction (Begin new)	5, 8, 13, 19, 24, 28
Consultants (Begin work with)	4, 5, 8, 9, 13, 14, 19, 25, 28, 30
Contracts (Bid on)	5, 8, 9, 11, 13, 14
Cultivate	no ideal dates
Decorating	7–9, 16–18
Demolition	3, 4, 21–24, 30, 31
Electronics (Buy)	8
Entertain Guests	26
Floor Covering (Laying new)	22–28
Habits (Break)	no ideal dates
Hair (Cut to increase growth)	4–6, 10, 14–18
Hair (Cut to decrease growth)	3, 21, 30, 31
Harvest (Grain for storage)	21–24
Harvest (Root crops)	21–23, 30, 31
Investments (New)	13, 24
Loan (Ask for)	14–16
Massage (Relaxing)	16
Mow Lawn (Decrease growth)	1, 2, 19–31
Mow Lawn (Increase growth)	5–17
Mushrooms (Pick)	17–19
Negotiate (Business for the elderly)	3, 12, 17, 31
Prune for Better Fruit	1–3, 29–31
Prune to Promote Healing	no ideal dates
Wean Children	3–9, 31
Wood Floors (Installing)	no ideal dates
Write Letters or Contracts	4, 6, 10, 20, 25

Choose the Best Time for Your Activities

When rules for elections refer to "favorable" and "unfavorable" aspects to your Sun or other planets, please refer to the Favorable and Unfavorable Days Tables and Lunar Aspectarian for more information. You'll find instructions beginning on page 129 and the tables beginning on page 136.

The material in this section came from several sources including: *The New A to Z Horoscope Maker and Delineator* by Llewellyn George (Llewellyn, 1999), *Moon Sign Book* (Llewellyn, 1945), and *Electional Astrology* by Vivian Robson (Slingshot Publishing, 2000). Robson's book was originally published in 1937.

Advertise (Internet)

The Moon should be conjunct, sextile, or trine Mercury or Uranus and in the sign of Gemini, Capricorn, or Aquarius.

Advertise (Print)

Write ads on a day favorable to your Sun The Moon should be conjunct, sextile, or trine Mercury or Venus. Avoid hard aspects to Mars and Saturn. Ad campaigns produce the best results when the Moon is well aspected in Gemini (to enhance communication) or Capricorn (to build business).

Animals

Take home new pets when the day is favorable to your Sun, or when the Moon is trine, sextile, or conjunct Mercury, Jupiter or Venus, or in the sign of Virgo or Pisces. However, avoid days when the Moon is either square or opposing the Sun, Mars, Saturn, Uranus, Neptune, or Pluto. When selecting a pet, have the Moon well aspected by the planet that rules the animal. Cats are ruled by the Sun, dogs by Mercury, birds by Venus, horses by Jupiter, and fish by Neptune. Buy large animals when the Moon is in Sagittarius or Pisces and making favorable aspects to Jupiter or Mercury. Buy animals smaller than sheep when the Moon is in Virgo with favorable aspects to Mercury or Venus.

Animals (Breed)

Animals are easiest to handle when the Moon is in Taurus, Cancer, Libra, or Pisces, but try to avoid the Full Moon. To encourage healthy births, animals should be mated so births occur when the Moon is increasing in Taurus, Cancer, Pisces, or Libra. Those born during a semi-fruitful sign (Taurus and Capricorn) will produce leaner meat. Libra yields beautiful animals for showing and racing.

Animals (Declaw)

Declaw cats for medical purposes in the dark of the Moon. Avoid the week before and after the Full Moon and the sign of Pisces.

Animals (Neuter or Spay)

Have livestock and pets neutered or spayed when the Moon is in Sagittarius, Capricorn, or Pisces, after it has passed through Scorpio, the sign that rules reproductive organs. Avoid the week before and after the Full Moon.

Animals (Sell or Buy)

In either buying or selling, it is important to keep the Moon and Mercury free from any aspect to Mars. Aspects to Mars will create discord and increase the likelihood of wrangling over price and quality. The Moon should be passing from the first quarter to full and sextile or trine Venus or Jupiter. When buying racehorses, let the Moon be in an air sign. The Moon should be in air signs when you buy birds. If the birds are to be pets, let the Moon be in good aspect to Venus.

Animals (Train)

Train pets when the Moon is in Virgo or trine to Mercury.

Animals (Train Dogs to Hunt)

Let the Moon be in Aries in conjunction with Mars, which makes them courageous and quick to learn. But let Jupiter also be in aspect to preserve them from danger in hunting.

Automobiles

When buying an automobile, select a time when the Moon is conjunct, sextile, or trine to Mercury, Saturn, or Uranus and in the sign of Gemini or Capricorn. Avoid times when Mercury is in retrograde motion.

Baking Cakes

Your cakes will have a lighter texture if you see that the Moon is in Gemini, Libra, or Aquarius and in good aspect to Venus or Mercury. If you are decorating a cake or confections are being made, have the Moon placed in Libra.

Beauty Treatments (Massage, etc.)

See that the Moon is in Taurus, Cancer, Leo, Libra, or Aquarius and in favorable aspect to Venus. In the case of plastic surgery, aspects to Mars should be avoided, and the Moon should not be in the sign ruling the part to be operated on.

Borrow (Money or Goods)

See that the Moon is not placed between 15 degrees Libra and 15 degrees Scorpio. Let the Moon be waning and in Leo, Scorpio (16 to 30 degrees), Sagittarius, or Pisces. Venus should be in good aspect to the Moon, and the Moon should not be square, opposing, or conjunct either Saturn or Mars.

Brewing

Start brewing during the third or fourth quarter, when the Moon is in Cancer, Scorpio, or Pisces.

Build (Start Foundation)

Turning the first sod for the foundation marks the beginning of the building. For best results, excavate the site when the Moon is in the first quarter of a fixed sign and making favorable aspects to Saturn.

Business (Start New)

When starting a business, have the Moon be in Taurus, Virgo, or Capricorn and increasing. The Moon should be sextile or trine Jupiter or Saturn, but avoid oppositions or squares. The planet ruling the business should be well aspected too.

Buy Goods

Buy during the third quarter, when the Moon is in Taurus for quality or in a mutable sign (Gemini, Sagittarius, Virgo, or Pisces) for savings. Good aspects to Venus or the Sun are desirable. If you are buying for yourself, it is good if the day is favorable for your Sun sign. You may also apply rules for buying specific items.

Canning

Can fruits and vegetables when the Moon is in either the third or fourth quarter and in the water sign Cancer or Pisces. Preserves and jellies use the same quarters and the signs Cancer, Pisces, or Taurus.

Clothing

Buy clothing on a day that is favorable for your Sun sign and when Venus or Mercury is well aspected. Avoid aspects to Mars and Saturn. Buy your clothing when the Moon is in Taurus if you want to remain satisfied. Do not buy clothing or jewelry when the Moon is in Scorpio or Aries. See that the Moon is sextile or trine the Sun during the first or second quarters.

Collections

Try to make collections on days when your natal Sun is well aspected. Avoid days when the Moon is opposing or square Mars or Saturn. If possible, the Moon should be in a cardinal sign (Aries, Cancer, Libra, or Capricorn). It is more difficult to collect when the Moon is in Taurus or Scorpio.

Concrete

Pour concrete when the Moon is in the third quarter of the fixed sign Taurus, Leo, or Aquarius.

Construction (Begin New)

The Moon should be sextile or trine Jupiter. According to Hermes, no building should be begun when the Moon is in Scorpio or Pisces. The best time to begin building is when the Moon is in Aquarius.

Consultants (Work with)

The Moon should be conjunct, sextile, or trine Mercury or Jupiter.

Contracts (Bid On)

The Moon should be in Gemini or Capricorn and either the Moon or Mercury should be conjunct, sextile, or trine Jupiter.

Copyrights/Patents

The Moon should be conjunct, trine, or sextile either Mercury or Jupiter.

Coronations and Installations

Let the Moon be in Leo and in favorable aspect to Venus, Jupiter, or Mercury. The Moon should be applying to these planets.

Cultivate

Cultivate when the Moon is in a barren sign and waning, ideally the fourth quarter in Aries, Gemini, Leo, Virgo, or Aquarius. The third quarter in the sign of Sagittarius will also work.

Cut Timber

Timber cut during the waning Moon does not become worm-eaten; it will season well and not warp, decay, or snap during burning. Cut when the Moon is in Taurus, Gemini, Virgo, or Capricorn—especially in August. Avoid the water signs. Look for favorable aspects to Mars.

Decorating or Home Repairs

Have the Moon waxing and in the sign of Libra, Gemini, or Aquarius. Avoid squares or oppositions to either Mars or Saturn. Venus in good aspect to Mars or Saturn is beneficial.

Demolition

Let the waning Moon be in Leo, Sagittarius, or Aries.

Dental and Dentists

Visit the dentist when the Moon is in Virgo, or pick a day marked favorable for your Sun sign. Mars should be marked sextile, conjunct, or trine; avoid squares or oppositions to Saturn, Uranus, or Jupiter.

Teeth are best removed when the Moon is in Gemini, Virgo, Sagittarius, or Pisces and during the first or second quarter. Avoid the Full Moon! The day should be favorable for your lunar cycle, and Mars and Saturn should be marked conjunct, trine, or sextile. Fillings should be done in the third or fourth quarters in the sign of Taurus, Leo, Scorpio, or Pisces. The same applies for dentures.

Dressmaking

William Lilly wrote in 1676: "Make no new clothes, or first put them on when the Moon is in Scorpio or afflicted by Mars, for they will be apt to be torn and quickly worn out." Design, repair, and sew clothes in the first and second quarters of Taurus, Leo, or Libra on a day marked favorable for your Sun sign. Venus, Jupiter, and Mercury should be favorably aspected, but avoid hard aspects to Mars or Saturn.

Egg-Setting (see p. 161)

Eggs should be set so chicks will hatch during fruitful signs. To set eggs, subtract the number of days given for incubation or gestation from the fruitful dates. Chickens incubate in twenty-one days, turkeys and geese in twenty-eight days.

A freshly laid egg loses quality rapidly if it is not handled properly. Use plenty of clean litter in the nests to reduce the number of dirty or cracked eggs. Gather eggs daily in mild weather and at least two times daily in hot or cold weather. The eggs should be placed in a cooler immediately after gathering and stored at 50 to 55°F. Do not store eggs with foods or products that give off pungent odors since eggs may absorb the odors.

Eggs saved for hatching purposes should not be washed. Only clean and slightly soiled eggs should be saved for hatching. Dirty eggs should not be incubated. Eggs should be stored in a cool place with the large ends up. It is not advisable to store the eggs longer than one week before setting them in an incubator.

Electricity and Gas (Install)

The Moon should be in a fire sign, and there should be no squares, oppositions, or conjunctions with Uranus (ruler of electricity), Neptune (ruler of gas), Saturn, or Mars. Hard aspects to Mars can cause fires.

Electronics (Buying)

Choose a day when the Moon is in an air sign (Gemini, Libra, Aquarius) and well aspected by Mercury and/or Uranus when buying electronics.

Electronics (Repair)

The Moon should be sextile or trine Mars or Uranus and in a fixed sign (Taurus, Leo, Scorpio, Aquarius).

Entertain Friends

Let the Moon be in Leo or Libra and making good aspects to Venus. Avoid squares or oppositions to either Mars or Saturn by the Moon or Venus.

Eyes and Eyeglasses

Have your eyes tested and glasses fitted on a day marked favorable for your Sun sign, and on a day that falls during your favorable lunar cycle. Mars should not be in aspect with the Moon. The same applies for any treatment of the eyes, which should also be started during the Moon's first or second quarter.

Fence Posts

Set posts when the Moon is in the third or fourth quarter of the fixed sign Taurus or Leo.

Fertilize and Compost

Fertilize when the Moon is in a fruitful sign (Cancer, Scorpio, Pisces). Organic fertilizers are best when the Moon is waning. Use chemical fertilizers when the Moon is waxing. Start compost when the Moon is in the fourth quarter in a water sign.

Find Hidden Treasure

Let the Moon be in good aspect to Jupiter or Venus. If you erect a horoscope for this election, place the Moon in the Fourth House.

Find Lost Articles

Search for lost articles during the first quarter and when your Sun sign is marked favorable. Also check to see that the planet ruling the lost item is trine, sextile, or conjunct the Moon. The Moon rules household utensils; Mercury rules letters and books; and Venus rules clothing, jewelry, and money.

Fishing

During the summer months, the best time of the day to fish is from sunrise to three hours after and from two hours before sunset until one hour after. Fish do not bite in cooler months until the air is warm, from noon to three pm. Warm, cloudy days are good. The most favorable winds are from the south and southwest.

Easterly winds are unfavorable. The best days of the month for fishing are when the Moon changes quarters, especially if the change occurs on a day when the Moon is in a water sign (Cancer, Scorpio, Pisces). The best period in any month is the day after the Full Moon.

Friendship

The need for friendship is greater when the Moon is in Aquarius or when Uranus aspects the Moon. Friendship prospers when Venus or Uranus is trine, sextile, or conjunct the Moon. The Moon in Gemini facilitates the chance meeting of acquaintances and friends.

Grafting or Budding

Grafting is the process of introducing new varieties of fruit on less desirable trees. For this process you should use the increasing phase of the Moon in fruitful signs such as Cancer, Scorpio, or Pisces. Capricorn may be used, too. Cut your grafts while trees are dormant, from December to March. Keep them in a cool, dark place, not too dry or too damp. Do the grafting before the sap starts to flow and while the Moon is waxing, preferably while it is

in Cancer, Scorpio, or Pisces. The type of plant should determine both cutting and planting times.

Habit (Breaking)

To end an undesirable habit, and this applies to ending everything from a bad relationship to smoking, start on a day when the Moon is in the fourth quarter and in the barren sign of Gemini, Leo, or Aquarius. Aries, Virgo, and Capricorn may be suitable as well, depending on the habit you want to be rid of. Make sure that your lunar cycle is favorable. Avoid lunar aspects to Mars or Jupiter. However, favorable aspects to Pluto are helpful.

Haircuts

Cut hair when the Moon is in Gemini, Sagittarius, Pisces, Taurus, or Capricorn, but not in Virgo. Look for favorable aspects to Venus. For faster growth, cut hair when the Moon is increasing in Cancer or Pisces. To make hair grow thicker, cut when the Moon is full in the signs of Taurus, Cancer, or Leo. If you want your hair to grow more slowly, have the Moon be decreasing in Aries, Gemini, or Virgo, and have the Moon square or opposing Saturn.

Permanents, straightening, and hair coloring will take well if the Moon is in Taurus or Leo and trine or sextile Venus. Avoid hair treatments if Mars is marked as square or in opposition, especially if heat is to be used. For permanents, a trine to Jupiter is helpful. The Moon also should be in the first quarter. Check the lunar cycle for a favorable day in relation to your Sun sign.

Harvest Crops

Harvest root crops when the Moon is in a dry sign (Aries, Leo, Sagittarius, Gemini, Aquarius) and waning. Harvest grain for storage just after the Full Moon, avoiding Cancer, Scorpio, or Pisces. Harvest in the third and fourth quarters in dry signs. Dry crops in the third quarter in fire signs.

Health

A diagnosis is more likely to be successful when the Moon is in Aries, Cancer, Libra, or Capricorn and less so when in Gemini, Sagittarius, Pisces, or Virgo. Begin a recuperation program or enter a hospital when the Moon is in a cardinal or fixed sign and the day is favorable to your Sun sign. For surgery, see "Surgical Procedures." Buy medicines when the Moon is in Virgo or Scorpio.

Home (Buy New)

If you desire a permanent home, buy when the New Moon is in a fixed sign—Taurus or Leo, for example. Each sign will affect your decision in a different way. A house bought when the Moon is in Taurus is likely to be more practical and have a country look—right down to the split-rail fence. A house purchased when the Moon is in Leo will more likely be a real showplace.

If you're buying for speculation and a quick turnover, be certain that the Moon is in a cardinal sign (Aries, Cancer, Libra, Capricorn). Avoid buying when the Moon is in a fixed sign (Leo, Scorpio, Aquarius, Taurus).

Home (Make Repairs)

In all repairs, avoid squares, oppositions, or conjunctions to the planet ruling the place or thing to be repaired. For example, bathrooms are ruled by Scorpio and Cancer. You would not want to start a project in those rooms when the Moon or Pluto is receiving hard aspects. The front entrance, hall, dining room, and porch are ruled by the Sun So you would want to avoid times when Saturn or Mars are square, opposing, or conjunct the Sun Also, let the Moon be waxing.

Home (Sell)

Make a strong effort to list your property for sale when the Sun is marked favorable in your sign and in good aspect to Jupiter. Avoid adverse aspects to as many planets as possible.

Home Furnishings (Buy New)

Saturn days (Saturday) are good for buying, and Jupiter days (Thursday) are good for selling. Items bought on days when Saturn is well aspected tend to wear longer and purchases tend to be more conservative.

Job (Start New)

Jupiter and Venus should be sextile, trine, or conjunct the Moon. A day when your Sun is receiving favorable aspects is preferred.

Legal Matters

Good Moon-Jupiter aspects improve the outcome in legal decisions. To gain damages through a lawsuit, begin the process during the increasing Moon. To avoid paying damages, a court date during the decreasing Moon is desirable. Good Moon-Sun aspects strengthen your chance of success. A well-aspected Moon in Cancer or Leo, making good aspects to the Sun, brings the best results in custody cases. In divorce cases, a favorable Moon-Venus aspect is best.

Loan (Ask For)

A first and second quarter phase favors the lender, the third and fourth quarters favor the borrower. Good aspects of Jupiter and Venus to the Moon are favorable to both, as is having the Moon in Leo or Taurus.

Machinery, Appliances, or Tools (Buy)

Tools, machinery, and other implements should be bought on days when your lunar cycle is favorable and when Mars and Uranus are trine, sextile, or conjunct the Moon. Any quarter of the Moon is suitable. When buying gas or electrical appliances, the Moon should be in Aquarius.

Make a Will

Let the Moon be in a fixed sign (Taurus, Leo, Scorpio, or Aquarius) to ensure permanence. If the Moon is in a cardinal sign (Aries, Cancer, Libra, or Capricorn), the will could be altered. Let the Moon be waxing—increasing in light—and in good aspect to Saturn, Venus, or Mercury. In case the will is made in an emergency during illness and the Moon is slow in motion, void-of-course, combust, or under the Sun's beams, the testator will die and the will remain unaltered. There is some danger that it will be lost or stolen, however.

Marriage

The best time for marriage to take place is when the Moon is increasing, but not yet full. Good signs for the Moon to be in are Taurus, Cancer, Leo, or Libra.

The Moon in Taurus produces the most steadfast marriages, but if the partners later want to separate, they may have a difficult time. Make sure that the Moon is well aspected, especially to Venus or Jupiter. Avoid aspects to Mars, Uranus, or Pluto and the signs Aries, Gemini, Virgo, Scorpio, or Aquarius.

The values of the signs are as follows:

- Aries is not favored for marriage
- Taurus from 0 to 19 degrees is good, the remaining degrees are less favorable
- Cancer is unfavorable unless you are marrying a widow
- Leo is favored, but it may cause one party to deceive the other as to his or her money or possessions
- Virgo is not favored except when marrying a widow
- Libra is good for engagements but not for marriage
- Scorpio from 0 to 15 degrees is good, but the last 15 degrees are entirely unfortunate. The woman may be fickle, envious, and quarrelsome
- Sagittarius is neutral
- Capricorn, from 0 to 10 degrees, is difficult for marriage;

however, the remaining degrees are favorable, especially when marrying a widow

- Aquarius is not favored
- Pisces is favored, although marriage under this sign can incline a woman to chatter a lot

These effects are strongest when the Moon is in the sign. If the Moon and Venus are in a cardinal sign, happiness between the couple may not continue long.

On no account should the Moon apply to Saturn or Mars, even by good aspect.

Medical Treatment for the Eyes

Let the Moon be increasing in light and motion and making favorable aspects to Venus or Jupiter and be unaspected by Mars. Keep the Moon out of Taurus, Capricorn, or Virgo. If an aspect between the Moon and Mars is unavoidable, let it be separating.

Medical Treatment for the Head

If possible, have Mars and Saturn free of hard aspects. Let the Moon be in Aries or Taurus, decreasing in light, in conjunction or aspect with Venus or Jupiter and free of hard aspects. The Sun should not be in any aspect to the Moon.

Medical Treatment for the Nose

Let the Moon be in Cancer, Leo, or Virgo and not aspecting Mars or Saturn and also not in conjunction with a retrograde or weak planet.

Mining

Saturn rules mining. Begin work when Saturn is marked conjunct, trine, or sextile. Mine for gold when the Sun is marked conjunct, trine, or sextile. Mercury rules quicksilver, Venus rules copper, Jupiter rules tin, Saturn rules lead and coal, Uranus rules radioactive elements, Neptune rules oil, the Moon rules water. Mine for these items when the ruling planet is marked conjunct, trine, or sextile.

Move to New Home

If you have a choice, and sometimes you don't, make sure that Mars is not aspecting the Moon. Move on a day favorable to your Sun sign or when the Moon is conjunct, sextile, or trine the Sun

Mow Lawn

Mow in the first and second quarters (waxing phase) to increase growth and lushness, and in the third and fourth quarters (waning phase) to decrease growth.

Negotiate

When you are choosing a time to negotiate, consider what the meeting is about and what you want to have happen. If it is agreement or compromise between two parties that you desire, have the Moon be in the sign of Libra. When you are making contracts, it is best to have the Moon in the same element. For example, if your concern is communication, then elect a time when the Moon is in an air sign. If, on the other hand, your concern is about possessions, an earth sign would be more appropriate. Fixed signs are unfavorable, with the exception of Leo; so are cardinal signs, except for Capricorn. If you are negotiating the end of something, use the rules that apply to ending habits.

Occupational Training

When you begin training, see that your lunar cycle is favorable that day and that the planet ruling your occupation is marked conjunct or trine.

Paint

Paint buildings during the waning Libra or Aquarius Moon. If the weather is hot, paint when the Moon is in Taurus. If the weather is cold, paint when the Moon is in Leo. Schedule the painting to start in the fourth quarter as the wood is drier and paint will penetrate wood better. Avoid painting around the New Moon, though, as the wood is likely to be damp, making the paint subject to scalding when hot weather hits it. If the temperature is below 70°F, it is not advisable to paint while the Moon is in Cancer, Scorpio, or Pisces as the paint is apt to creep, check, or run.

Party (Host or Attend)

A party timed so the Moon is in Gemini, Leo, Libra, or Sagittarius, with good aspects to Venus and Jupiter, will be fun and well attended. There should be no aspects between the Moon and Mars or Saturn.

Pawn

Do not pawn any article when Jupiter is receiving a square or opposition from Saturn or Mars or when Jupiter is within 17 degrees of the Sun, for you will have little chance to redeem the items.

Pick Mushrooms

Mushrooms, one of the most promising traditional medicines in the world, should be gathered at the Full Moon.

Plant

Root crops, like carrots and potatoes, are best if planted in the sign Taurus or Capricorn. Beans, peas, tomatoes, peppers, and other fruit-bearing plants are best if planted in a sign that supports seed growth. Leaf plants, like lettuce, broccoli, or cauliflower, are best planted when the Moon is in a water sign.

It is recommended that you transplant during a decreasing Moon, when forces are streaming into the lower part of the plant. This helps root growth.

Promotion (Ask For)

Choose a day favorable to your Sun sign. Mercury should be marked conjunct, trine, or sextile. Avoid days when Mars or Saturn is aspected.

Prune

Prune during the third and fourth quarter of a Scorpio Moon to retard growth and to promote better fruit. Prune when the Moon is in cardinal Capricorn to promote healing.

Reconcile with People

If the reconciliation is with a woman, let Venus be strong and well aspected. If elders or superiors are involved, see that Saturn is receiving good aspects; if the reconciliation is between young people or between an older and younger person, see that Mercury is well aspected.

Romance

There is less control of when a romance starts, but romances begun under an increasing Moon are more likely to be permanent or satisfying, while those begun during the decreasing Moon tend to transform the participants. The tone of the relationship can be guessed from the sign the Moon is in. Romances begun with the Moon in Aries may be impulsive. Those begun in Capricorn will take greater effort to bring to a desirable conclusion, but they may be very rewarding. Good aspects between the Moon and Venus will have a positive influence on the relationship. Avoid unfavorable aspects to Mars, Uranus, and Pluto. A decreasing Moon, particularly the fourth quarter, facilitates ending a relationship and causes the least pain.

Roof a Building

Begin roofing a building during the third or fourth quarter, when the Moon is in Aries or Aquarius. Shingles laid during the New Moon have a tendency to curl at the edges.

Sauerkraut

The best-tasting sauerkraut is made just after the Full Moon in the fruitful signs of Cancer, Scorpio, or Pisces.

Select a Child's Sex

Count from the last day of menstruation to the first day of the next cycle and divide the interval between the two dates in half. Pregnancy in the first half produces females, but copulation should take place with the Moon in a feminine sign. Pregnancy in the latter half, up to three days before the beginning of menstruation, produces males, but copulation should take place with the Moon in a masculine sign. The three-day period before the next period again produces females.

Sell or Canvass

Begin these activities during a day favorable to your Sun sign. Otherwise, sell on days when Jupiter, Mercury, or Mars is trine, sextile, or conjunct the Moon. Avoid days when Saturn is square or opposing the Moon, for that always hinders business and causes discord. If the Moon is passing from the first quarter to full, it is best to have the Moon swift in motion and in good aspect with Venus and/or Jupiter.

Sign Papers

Sign contracts or agreements when the Moon is increasing in a fruitful sign and on a day when the Moon is making favorable aspects to Mercury. Avoid days when Mars, Saturn, or Neptune are square or opposite the Moon.

Spray and Weed

Spray pests and weeds during the fourth quarter when the Moon is in the barren sign Leo or Aquarius and making favorable aspects to Pluto. Weed during a waning Moon in a barren sign.

Staff (Fire)

Have the Moon in the third or fourth quarter, but not full. The Moon should not be square any planets.

Staff (Hire)

The Moon should be in the first or second quarter, and preferably in the sign of Gemini or Virgo. The Moon should be conjunct, trine, or sextile Mercury or Jupiter.

Stocks (Buy)

The Moon should be in Taurus or Capricorn, and there should be a sextile or trine to Jupiter or Saturn.

Surgical Procedures

Blood flow, like ocean tides, appears to be related to Moon phases. To reduce hemorrhage after a surgery, schedule it within one week before or after a New Moon. Schedule surgery to occur during the increase of the Moon if possible, as wounds heal better and vitality is greater than during the decrease of the Moon. Avoid surgery within one week before or after the Full Moon. Select a date when the Moon is past the sign governing the part of the body involved in the operation. For example, abdominal operations should be done when the Moon is in Sagittarius, Capricorn, or Aquarius.

The further removed the Moon sign is from the sign ruling the afflicted part of the body, the better.

For successful operations, avoid times when the Moon is applying to any aspect of Mars. (This tends to promote inflammation and complications.) See the Lunar Aspectarian on odd pages 137–159 to find days with negative Mars aspects and positive Venus and Jupiter aspects. Never operate with the Moon in the same sign as a person's Sun sign or Ascendant. Let the Moon be in a fixed sign and avoid square or opposing aspects. The Moon should not be void-of-course. Cosmetic surgery should be done in the increase of the Moon, when the Moon is not square or in opposition to Mars. Avoid days when the Moon is square or opposing Saturn or the Sun

Travel (Air)

Start long trips when the Moon is making favorable aspects to the Sun For enjoyment, aspects to Jupiter are preferable; for visiting, look for favorable aspects to Mercury. To prevent accidents, avoid squares or oppositions to Mars, Saturn, Uranus, or Pluto. Choose a day when the Moon is in Sagittarius or Gemini and well aspected to Mercury, Jupiter, or Uranus. Avoid adverse aspects of Mars, Saturn, or Uranus.

Visit

On setting out to visit a person, let the Moon be in aspect with any retrograde planet, for this ensures that the person you're visiting will be at home. If you desire to stay a long time in a place, let the Moon be in good aspect to Saturn. If you desire to leave the place quickly, let the Moon be in a cardinal sign.

Wean Children

To wean a child successfully, do so when the Moon is in Sagittarius, Capricorn, Aquarius, or Pisces—signs that do not rule vital human organs. By observing this astrological rule, much trouble for parents and child may be avoided.

Weight (Reduce)

If you want to lose weight, the best time to get started is when the Moon is in the third or fourth quarter and in the barren sign of Virgo. Review the section on How to Use the Moon Tables and Lunar Aspectarian beginning on page 136 to help you select a date that is favorable to begin your weight-loss program.

Wine and Drink Other Than Beer

Start brewing when the Moon is in Pisces or Taurus. Sextiles or trines to Venus are favorable, but avoid aspects to Mars or Saturn.

Write

Write for pleasure or publication when the Moon is in Gemini. Mercury should be making favorable aspects to Uranus and Neptune.

How to Use the Moon Tables and Lunar Aspectarian

Timing activities is one of the most important things you can do to ensure success. In many Eastern countries, timing by the planets is so important that practically no event takes place without first setting up a chart for it. Weddings have occurred in the middle of the night because the influences were at the best then. You may not want to take it that far, but you can still make use of the influences of the Moon whenever possible. It's easy and it works!

Llewellyn's Moon Sign Book has information to help you plan just about any activity: weddings, fishing, making purchases, cutting your hair, traveling, and more. We provide the guidelines you need to pick the best day out of the several from which you have to choose. The Moon Tables are the *Moon Sign Book's* primary method for choosing dates. Following are instructions, examples, and directions on how to read the Moon Tables. More advanced information on using the tables containing the Lunar Aspectarian and favorable and unfavorable days (found on odd-numbered pages opposite the Moon Tables), Moon void-of-course and retrograde information to choose the dates best for you is also included.

The Five Basic Steps

Step 1: Directions for Choosing Dates

Look up the directions for choosing dates for the activity that you wish to begin, then go to step 2.

Step 2: Check the Moon Tables

You'll find two tables for each month of the year beginning on page 136. The Moon Tables (on the left-hand pages) include the day, date, and sign the Moon is in; the element and nature of the sign; the Moon's phase; and when it changes sign or phase. If there is a time listed after a date, that time is the time when the Moon moves into that zodiac sign. Until then, the Moon is considered to be in the sign for the previous day.

The abbreviation Full signifies Full Moon and New signifies New Moon. The times listed with dates indicate when the Moon changes sign. The times listed after the phase indicate when the Moon changes phase.

Turn to the month you would like to begin your activity. You will be using the Moon's sign and phase information most often when you begin choosing your own dates. Use the Time Zone Map on page 164 and the Time Zone Conversions table on page 165 to convert time to your own time zone.

When you find dates that meet the criteria for the correct Moon phase and sign for your activity, you may have completed the process. For certain simple activities, such as getting a haircut, the phase and sign information is all that is needed. If the directions for your activity include information on certain lunar aspects, however, you should consult the Lunar Aspectarian. An example of this would be if the directions told you not to perform a certain activity when the Moon is square (Q) Jupiter.

Step 3: Check the Lunar Aspectarian

On the pages opposite the Moon Tables you will find tables containing the Lunar Aspectarian and Favorable and Unfavorable Days. The Lunar Aspectarian gives the aspects (or angles) of the Moon to other planets. Some aspects are favorable, while others are not. To use the Lunar Aspectarian, find the planet that the directions list as favorable for your activity, and run down the column to the date desired. For example, you should avoid aspects to Mars if you are planning surgery. So you would look for Mars across the top and then run down that column looking for days where there are no aspects to Mars (as signified by empty boxes). If you want to find a **favorable** aspect (sextile (X) or trine (T)) to Mercury, run your finger down the column under Mercury until you find an X or T. **Adverse** aspects to planets are squares (Q) or oppositions (O). A conjunction (C) is sometimes beneficial, sometimes not, depending on the activity or planets involved.

Step 4: Favorable and Unfavorable Days

The tables listing favorable and unfavorable days are helpful when you want to choose your personal best dates because your Sun sign is taken into consideration. The twelve Sun signs are listed on the right side of the tables. Once you have determined which days meet your criteria for phase, sign, and aspects, you can determine whether or not those days are positive for you by checking the favorable and unfavorable days for your Sun sign.

To find out if a day is positive for you, find your Sun sign and then look down the column. If it is marked F, it is very favorable. The Moon is in the same sign as your Sun on a favorable day. If it is marked f, it is slightly favorable; U is very unfavorable; and u means slightly unfavorable. A day marked very unfavorable (U) indicates that the Moon is in the sign opposing your Sun

Once you have selected good dates for the activity you are about to begin, you can go straight to "Using What You've Learned," beginning on the next page. To learn how to fine-tune your selections even further, read on.

Step 5: Void-of-Course Moon and Retrogrades

This last step is perhaps the most advanced portion of the procedure. It is generally considered poor timing to make decisions, sign important papers, or start special activities during a Moon void-of-course period or during a Mercury retrograde. Once you have chosen the best date for your activity based on steps one through four, you can check the Void-of-Course tables, beginning on page 76, to find out if any of the dates you have chosen have void periods.

The Moon is said to be void-of-course after it has made its last aspect to a planet within a particular sign, but before it has moved into the next sign. Put simply, the Moon is "resting" during the void-of-course period, so activities initiated at this time generally don't come to fruition. You will notice that there are many void periods during the year, and it is nearly impossible to avoid all of them. Some people choose to ignore these altogether and do not take them into consideration when planning activities.

Next, you can check the Retrograde Planets tables on page 160 to see what planets are retrograde during your chosen date(s).

A planet is said to be retrograde when it appears to move backward in the sky as viewed from Earth. Generally, the farther a planet is away from the Sun, the longer it can stay retrograde. Some planets will retrograde for several months at a time. Avoiding retrogrades is not as important in lunar planning as avoiding the Moon void-of-course, with the exception of the planet Mercury.

Mercury rules thought and communication, so it is advisable not to sign important papers, initiate important business or legal work, or make crucial decisions during these times. As with the Moon void-of-course, it is difficult to avoid all planetary retrogrades when beginning events, and you may choose to ignore this step of the process. Following are some examples using some or all of the steps outlined above.

Using What You've Learned

Let's say it's a new year and you want to have your hair cut. It's thin and you would like it to look fuller, so you find the directions for hair care and you see that for thicker hair you should cut hair while the Moon is Full and in the sign of Taurus, Cancer, or Leo. You should avoid the Moon in Aries, Gemini, or Virgo. Look at the January Moon Table on page 136. You see that the Full Moon is on January 28 at 2:16 pm. The Moon is in Leo from on January 27 and moves into Virgo on January 30 at 3:02 am, so January 28–29 meets both the phase and sign criteria.

Let's move on to a more difficult example using the sign and phase of the Moon. You want to buy a permanent home. After checking the instructions for purchasing a house: "Home (Buy New)" on page 118, you see that you should buy a home when the Moon is in Taurus, Cancer, or Leo. You need to get a loan, so you should also look under "Loan (Ask For)" on page 119. Here it says that the third and fourth quarters favor the borrower (you). You are going to buy the house in October, so go to page 154. The Moon is in the fourth quarter October 1–5, third quarter Oct 20–27, and fourth quarter Oct 28–31. The Moon is in Leo on Oct 1 until Oct 3 at 4:38 am; in Taurus from 3:59 pm Oct 20 until Oct 23 at 3:57 am; in Cancer from 5:00 pm Oct 25 to 5:07 am Oct 28 and in Leo from Oct 28 at 5:07 am until Oct 30 at 2:09 pm. The best days for obtaining a loan would be October 1–3, 20–23, and 25–30.

Just match up the best sign and phase (quarter) to come up with the best date. With all activities, be sure to check the favorable and unfavorable days for your Sun sign in the table adjoining the Lunar Aspectarian. If there is a choice between several dates, pick the one most favorable for you. Because buying a home is an important business decision, you may also wish to see if the Moon is void or if Mercury is retrograde during these dates.

Now let's look at an example that uses signs, phases, and aspects. Our example is starting new home construction. We will use the month of February. Look under "Build (Start Foundation)" on page 110 and you'll see that the Moon should be in the first quarter of a fixed sign—Leo, Taurus, Aquarius, or Scorpio. You should select a time when the Moon is not making unfavorable aspects to Saturn. (Conjunctions are usually considered unfavorable if they are to Mars, Saturn, or Neptune.) Look in the February Moon Table on page 138. You will see that the Moon is in the first quarter Feb 11–18 and in Aquarius from 8:20 pm Feb 9 until 2:23 am Feb 12 and Taurus from 10:12 pm on Feb 16 until 11:04 am on Feb 19. Now, look to the February Lunar Aspectarian. We see that there is one unfavorable square to Saturn on Feb 17; therefore, Feb 11–12, Feb 16, and Feb 18-19 would be the best dates to start a foundation.

A Note About Time and Time Zones

All tables in the Moon Sign Book use Eastern Time. You must calculate the difference between your time zone and the Eastern Time Zone. Please refer to the Time Zone Conversions chart on page 165 for help with time conversions. The sign the Moon is in at midnight is the sign shown in the Aspectarian and Favorable and Unfavorable Days tables.

How Does the Time Matter?

Due to the three-hour time difference between the East and West Coasts of the United States, those of you living on the East Coast may be, for example, under the influence of a Virgo

Moon, while those of you living on the West Coast will still have a Leo Moon influence.

We follow a commonly held belief among astrologers: whatever sign the Moon is in at the start of a day—12:00 am Eastern Time— is considered the dominant influence of the day. That sign is indicated in the Moon Tables. If the date you select for an activity shows the Moon changing signs, you can decide how important the sign change may be for your specific election and adjust your election date and time accordingly.

Use Common Sense

Some activities depend on outside factors. Obviously, you can't go out and plant when there is a foot of snow on the ground. You should adjust to the conditions at hand. If the weather was bad during the first quarter, when it was best to plant crops, do it during the second quarter while the Moon is in a fruitful sign. If the Moon is not in a fruitful sign during the first or second quarter, choose a day when it is in a semi-fruitful sign. The best advice is to choose either the sign or phase that is most favorable, when the two don't coincide.

To Summarize

First, look up the activity under the proper heading, then look for the information given in the tables. Choose the best date considering the number of positive factors in effect. If most of the dates are favorable, there is no problem choosing the one that will fit your schedule. However, if there aren't any really good dates, pick the ones with the least number of negative influences. Please keep in mind that the information found here applies in the broadest sense to the events you want to plan or are considering. To be the most effective, when you use electional astrology, you should also consider your own birth chart in relation to a chart drawn for the time or times you have under consideration. The best advice we can offer you is: read the entire introduction to each section.

January Moon Table

Date	Sign	Element	Nature	Phase
1 Fri	Leo	Fire	Barren	3rd
2 Sat 8:13 pm	Virgo	Earth	Barren	3rd
3 Sun	Virgo	Earth	Barren	3rd
4 Mon	Virgo	Earth	Barren	3rd
5 Tue 12:42 am	Libra	Air	Semi-fruitful	3rd
6 Wed	Libra	Air	Semi-fruitful	4th 4:37 am
7 Thu 3:53 am	Scorpio	Water	Fruitful	4th
8 Fri	Scorpio	Water	Fruitful	4th
9 Sat 6:15 am	Sagittarius	Fire	Barren	4th
10 Sun	Sagittarius	Fire	Barren	4th
11 Mon 8:30 am	Capricorn	Earth	Semi-fruitful	4th
12 Tue	Capricorn	Earth	Semi-fruitful	4th
13 Wed 11:44 am	Aquarius	Air	Barren	New 12:00 am
14 Thu	Aquarius	Air	Barren	1st
15 Fri 5:17 pm	Pisces	Water	Fruitful	1st
16 Sat	Pisces	Water	Fruitful	1st
17 Sun	Pisces	Water	Fruitful	1st
18 Mon 2:07 am	Aries	Fire	Barren	1st
19 Tue	Aries	Fire	Barren	1st
20 Wed 1:56 pm	Taurus	Earth	Semi-fruitful	2nd 4:02 pm
21 Thu	Taurus	Earth	Semi-fruitful	2nd
22 Fri	Taurus	Earth	Semi-fruitful	2nd
23 Sat 2:43 am	Gemini	Air	Barren	2nd
24 Sun	Gemini	Air	Barren	2nd
25 Mon 1:52 pm	Cancer	Water	Fruitful	2nd
26 Tue	Cancer	Water	Fruitful	2nd
27 Wed 9:54 pm	Leo	Fire	Barren	2nd
28 Thu	Leo	Fire	Barren	Full 2:16 pm
29 Fri	Leo	Fire	Barren	3rd
30 Sat 3:02 am	Virgo	Earth	Barren	3rd
31 Sun	Virgo	Earth	Barren	3rd

January Aspectarian/Favorable & Unfavorable Days

Date	Sun	Mercury	Venus	Mars	Jupiter	Saturn	Uranus	Neptune	Pluto
1								Q	
2			T	T					
3	T							T	
4		T	Q					O	T
5					T	T			
6	Q								Q
7		Q	X	O	Q	Q	O		
8	X							T	X
9		X			X	X			
10								Q	
11			C	T			T		
12								X	
13	C			Q	C	C	Q		C
14		C							
15									
16			X	X			X		
17	X							C	X
18					X	X			
19		X	Q						
20	Q					Q			Q
21			C	Q			C		
22		Q	T					X	T
23	T				T	T			
24								Q	
25		T							
26			X				X		
27			O					T	O
28	O				Q	O	O	Q	
29		O							
30				T			T		
31								O	T

Date	Aries	Taurus	Gemini	Cancer	Leo	Virgo	Libra	Scorpio	Sagittarius	Capricorn	Aquarius	Pisces
1	f	u	f		F		f	u	f		U	
2	f	u	f		F		f	u	f		U	
3		f	u	f		F		f	u	f		U
4		f	u	f		F		f	u	f		U
5	U		f	u	f		F		f	u	f	
6	U		f	u	f		F		f	u	f	
7	U		f	u	f		F		f	u	f	
8		U		f	u	f		F		f	u	f
9		U		f	u	f		F		f	u	f
10	f		U		f	u	f		F		f	u
11	f		U		f	u	f		F		f	u
12	u	f		U		f	u	f		F		f
13	u	f		U		f	u	f		F		f
14	f	u	f		U		f	u	f		F	
15	f	u	f		U		f	u	f		F	
16		f	u	f		U		f	u	f		F
17		f	u	f		U		f	u	f		F
18	F		f	u	f		U		f	u	f	
19	F		f	u	f		U		f	u	f	
20	F		f	u	f		U		f	u	f	
21		F		f	u	f		U		f	u	f
22		F		f	u	f		U		f	u	f
23	f		F		f	u	f		U		f	u
24	f		F		f	u	f		U		f	u
25	f		F		f	u	f		U		f	u
26	u	f		F		f	u	f		U		f
27	u	f		F		f	u	f		U		f
28	f	u	f		F		f	u	f		U	
29	f	u	f		F		f	u	f		U	
30	f	u	f		F		f	u	f		U	
31		f	u	f		F		f	u	f		U

February Moon Table

Date	Sign	Element	Nature	Phase
1 Mon 6:25 am	Libra	Air	Semi-fruitful	3rd
2 Tue	Libra	Air	Semi-fruitful	3rd
3 Wed 9:15 am	Scorpio	Water	Fruitful	3rd
4 Thu	Scorpio	Water	Fruitful	4th 12:37 pm
5 Fri 12:16 pm	Sagittarius	Fire	Barren	4th
6 Sat	Sagittarius	Fire	Barren	4th
7 Sun 3:52 pm	Capricorn	Earth	Semi-fruitful	4th
8 Mon	Capricorn	Earth	Semi-fruitful	4th
9 Tue 8:20 pm	Aquarius	Air	Barren	4th
10 Wed	Aquarius	Air	Barren	4th
11 Thu	Aquarius	Air	Barren	New 2:06 pm
12 Fri 2:23 am	Pisces	Water	Fruitful	1st
13 Sat	Pisces	Water	Fruitful	1st
14 Sun 10:54 am	Aries	Fire	Barren	1st
15 Mon	Aries	Fire	Barren	1st
16 Tue 10:12 pm	Taurus	Earth	Semi-fruitful	1st
17 Wed	Taurus	Earth	Semi-fruitful	1st
18 Thu	Taurus	Earth	Semi-fruitful	1st
19 Fri 11:04 am	Gemini	Air	Barren	2nd 1:47 pm
20 Sat	Gemini	Air	Barren	2nd
21 Sun 10:53 pm	Cancer	Water	Fruitful	2nd
22 Mon	Cancer	Water	Fruitful	2nd
23 Tue	Cancer	Water	Fruitful	2nd
24 Wed 7:23 am	Leo	Fire	Barren	2nd
25 Thu	Leo	Fire	Barren	2nd
26 Fri 12:07 pm	Virgo	Earth	Barren	2nd
27 Sat	Virgo	Earth	Barren	Full 3:17 am
28 Sun 2:17 pm	Libra	Air	Semi-fruitful	3rd

February Aspectarian/Favorable & Unfavorable Days

Date	Sun	Mercury	Venus	Mars	Jupiter	Saturn	Uranus	Neptune	Pluto
1			T		T	T			
2	T								
3		T	Q			Q	O		Q
4	Q			O	Q			T	
5		Q	X			X			X
6	X				X			Q	
7		X							
8				T				T	
9								X	C
10			C		C	C	Q		
11	C	C		Q					
12								X	
13				X				C	
14									X
15		X	X		X	X			
16	X								Q
17		Q				Q	C		
18			Q	C	Q			X	
19	Q								T
20		T			T	T			
21			T					Q	
22	T						X		
23				X				T	O
24					O	Q			
25		O			O				
26			O	Q					
27	O						T	O	
28				T					T

Date	Aries	Taurus	Gemini	Cancer	Leo	Virgo	Libra	Scorpio	Sagittarius	Capricorn	Aquarius	Pisces
1		f	u	f		F		f	u	f		U
2	U		f	u	f		F		f	u	f	
3	U		f	u	f		F		f	u	f	
4		U		f	u	f		F		f	u	f
5		U		f	u	f		F		f	u	f
6	f		U		f	u	f		F		f	u
7	f		U		f	u	f		F		f	u
8	u	f		U		f	u	f		F		f
9	u	f		U		f	u	f		F		f
10	f	u	f		U		f	u	f		F	
11	f	u	f		U		f	u	f		F	U
12		f	u	f		U		f	u	f		F
13		f	u	f		U		f	u	f		F
14		f	u	f		U		f	u	f		F
15	F		f	u	f		U		f	u	f	
16	F		f	u	f		U		f	u	f	
17		F		f	u	f		U		f	u	f
18		F		f	u	f		U		f	u	f
19		F		f	u	f		U		f	u	f
20	f		F		f	u	f		U		f	u
21	f		F		f	u	f		U		f	u
22	u	f		F		f	u	f		U		f
23	u	f		F		f	u	f		U		f
24	u	f		F		f	u	f		U		f
25	f	u	f		F		f	u	f		U	
26	f	u	f		F		f	u	f		U	
27		f	u	f		F		f	u	f		U
28		f	u	f		F		f	u	f		U

March Moon Table

Date	Sign	Element	Nature	Phase
1 Mon	Libra	Air	Semi-fruitful	3rd
2 Tue 3:38 pm	Scorpio	Water	Fruitful	3rd
3 Wed	Scorpio	Water	Fruitful	3rd
4 Thu 5:43 pm	Sagittarius	Fire	Barren	3rd
5 Fri	Sagittarius	Fire	Barren	4th 8:30 pm
6 Sat 9:20 pm	Capricorn	Earth	Semi-fruitful	4th
7 Sun	Capricorn	Earth	Semi-fruitful	4th
8 Mon	Capricorn	Earth	Semi-fruitful	4th
9 Tue 2:41 am	Aquarius	Air	Barren	4th
10 Wed	Aquarius	Air	Barren	4th
11 Thu 9:44 am	Pisces	Water	Fruitful	4th
12 Fri	Pisces	Water	Fruitful	4th
13 Sat 6:44 pm	Aries	Fire	Barren	New 5:21 am
14 Sun	Aries	Fire	Barren	1st
15 Mon	Aries	Fire	Barren	1st
16 Tue 6:56 am	Taurus	Earth	Semi-fruitful	1st
17 Wed	Taurus	Earth	Semi-fruitful	1st
18 Thu 7:47 pm	Gemini	Air	Barren	1st
19 Fri	Gemini	Air	Barren	1st
20 Sat	Gemini	Air	Barren	1st
21 Sun 8:18 am	Cancer	Water	Fruitful	2nd 10:40 am
22 Mon	Cancer	Water	Fruitful	2nd
23 Tue 5:56 pm	Leo	Fire	Barren	2nd
24 Wed	Leo	Fire	Barren	2nd
25 Thu 11:25 pm	Virgo	Earth	Barren	2nd
26 Fri	Virgo	Earth	Barren	2nd
27 Sat	Virgo	Earth	Barren	2nd
28 Sun 1:22 am	Libra	Air	Semi-fruitful	Full 2:48 pm
29 Mon	Libra	Air	Semi-fruitful	3rd
30 Tue 1:33 am	Scorpio	Water	Fruitful	3rd
31 Wed	Scorpio	Water	Fruitful	3rd

March Aspectarian/Favorable & Unfavorable Days

Date	Sun	Mercury	Venus	Mars	Jupiter	Saturn	Uranus	Neptune	Pluto
1		T			T	T			
2									Q
3	T	Q	T		Q	Q	O		
4				O				T	X
5	Q		Q			X			
6		X			X			Q	
7			X				T		
8	X							X	C
9				T		C	Q		
10		C			C				
11				Q					
12			C			X			
13	C						C	X	
14				X		X			
15					X				Q
16		X					C		
17					Q				
18	X		X		Q		X	T	
19		Q		C		T			
20					T		Q		
21	Q		Q						
22		T				X			
23			T				T	O	
24	T			X		O	Q		
25					O				
26				Q			T		
27		O					O	T	
28	O		O			T			
29				T	T				Q
30						Q	O		
31		T			Q			T	X

Date	Aries	Taurus	Gemini	Cancer	Leo	Virgo	Libra	Scorpio	Sagittarius	Capricorn	Aquarius	Pisces
1	U		f	u	f		F		f	u	f	
2	U		f	u	f		F		f	u	f	u
3		U		f	u	f		F		f	u	f
4		U		f	u	f		F		f	u	f
5	f		U		f	u	f		F		f	u
6	f		U		f	u	f		F		f	u
7	u	f		U		f	u	f		F		f
8	u	f		U		f	u	f		F		f
9	f	u	f		U		f	u	f		F	
10	f	u	f		U		f	u	f		F	
11	f	u	f		U		f	u	f		F	
12		f	u	f		U		f	u	f		F
13		f	u	f		U		f	u	f		F
14	F		f	u	f		U		f	u	f	
15	F		f	u	f		U		f	u	f	
16	F		f	u	f		U		f	u	f	
17		F		f	u	f		U		f	u	f
18		F		f	u	f		U		f	u	f
19	f		F		f	u	f		U		f	u
20	f		F		f	u	f		U		f	u
21	f		F		f	u	f		U		f	u
22	u	f		F		f	u	f		U		f
23	u	f		F		f	u	f		U		f
24	f	u	f		F		f	u	f		U	
25	f	u	f		F		f	u	f		U	
26		f	u	f		F		f	u	f		U
27		f	u	f		F		f	u	f		U
28	U		f	u	f		F		f	u	f	
29	U		f	u	f		F		f	u	f	
30		U		f	u	f		F		f	u	f
31		U		f	u	f		F		f	u	f

141

April Moon Table

Date	Sign	Element	Nature	Phase
1 Thu 1:59 am	Sagittarius	Fire	Barren	3rd
2 Fri	Sagittarius	Fire	Barren	3rd
3 Sat 4:13 am	Capricorn	Earth	Semi-fruitful	3rd
4 Sun	Capricorn	Earth	Semi-fruitful	4th 6:02 am
5 Mon 9:04 am	Aquarius	Air	Barren	4th
6 Tue	Aquarius	Air	Barren	4th
7 Wed 4:30 pm	Pisces	Water	Fruitful	4th
8 Thu	Pisces	Water	Fruitful	4th
9 Fri	Pisces	Water	Fruitful	4th
10 Sat 2:11 am	Aries	Fire	Barren	4th
11 Sun	Aries	Fire	Barren	New 10:31 pm
12 Mon 1:44 pm	Taurus	Earth	Semi-fruitful	1st
13 Tue	Taurus	Earth	Semi-fruitful	1st
14 Wed	Taurus	Earth	Semi-fruitful	1st
15 Thu 2:35 am	Gemini	Air	Barren	1st
16 Fri	Gemini	Air	Barren	1st
17 Sat 3:25 pm	Cancer	Water	Fruitful	1st
18 Sun	Cancer	Water	Fruitful	1st
19 Mon	Cancer	Water	Fruitful	1st
20 Tue 2:11 am	Leo	Fire	Barren	2nd 2:59 am
21 Wed	Leo	Fire	Barren	2nd
22 Thu 9:08 am	Virgo	Earth	Barren	2nd
23 Fri	Virgo	Earth	Barren	2nd
24 Sat 12:06 pm	Libra	Air	Semi-fruitful	2nd
25 Sun	Libra	Air	Semi-fruitful	2nd
26 Mon 12:18 pm	Scorpio	Water	Fruitful	Full 11:32 pm
27 Tue	Scorpio	Water	Fruitful	3rd
28 Wed 11:42 am	Sagittarius	Fire	Barren	3rd
29 Thu	Sagittarius	Fire	Barren	3rd
30 Fri 12:16 pm	Capricorn	Earth	Semi-fruitful	3rd

April Aspectarian/Favorable & Unfavorable Days

Date	Sun	Mercury	Venus	Mars	Jupiter	Saturn	Uranus	Neptune	Pluto
1	T					X			
2			T	O	X			Q	
3		Q					T		
4	Q		Q					X	
5		X							C
6	X		X	T		C	Q		
7					C				
8							X		
9			Q					C	X
10									
11	C	C				X			
12			C	X	X				Q
13					Q	C			
14				Q				X	T
15									
16						T		Q	
17	X	X	X	C	T				
18							X		
19								T	O
20	Q	Q	Q				Q		
21						O			
22	T	T		X	O				
23			T				T	O	
24			Q						T
25						T			
26	O			T	T				Q
27		O	O			Q	O	T	
28					Q				X
29				X			Q		
30				O	X				

Date	Aries	Taurus	Gemini	Cancer	Leo	Virgo	Libra	Scorpio	Sagittarius	Capricorn	Aquarius	Pisces
1	f		U		f	u	f		F		f	u
2	f		U		f	u	f		F		f	u
3	f		U		f	u	f		F		f	u
4	u	f		U		f	u	f		F		f
5	u	f		U		f	u	f		F		f
6	f	u	f		U		f	u	f		F	
7	f	u	f		U		f	u	f		F	
8		f	u	f		U		f	u	f		F
9		f	u	f		U		f	u	f		F
10	F		f	u	f		U		f	u	f	
11	F		f	u	f		U		f	u	f	
12	F		f	u	f		U		f	u	f	
13		F		f	u	f		U		f	u	f
14		F		f	u	f		U		f	u	f
15	f		F		f	u	f		U		f	u
16	f		F		f	u	f		U		f	u
17	f		F		f	u	f		U		f	u
18	u	f		F		f	u	f		U		f
19	u	f		F		f	u	f		U		f
20	f	u	f		F		f	u	f		U	
21	f	u	f		F		f	u	f		U	
22	f	u	f		F		f	u	f		U	
23		f	u	f		F		f	u	f		U
24		f	u	f		F		f	u	f		U
25	U		f	u	f		F		f	u	f	
26	U		f	u	f		F		f	u	f	
27		U		f	u	f		F		f	u	f
28		U		f	u	f		F		f	u	f
29	f		U		f	u	f		F		f	u
30	f		U		f	u	f		F		f	u

May Moon Table

Date	Sign	Element	Nature	Phase
1 Sat	Capricorn	Earth	Semi-fruitful	3rd
2 Sun 3:31 pm	Aquarius	Air	Barren	3rd
3 Mon	Aquarius	Air	Barren	4th 3:50 pm
4 Tue 10:09 pm	Pisces	Water	Fruitful	4th
5 Wed	Pisces	Water	Fruitful	4th
6 Thu	Pisces	Water	Fruitful	4th
7 Fri 7:52 am	Aries	Fire	Barren	4th
8 Sat	Aries	Fire	Barren	4th
9 Sun 7:46 pm	Taurus	Earth	Semi-fruitful	4th
10 Mon	Taurus	Earth	Semi-fruitful	4th
11 Tue	Taurus	Earth	Semi-fruitful	New 3:00 pm
12 Wed 8:43 am	Gemini	Air	Barren	1st
13 Thu	Gemini	Air	Barren	1st
14 Fri 9:30 pm	Cancer	Water	Fruitful	1st
15 Sat	Cancer	Water	Fruitful	1st
16 Sun	Cancer	Water	Fruitful	1st
17 Mon 8:44 am	Leo	Fire	Barren	1st
18 Tue	Leo	Fire	Barren	1st
19 Wed 4:59 pm	Virgo	Earth	Barren	2nd 3:13 pm
20 Thu	Virgo	Earth	Barren	2nd
21 Fri 9:35 pm	Libra	Air	Semi-fruitful	2nd
22 Sat	Libra	Air	Semi-fruitful	2nd
23 Sun 11:00 pm	Scorpio	Water	Fruitful	2nd
24 Mon	Scorpio	Water	Fruitful	2nd
25 Tue 10:39 pm	Sagittarius	Fire	Barren	2nd
26 Wed	Sagittarius	Fire	Barren	Full 7:14 am
27 Thu 10:23 pm	Capricorn	Earth	Semi-fruitful	3rd
28 Fri	Capricorn	Earth	Semi-fruitful	3rd
29 Sat	Capricorn	Earth	Semi-fruitful	3rd
30 Sun 12:04 am	Aquarius	Air	Barren	3rd
31 Mon	Aquarius	Air	Barren	3rd

May Aspectarian/Favorable & Unfavorable Days

Date	Sun	Mercury	Venus	Mars	Jupiter	Saturn	Uranus	Neptune	Pluto
1	T							T	
2		T	T					X	C
3	Q						C	Q	
4			Q		C				
5		Q		T			X		
6	X							C	
7		X	X						X
8				Q		X			
9					X				Q
10				X		Q	C		
11	C						X		
12			C		Q				T
13		C				T			
14					T			Q	
15							X		
16			C					T	
17	X								O
18		X	X			O	Q		
19	Q				O				
20			Q	X			T		
21	T	Q						O	T
22						T			
23		T	T	Q					Q
24					T	Q	O		
25				T				T	X
26	O				Q	X			
27		O	O					Q	
28					X		T		
29				O				X	C
30	T					C	Q		
31		T							

Date	Aries	Taurus	Gemini	Cancer	Leo	Virgo	Libra	Scorpio	Sagittarius	Capricorn	Aquarius	Pisces
1	u	f		U		f	u	f		F		f
2	u	f		U		f	u	f		F		f
3	f	u	f		U		f	u	f		F	
4	f	u	f		U		f	u	f		F	U
5		f	u	f		U		f	u	f		F
6		f	u	f		U		f	u	f		F
7		f	u	f		U		f	u	f		F
8	F		f	u	f		U		f	u	f	
9	F		f	u	f		U		f	u	f	
10		F		f	u	f		U		f	u	f
11		F		f	u	f		U		f	u	f
12		F		f	u	f		U		f	u	f
13	f		F		f	u	f		U		f	u
14	f		F		f	u	f		U		f	u
15	u	f		F		f	u	f		U		f
16	u	f		F		f	u	f		U		f
17	u	f		F		f	u	f		U		f
18	f	u	f		F		f	u	f		U	
19	f	u	f		F		f	u	f		U	
20		f	u	f		F		f	u	f		U
21		f	u	f		F		f	u	f		U
22	U		f	u	f		F		f	u	f	
23	U		f	u	f		F		f	u	f	
24		U		f	u	f		F		f	u	f
25		U		f	u	f		F		f	u	f
26	f		U		f	u	f		F		f	u
27	f		U		f	u	f		F		f	u
28	u	f		U		f	u	f		F		f
29	u	f		U		f	u	f		F		f
30	f	u	f		U		f	u	f		F	
31	f	u	f		U		f	u	f		F	

June Moon Table

Date	Sign	Element	Nature	Phase
1 Tue 5:07 am	Pisces	Water	Fruitful	3rd
2 Wed	Pisces	Water	Fruitful	4th 3:24 am
3 Thu 1:59 pm	Aries	Fire	Barren	4th
4 Fri	Aries	Fire	Barren	4th
5 Sat	Aries	Fire	Barren	4th
6 Sun 1:46 am	Taurus	Earth	Semi-fruitful	4th
7 Mon	Taurus	Earth	Semi-fruitful	4th
8 Tue 2:47 pm	Gemini	Air	Barren	4th
9 Wed	Gemini	Air	Barren	4th
10 Thu	Gemini	Air	Barren	New 6:53 am
11 Fri 3:23 am	Cancer	Water	Fruitful	1st
12 Sat	Cancer	Water	Fruitful	1st
13 Sun 2:22 pm	Leo	Fire	Barren	1st
14 Mon	Leo	Fire	Barren	1st
15 Tue 11:02 pm	Virgo	Earth	Barren	1st
16 Wed	Virgo	Earth	Barren	1st
17 Thu	Virgo	Earth	Barren	2nd 11:54 pm
18 Fri 4:54 am	Libra	Air	Semi-fruitful	2nd
19 Sat	Libra	Air	Semi-fruitful	2nd
20 Sun 7:58 am	Scorpio	Water	Fruitful	2nd
21 Mon	Scorpio	Water	Fruitful	2nd
22 Tue 8:55 am	Sagittarius	Fire	Barren	2nd
23 Wed	Sagittarius	Fire	Barren	2nd
24 Thu 9:05 am	Capricorn	Earth	Semi-fruitful	Full 2:40 pm
25 Fri	Capricorn	Earth	Semi-fruitful	3rd
26 Sat 10:09 am	Aquarius	Air	Barren	3rd
27 Sun	Aquarius	Air	Barren	3rd
28 Mon 1:51 pm	Pisces	Water	Fruitful	3rd
29 Tue	Pisces	Water	Fruitful	3rd
30 Wed 9:21 pm	Aries	Fire	Barren	3rd

June Aspectarian/Favorable & Unfavorable Days

Date	Sun	Mercury	Venus	Mars	Jupiter	Saturn	Uranus	Neptune	Pluto
1			T		C				
2	Q							X	
3		Q	Q	T				C	X
4	X					X			
5		X		Q					Q
6			X		X				
7						Q	C		
8				X	Q			X	T
9						T			
10	C	C						Q	
11					T				
12			C				X		
13			C					T	O
14						O	Q		
15	X	X							
16						O		T	
17	Q	Q	X					O	T
18				X					
19		T	Q			T			
20	T			Q	T				Q
21			T			Q	O	T	
22				T	Q				X
23		O				X		Q	
24	O				X				
25								T	X
26			O						C
27		T		O		C	Q		
28					C				
29	T	Q						X	
30								C	X

Date	Aries	Taurus	Gemini	Cancer	Leo	Virgo	Libra	Scorpio	Sagittarius	Capricorn	Aquarius	Pisces
1	f	u	f		U		f	u	f		F	
2		f	u	f		U		f	u	f		F
3		f	u	f		U		f	u	f		F
4	F		f	u	f		U		f	u	f	
5	F		f	u	f		U		f	u	f	
6		F		f	u	f		U		f	u	f
7		F		f	u	f		U		f	u	f
8		F		f	u	f		U		f	u	f
9	f		F		f	u	f		U		f	u
10	f		F		f	u	f		U		f	u
11	f		F		f	u	f		U		f	u
12	u	f		F		f	u	f		U		f
13	u	f		F		f	u	f		U		f
14	f	u	f		F		f	u	f		U	
15	f	u	f		F		f	u	f		U	
16		f	u	f		F		f	u	f		U
17		f	u	f		F		f	u	f		U
18		f	u	f		F		f	u	f		U
19	U		f	u	f		F		f	u	f	
20	U		f	u	f		F		f	u	f	
21		U		f	u	f		F		f	u	f
22		U		f	u	f		F		f	u	f
23	f		U		f	u	f		F		f	u
24	f		U		f	u	f		F		f	u
25	u	f		U		f	u	f		F		f
26	u	f		U		f	u	f		F		f
27	f	u	f		U		f	u	f		F	
28	f	u	f		U		f	u	f		F	
29		f	u	f		U		f	u	f		F
30		f	u	f		U		f	u	f		F

147

July Moon Table

Date	Sign	Element	Nature	Phase
1 Thu	Aries	Fire	Barren	4th 5:11 pm
2 Fri	Aries	Fire	Barren	4th
3 Sat 8:28 am	Taurus	Earth	Semi-fruitful	4th
4 Sun	Taurus	Earth	Semi-fruitful	4th
5 Mon 9:24 pm	Gemini	Air	Barren	4th
6 Tue	Gemini	Air	Barren	4th
7 Wed	Gemini	Air	Barren	4th
8 Thu 9:51 am	Cancer	Water	Fruitful	4th
9 Fri	Cancer	Water	Fruitful	New 9:17 pm
10 Sat 8:21 pm	Leo	Fire	Barren	1st
11 Sun	Leo	Fire	Barren	1st
12 Mon	Leo	Fire	Barren	1st
13 Tue 4:30 am	Virgo	Earth	Barren	1st
14 Wed	Virgo	Earth	Barren	1st
15 Thu 10:32 am	Libra	Air	Semi-fruitful	1st
16 Fri	Libra	Air	Semi-fruitful	1st
17 Sat 2:38 pm	Scorpio	Water	Fruitful	2nd 6:11 am
18 Sun	Scorpio	Water	Fruitful	2nd
19 Mon 5:08 pm	Sagittarius	Fire	Barren	2nd
20 Tue	Sagittarius	Fire	Barren	2nd
21 Wed 6:36 pm	Capricorn	Earth	Semi-fruitful	2nd
22 Thu	Capricorn	Earth	Semi-fruitful	2nd
23 Fri 8:12 pm	Aquarius	Air	Barren	Full 10:37 pm
24 Sat	Aquarius	Air	Barren	3rd
25 Sun 11:30 pm	Pisces	Water	Fruitful	3rd
26 Mon	Pisces	Water	Fruitful	3rd
27 Tue	Pisces	Water	Fruitful	3rd
28 Wed 5:58 am	Aries	Fire	Barren	3rd
29 Thu	Aries	Fire	Barren	3rd
30 Fri 4:08 pm	Taurus	Earth	Semi-fruitful	3rd
31 Sat	Taurus	Earth	Semi-fruitful	4th 9:16 am

July Aspectarian/Favorable & Unfavorable Days

Date	Sun	Mercury	Venus	Mars	Jupiter	Saturn	Uranus	Neptune	Pluto
1	Q		T	T		X			
2		X							
3					X				Q
4	X		Q	Q		Q	C		
5								X	T
6			X			Q	T		
7				X				Q	
8		C				T			
9	C						X		
10								T	O
11						O	Q		
12			C	C					
13		X			O				
14	X							T	O
15		Q							T
16						T			
17	Q		X	X	T				Q
18		T				Q	O		
19	T		Q	Q	Q			T	X
20						X			
21			T	T	X			Q	
22							T		
23	O	O						X	C
24						C	Q		
25				O	C				
26			O						
27							X	C	X
28	T	T							
29						X			
30				T	X				Q
31	Q	Q	T			Q	C		

Date	Aries	Taurus	Gemini	Cancer	Leo	Virgo	Libra	Scorpio	Sagittarius	Capricorn	Aquarius	Pisces
1	F		f	u	f		U		f	u	f	
2	F		f	u	f		U		f	u	f	
3	F		f	u	f		U		f	u	f	
4		F		f	u	f		U		f	u	f
5		F		f	u	f		U		f	u	f
6	f		F		f	u	f		U		f	u
7	f		F		f	u	f		U		f	u
8	f		F		f	u	f		U		f	u
9	u	f		F		f	u	f		U		f
10	u	f		F		f	u	f		U		f
11	f	u	f		F		f	u	f		U	
12	f	u	f		F		f	u	f		U	
13	f	u	f		F		f	u	f		U	
14		f	u	f		F		f	u	f		U
15		f	u	f		F		f	u	f		U
16	U		f	u	f		F		f	u	f	
17	U		f	u	f		F		f	u	f	
18		U		f	u	f		F		f	u	f
19		U		f	u	f		F		f	u	f
20	f		U		f	u	f		F		f	u
21	f		U		f	u	f		F		f	u
22	u	f		U		f	u	f		F		f
23	u	f		U		f	u	f		F		f
24	f	u	f		U		f	u	f		F	
25	f	u	f		U		f	u	f		F	
26		f	u	f		U		f	u	f		F
27		f	u	f		U		f	u	f		F
28		f	u	f		U		f	u	f		F
29	F		f	u	f		U		f	u	f	
30	F		f	u	f		U		f	u	f	u
31		F		f	u	f		U		f	u	f

August Moon Table

Date	Sign	Element	Nature	Phase
1 Sun	Taurus	Earth	Semi-fruitful	4th
2 Mon 4:46 am	Gemini	Air	Barren	4th
3 Tue	Gemini	Air	Barren	4th
4 Wed 5:17 pm	Cancer	Water	Fruitful	4th
5 Thu	Cancer	Water	Fruitful	4th
6 Fri	Cancer	Water	Fruitful	4th
7 Sat 3:31 am	Leo	Fire	Barren	4th
8 Sun	Leo	Fire	Barren	New 9:50 am
9 Mon 10:56 am	Virgo	Earth	Barren	1st
10 Tue	Virgo	Earth	Barren	1st
11 Wed 4:08 pm	Libra	Air	Semi-fruitful	1st
12 Thu	Libra	Air	Semi-fruitful	1st
13 Fri 8:01 pm	Scorpio	Water	Fruitful	1st
14 Sat	Scorpio	Water	Fruitful	1st
15 Sun 11:12 pm	Sagittarius	Fire	Barren	2nd 11:20 am
16 Mon	Sagittarius	Fire	Barren	2nd
17 Tue	Sagittarius	Fire	Barren	2nd
18 Wed 1:58 am	Capricorn	Earth	Semi-fruitful	2nd
19 Thu	Capricorn	Earth	Semi-fruitful	2nd
20 Fri 4:49 am	Aquarius	Air	Barren	2nd
21 Sat	Aquarius	Air	Barren	2nd
22 Sun 8:43 am	Pisces	Water	Fruitful	Full 8:02 am
23 Mon	Pisces	Water	Fruitful	3rd
24 Tue 2:57 pm	Aries	Fire	Barren	3rd
25 Wed	Aries	Fire	Barren	3rd
26 Thu	Aries	Fire	Barren	3rd
27 Fri 12:27 am	Taurus	Earth	Semi-fruitful	3rd
28 Sat	Taurus	Earth	Semi-fruitful	3rd
29 Sun 12:42 pm	Gemini	Air	Barren	3rd
30 Mon	Gemini	Air	Barren	4th 3:13 am
31 Tue	Gemini	Air	Barren	4th

August Aspectarian/Favorable & Unfavorable Days

Date	Sun	Mercury	Venus	Mars	Jupiter	Saturn	Uranus	Neptune	Pluto
1								X	T
2				Q	Q				
3	X	X	Q			T			
4					T			Q	
5				X			X		
6		X						T	O
7							O		
8	C						Q		
9		C		C	O				
10							T		
11			C					O	T
12						T			
13	X				T				Q
14		X		X		Q	O		
15	Q		X		Q			T	X
16		Q		Q		X			
17	T				X			Q	
18		T	Q	T					
19							T	X	C
20			T			C			
21								Q	
22	O				C				
23		O		O			X		
24								C	X
25			O			X			
26					X				Q
27	T					Q			
28				T			C	X	
29		T			Q				T
30	Q					T			
31			T	Q	T			Q	

Date	Aries	Taurus	Gemini	Cancer	Leo	Virgo	Libra	Scorpio	Sagittarius	Capricorn	Aquarius	Pisces
1		F		f	u	f		U		f	u	f
2		F		f	u	f		U		f	u	f
3	f		F		f	u	f		U		f	u
4	f		F		f	u	f		U		f	u
5	u	f		F		f	u	f		U		f
6	u	f		F		f	u	f		U		f
7	u	f		F		f	u	f		U		f
8	f	u	f		F		f	u	f		U	
9	f	u	f		F		f	u	f		U	
10		f	u	f		F		f	u	f		U
11		f	u	f		F		f	u	f		U
12	U		f	u	f		F		f	u	f	
13	U		f	u	f		F		f	u	f	
14		U		f	u	f		F		f	u	f
15		U		f	u	f		F		f	u	f
16	f		U		f	u	f		F		f	u
17	f		U		f	u	f		F		f	u
18	u	f		U		f	u	f		F		f
19	u	f		U		f	u	f		F		f
20	u	f		U		f	u	f		F		f
21	f	u	f		U		f	u	f		F	
22	f	u	f		U		f	u	f		F	
23		f	u	f		U		f	u	f		F
24		f	u	f		U		f	u	f		F
25	F		f	u	f		U		f	u	f	
26	F		f	u	f		U		f	u	f	
27		F		f	u	f		U		f	u	f
28		F		f	u	f		U		f	u	f
29		F		f	u	f		U		f	u	f
30	f		F		f	u	f		U		f	u
31	f		F		f	u	f		U		f	u

September Moon Table

Date	Sign	Element	Nature	Phase
1 Wed 1:26 am	Cancer	Water	Fruitful	4th
2 Thu	Cancer	Water	Fruitful	4th
3 Fri 11:58 am	Leo	Fire	Barren	4th
4 Sat	Leo	Fire	Barren	4th
5 Sun 7:06 pm	Virgo	Earth	Barren	4th
6 Mon	Virgo	Earth	Barren	New 8:52 pm
7 Tue 11:20 pm	Libra	Air	Semi-fruitful	1st
8 Wed	Libra	Air	Semi-fruitful	1st
9 Thu	Libra	Air	Semi-fruitful	1st
10 Fri 2:05 am	Scorpio	Water	Fruitful	1st
11 Sat	Scorpio	Water	Fruitful	1st
12 Sun 4:34 am	Sagittarius	Fire	Barren	1st
13 Mon	Sagittarius	Fire	Barren	2nd 4:39 pm
14 Tue 7:34 am	Capricorn	Earth	Semi-fruitful	2nd
15 Wed	Capricorn	Earth	Semi-fruitful	2nd
16 Thu 11:23 am	Aquarius	Air	Barren	2nd
17 Fri	Aquarius	Air	Barren	2nd
18 Sat 4:22 pm	Pisces	Water	Fruitful	2nd
19 Sun	Pisces	Water	Fruitful	2nd
20 Mon 11:13 pm	Aries	Fire	Barren	Full 7:55 pm
21 Tue	Aries	Fire	Barren	3rd
22 Wed	Aries	Fire	Barren	3rd
23 Thu 8:38 am	Taurus	Earth	Semi-fruitful	3rd
24 Fri	Taurus	Earth	Semi-fruitful	3rd
25 Sat 8:36 pm	Gemini	Air	Barren	3rd
26 Sun	Gemini	Air	Barren	3rd
27 Mon	Gemini	Air	Barren	3rd
28 Tue 9:34 am	Cancer	Water	Fruitful	4th 9:57 pm
29 Wed	Cancer	Water	Fruitful	4th
30 Thu 8:53 pm	Leo	Fire	Barren	4th

September Aspectarian/Favorable & Unfavorable Days

Date	Sun	Mercury	Venus	Mars	Jupiter	Saturn	Uranus	Neptune	Pluto
1	X	Q							
2			Q	X			X	T	
3									O
4		X				O	Q		
5			X		O				
6	C						T		
7				C				O	T
8		C				T			
9					T				Q
10			C			Q			
11	X				Q		O	T	X
12				X		X			
13	Q	X			X			Q	
14			X	Q					
15		Q					T	X	
16	T			T					C
17			Q			C	Q		
18		T				C			
19			T				X		
20	O							C	X
21				O		X			
22		O		X					Q
23						Q			
24			O				C		
25					Q			X	T
26	T			T		T			
27					T			Q	
28	Q	T							
29				Q			X		
30		Q	T					T	O

Date	Aries	Taurus	Gemini	Cancer	Leo	Virgo	Libra	Scorpio	Sagittarius	Capricorn	Aquarius	Pisces
1	u	f		F		f	u	f		U		f
2	u	f		F		f	u	f		U		f
3	u	f		F		f	u	f		U		f
4	f	u	f		F		f	u	f		U	
5	f	u	f		F		f	u	f		U	
6		f	u	f		F		f	u	f		U
7		f	u	f		F		f	u	f		U
8	U		f	u	f		F		f	u	f	
9	U		f	u	f		F		f	u	f	u
10		U		f	u	f		F		f	u	f
11		U		f	u	f		F		f	u	f
12		U		f	u	f		F		f	u	f
13	f		U		f	u	f		F		f	u
14	f		U		f	u	f		F		f	u
15	u	f		U		f	u	f		F		f
16	u	f		U		f	u	f		F		f
17	f	u	f		U		f	u	f		F	
18	f	u	f		U		f	u	f		F	
19		f	u	f		U		f	u	f		F
20		f	u	f		U		f	u	f		F
21	F		f	u	f		U		f	u	f	
22	F		f	u	f		U		f	u	f	
23	F		f	u	f		U		f	u	f	
24		F		f	u	f		U		f	u	f
25		F		f	u	f		U		f	u	f
26	f		F		f	u	f		U		f	u
27	f		F		f	u	f		U		f	u
28	f		F		f	u	f		U		f	u
29	u	f		F		f	u	f		U		f
30	u	f		F		f	u	f		U		f

October Moon Table

Date	Sign	Element	Nature	Phase
1 Fri	Leo	Fire	Barren	4th
2 Sat	Leo	Fire	Barren	4th
3 Sun 4:38 am	Virgo	Earth	Barren	4th
4 Mon	Virgo	Earth	Barren	4th
5 Tue 8:41 am	Libra	Air	Semi-fruitful	4th
6 Wed	Libra	Air	Semi-fruitful	New 7:05 am
7 Thu 10:22 am	Scorpio	Water	Fruitful	1st
8 Fri	Scorpio	Water	Fruitful	1st
9 Sat 11:24 am	Sagittarius	Fire	Barren	1st
10 Sun	Sagittarius	Fire	Barren	1st
11 Mon 1:15 pm	Capricorn	Earth	Semi-fruitful	1st
12 Tue	Capricorn	Earth	Semi-fruitful	2nd 11:25 pm
13 Wed 4:47 pm	Aquarius	Air	Barren	2nd
14 Thu	Aquarius	Air	Barren	2nd
15 Fri 10:22 pm	Pisces	Water	Fruitful	2nd
16 Sat	Pisces	Water	Fruitful	2nd
17 Sun	Pisces	Water	Fruitful	2nd
18 Mon 6:04 am	Aries	Fire	Barren	2nd
19 Tue	Aries	Fire	Barren	2nd
20 Wed 3:59 pm	Taurus	Earth	Semi-fruitful	Full 10:57 am
21 Thu	Taurus	Earth	Semi-fruitful	3rd
22 Fri	Taurus	Earth	Semi-fruitful	3rd
23 Sat 3:57 am	Gemini	Air	Barren	3rd
24 Sun	Gemini	Air	Barren	3rd
25 Mon 5:00 pm	Cancer	Water	Fruitful	3rd
26 Tue	Cancer	Water	Fruitful	3rd
27 Wed	Cancer	Water	Fruitful	3rd
28 Thu 5:07 am	Leo	Fire	Barren	4th 4:05 pm
29 Fri	Leo	Fire	Barren	4th
30 Sat 2:09 pm	Virgo	Earth	Barren	4th
31 Sun	Virgo	Earth	Barren	4th

October Aspectarian/Favorable & Unfavorable Days

Date	Sun	Mercury	Venus	Mars	Jupiter	Saturn	Uranus	Neptune	Pluto
1	X			X		O	Q		
2		X	Q		O				
3									
4						T	O	T	
5			X		T				
6	C	C		C	T				
7						Q			Q
8					Q		O	T	
9			C			X			X
10	X	X		X				Q	
11					X				
12	Q	Q		Q			T		
13								X	C
14		T	X			C	Q		
15	T			T	C				
16			Q				X		
17								C	X
18						X			
19		O	T						
20	O			O	X				Q
21						Q	C		
22					Q			X	T
23						T			
24		T	O					Q	
25	T			T	T				
26							X		
27		Q						T	O
28	Q			Q	O				
29		X					Q		
30			T	X	O				
31	X					T			

Date	Aries	Taurus	Gemini	Cancer	Leo	Virgo	Libra	Scorpio	Sagittarius	Capricorn	Aquarius	Pisces
1	f	u	f		F		f	u	f		U	
2	f	u	f		F		f	u	f		U	
3	f	u	f		F		f	u	f		U	
4		f	u	f		F		f	u	f		U
5		f	u	f		F		f	u	f		U
6	U		f	u	f		F		f	u	f	
7	U		f	u	f		F		f	u	f	
8		U		f	u	f		F		f	u	f
9		U		f	u	f		F		f	u	f
10	f		U		f	u	f		F		f	u
11	f		U		f	u	f		F		f	u
12	u	f		U		f	u	f		F		f
13	u	f		U		f	u	f		F		f
14	f	u	f		U		f	u	f		F	
15	f	u	f		U		f	u	f		F	
16		f	u	f		U		f	u	f		F
17		f	u	f		U		f	u	f		F
18		f	u	f		U		f	u	f		F
19	F		f	u	f		U		f	u	f	
20	F		f	u	f		U		f	u	f	
21		F		f	u	f		U		f	u	f
22		F		f	u	f		U		f	u	f
23		F		f	u	f		U		f	u	f
24	f		F		f	u	f		U		f	u
25	f		F		f	u	f		U		f	u
26	u	f		F		f	u	f		U		f
27	u	f		F		f	u	f		U		f
28	u	f		F		f	u	f		U		f
29	f	u	f		F		f	u	f		U	
30	f	u	f		F		f	u	f		U	
31		f	u	f		F		f	u	f		U

November Moon Table

Date	Sign	Element	Nature	Phase
1 Mon 7:11 pm	Libra	Air	Semi-fruitful	4th
2 Tue	Libra	Air	Semi-fruitful	4th
3 Wed 8:52 pm	Scorpio	Water	Fruitful	4th
4 Thu	Scorpio	Water	Fruitful	New 5:15 pm
5 Fri 8:52 pm	Sagittarius	Fire	Barren	1st
6 Sat	Sagittarius	Fire	Barren	1st
7 Sun 8:03 pm	Capricorn	Earth	Semi-fruitful	1st
8 Mon	Capricorn	Earth	Semi-fruitful	1st
9 Tue 10:03 pm	Aquarius	Air	Barren	1st
10 Wed	Aquarius	Air	Barren	1st
11 Thu	Aquarius	Air	Barren	2nd 7:46 am
12 Fri 2:54 am	Pisces	Water	Fruitful	2nd
13 Sat	Pisces	Water	Fruitful	2nd
14 Sun 10:48 am	Aries	Fire	Barren	2nd
15 Mon	Aries	Fire	Barren	2nd
16 Tue 9:18 pm	Taurus	Earth	Semi-fruitful	2nd
17 Wed	Taurus	Earth	Semi-fruitful	2nd
18 Thu	Taurus	Earth	Semi-fruitful	2nd
19 Fri 9:33 am	Gemini	Air	Barren	Full 3:57 am
20 Sat	Gemini	Air	Barren	3rd
21 Sun 10:33 pm	Cancer	Water	Fruitful	3rd
22 Mon	Cancer	Water	Fruitful	3rd
23 Tue	Cancer	Water	Fruitful	3rd
24 Wed 10:59 am	Leo	Fire	Barren	3rd
25 Thu	Leo	Fire	Barren	3rd
26 Fri 9:12 pm	Virgo	Earth	Barren	3rd
27 Sat	Virgo	Earth	Barren	4th 7:28 am
28 Sun	Virgo	Earth	Barren	4th
29 Mon 3:55 am	Libra	Air	Semi-fruitful	4th
30 Tue	Libra	Air	Semi-fruitful	4th

November Aspectarian/Favorable & Unfavorable Days

Date	Sun	Mercury	Venus	Mars	Jupiter	Saturn	Uranus	Neptune	Pluto
1			Q					O	T
2						T			
3		C	X		T				Q
4	C			C		Q	O		
5					Q			T	X
6						X			
7					X			Q	
8		X	C	X			T		
9	X							X	C
10		Q		Q	C	Q			
11	Q				C				
12			X	T					
13	T	T						X	C
14									X
15			Q			X			
16					X				Q
17			T	O		Q	C		
18		O			Q			X	T
19	O								
20						T			
21						T		Q	
22							X		
23			O	T				T	
24	T	T							O
25					Q	O	Q		
26						O			
27	Q	Q					T		
28			T	X				O	T
29	X	X				T			
30			Q		T				Q

Date	Aries	Taurus	Gemini	Cancer	Leo	Virgo	Libra	Scorpio	Sagittarius	Capricorn	Aquarius	Pisces
1		f	u	f		F		f	u	f		U
2	U		f	u	f		F		f	u	f	
3	U		f	u	f		F		f	u	f	
4		U		f	u	f		F		f	u	f
5		U		f	u	f		F		f	u	f
6	f		U		f	u	f		F		f	u
7	f		U		f	u	f		F		f	u
8	u	f		U		f	u	f		F		f
9	u	f		U		f	u	f		F		f
10	f	u	f		U		f	u	f		F	
11	f	u	f		U		f	u	f		F	
12		f	u	f		U		f	u	f		F
13		f	u	f		U		f	u	f		F
14		f	u	f		U		f	u	f		F
15	F		f	u	f		U		f	u	f	
16	F		f	u	f		U		f	u	f	
17		F		f	u	f		U		f	u	f
18		F		f	u	f		U		f	u	f
19		F		f	u	f		U		f	u	f
20	f		F		f	u	f		U		f	u
21	f		F		f	u	f		U		f	u
22	u	f		F		f	u	f		U		f
23	u	f		F		f	u	f		U		f
24	u	f		F		f	u	f		U		f
25	f	u	f		F		f	u	f		U	
26	f	u	f		F		f	u	f		U	
27		f	u	f		F		f	u	f		U
28		f	u	f		F		f	u	f		U
29		f	u	f		F		f	u	f		U
30	U		f	u	f		F		f	u	f	u

December Moon Table

Date	Sign	Element	Nature	Phase
1 Wed 6:55 am	Scorpio	Water	Fruitful	4th
2 Thu	Scorpio	Water	Fruitful	4th
3 Fri 7:13 am	Sagittarius	Fire	Barren	4th
4 Sat	Sagittarius	Fire	Barren	New 2:43 am
5 Sun 6:31 am	Capricorn	Earth	Semi-fruitful	1st
6 Mon	Capricorn	Earth	Semi-fruitful	1st
7 Tue 6:49 am	Aquarius	Air	Barren	1st
8 Wed	Aquarius	Air	Barren	1st
9 Thu 9:53 am	Pisces	Water	Fruitful	1st
10 Fri	Pisces	Water	Fruitful	2nd 8:36 pm
11 Sat 4:46 pm	Aries	Fire	Barren	2nd
12 Sun	Aries	Fire	Barren	2nd
13 Mon	Aries	Fire	Barren	2nd
14 Tue 3:11 am	Taurus	Earth	Semi-fruitful	2nd
15 Wed	Taurus	Earth	Semi-fruitful	2nd
16 Thu 3:43 pm	Gemini	Air	Barren	2nd
17 Fri	Gemini	Air	Barren	2nd
18 Sat	Gemini	Air	Barren	Full 11:36 pm
19 Sun 4:42 am	Cancer	Water	Fruitful	3rd
20 Mon	Cancer	Water	Fruitful	3rd
21 Tue 4:54 pm	Leo	Fire	Barren	3rd
22 Wed	Leo	Fire	Barren	3rd
23 Thu	Leo	Fire	Barren	3rd
24 Fri 3:24 am	Virgo	Earth	Barren	3rd
25 Sat	Virgo	Earth	Barren	3rd
26 Sun 11:24 am	Libra	Air	Semi-fruitful	4th 9:24 pm
27 Mon	Libra	Air	Semi-fruitful	4th
28 Tue 4:16 pm	Scorpio	Water	Fruitful	4th
29 Wed	Scorpio	Water	Fruitful	4th
30 Thu 6:08 pm	Sagittarius	Fire	Barren	4th
31 Fri	Sagittarius	Fire	Barren	4th

December Aspectarian/Favorable & Unfavorable Days

Date	Sun	Mercury	Venus	Mars	Jupiter	Saturn	Uranus	Neptune	Pluto
1						Q			
2			X	C			O	T	X
3					Q	X			
4	C	C						Q	
5						X			
6			C	X			T	X	C
7						C			
8	X	X						Q	
9				Q	C				
10	Q						X	C	
11		Q	X	T					X
12						X			
13	T		Q		X				Q
14		T				Q			
15							C	X	
16			T	O	Q				T
17						T			
18	O							Q	
19				T					
20		O					X	T	
21			O						O
22				T	O	Q			
23									
24	T			Q	O				
25		T					T	O	
26	Q		T						T
27				X	T				
28		Q	Q		T				Q
29	X					Q	O		
30		X	X		Q			T	X
31				C		X			

Date	Aries	Taurus	Gemini	Cancer	Leo	Virgo	Libra	Scorpio	Sagittarius	Capricorn	Aquarius	Pisces
1	U		f	u	f		F		f	u	f	u
2		U		f	u	f		F		f	u	f
3		U		f	u	f		F		f	u	f
4	f		U		f	u	f		F		f	u
5	f		U		f	u	f		F		f	u
6	u	f		U		f	u	f		F		f
7	u	f		U		f	u	f		F		f
8	f	u	f		U		f	u	f		F	
9	f	u	f		U		f	u	f		F	
10		f	u	f		U		f	u	f		F
11		f	u	f		U		f	u	f		F
12	F		f	u	f		U		f	u	f	
13	F		f	u	f		U		f	u	f	
14	F		f	u	f		U		f	u	f	
15		F		f	u	f		U		f	u	f
16		F		f	u	f		U		f	u	f
17	f		F		f	u	f		U		f	u
18	f		F		f	u	f		U		f	u
19	f		F		f	u	f		U		f	u
20	u	f		F		f	u	f		U		f
21	u	f		F		f	u	f		U		f
22	f	u	f		F		f	u	f		U	
23	f	u	f		F		f	u	f		U	
24	f	u	f		F		f	u	f		U	
25		f	u	f		F		f	u	f		U
26		f	u	f		F		f	u	f		U
27	U		f	u	f		F		f	u	f	
28	U		f	u	f		F		f	u	f	
29		U		f	u	f		F		f	u	f
30		U		f	u	f		F		f	u	f
31	f		U		f	u	f		F		f	u

2021 Retrograde Planets

Planet	Begin	Eastern	Pacific	End	Eastern	Pacific
Uranus	8/15/20	10:25 am	**7:25 am**	1/14/21	3:36 am	**12:36 am**
Mercury	1/30	10:52 am	**7:52 am**	2/20	7:52 pm	**4:52 pm**
Pluto	4/27	4:04 pm	**1:04 pm**	10/6	2:29 pm	**11:29 am**
Saturn	5/23	5:21 am	**2:21 am**	10/10	10:17 pm	**7:17 pm**
Mercury	5/29	6:34 pm	**3:34 pm**	6/22	6:00 pm	**3:00 pm**
Jupiter	6/20	11:06 am	**8:06 am**	10/17		**10:30 pm**
Jupiter	6/20	11:06 am	**8:06 am**	10/18	1:30 am	
Neptune	6/25	3:21 pm	**12:21 pm**	12/1	8:22 am	**5:22 am**
Uranus	8/19	9:40 pm	**6:40 pm**	1/18/22	10:27 am	**7:27 am**
Mercury	9/26		**10:10 pm**	10/18	11:17 am	**8:17 am**
Mercury	9/27	1:10 am		10/18	11:17 am	**8:17 am**
Venus	12/19	5:36 am	**2:36 am**	1/29/22	3:46 am	**12:46 am**

Eastern Time in plain type, **Pacific Time in bold type**

	Dec 20	Jan 21	Feb	Mar	Apr	May	Jun	Jul	Aug	Sep	Oct	Nov	Dec	Jan 21
☿														
♃														
♀														
♄														
♇														
♆														
♅														
♂														

Egg-Setting Dates

To Have Eggs by this Date	Sign	Qtr.	Date to Set Eggs
Jan 15, 5:17 pm–Jan 18, 2:07 am	Pisces	1st	Dec 25, 2020
Jan 20, 1:56 pm–Jan 23, 2:43 am	Taurus	1st	Dec 30, 2020
Jan 25, 1:52 pm–Jan 27, 9:54 pm	Cancer	2nd	Jan 04, 2021
Feb 12, 2:23 am–Feb 14, 10:54 am	Pisces	1st	Jan 22
Feb 16, 10:12 pm–Feb 19, 11:04 am	Taurus	1st	Jan 26
Feb 21, 10:53 pm–Feb 24, 7:23 am	Cancer	2nd	Jan 31
Mar 13, 5:21 am–Mar 13, 6:44 pm	Pisces	1st	Feb 20
Mar 16, 6:56 am–Mar 18, 7:47 pm	Taurus	1st	Feb 23
Mar 21, 8:18 am–Mar 23, 5:56 pm	Cancer	1st	Feb 28
Mar 28, 1:22 am–Mar 28, 2:48 pm	Libra	2nd	Mar 07
Apr 12, 1:44 pm–Apr 15, 2:35 am	Taurus	1st	Mar 22
Apr 17, 3:25 pm–Apr 20, 2:11 am	Cancer	1st	Mar 27
Apr 24, 12:06 pm–Apr 26, 12:18 pm	Libra	2nd	Apr 03
May 11, 3:00 pm–May 12, 8:43 am	Taurus	1st	Apr 20
May 14, 9:30 pm–May 17, 8:44 am	Cancer	1st	Apr 23
May 21, 9:35 pm–May 23, 11:00 pm	Libra	2nd	Apr 30
Jun 11, 3:23 am–Jun 13, 2:22 pm	Cancer	1st	May 21
Jun 18, 4:54 am–Jun 20, 7:58 am	Libra	2nd	May 28
Jul 9, 9:17 pm–Jul 10, 8:21 pm	Cancer	1st	Jun 18
Jul 15, 10:32 am–Jul 17, 2:38 pm	Libra	1st	Jun 24
Aug 11, 4:08 pm–Aug 13, 8:01 pm	Libra	1st	Jul 21
Sep 7, 11:20 pm–Sep 10, 2:05 am	Libra	1st	Aug 17
Sep 18, 4:22 pm–Sep 20, 7:55 pm	Pisces	2nd	Aug 28
Oct 6, 7:05 am–Oct 7, 10:22 am	Libra	1st	Sep 15
Oct 15, 10:22 pm–Oct 18, 6:04 am	Pisces	2nd	Sep 24
Nov 12, 2:54 am–Nov 14, 10:48 am	Pisces	2nd	Oct 22
Nov 16, 9:18 pm–Nov 19, 3:57 am	Taurus	2nd	Oct 26
Dec 9, 9:53 am–Dec 11, 4:46 pm	Pisces	1st	Nov 18
Dec 14, 3:11 am–Dec 16, 3:43 pm	Taurus	2nd	Nov 23

Dates to Hunt and Fish

Date	Quarter	Sign
Jan 7, 3:53 am–Jan 9, 6:15 am	4th	Scorpio
Jan 15, 5:17 pm–Jan 18, 2:07 am	1st	Pisces
Jan 25, 1:52 pm–Jan 27, 9:54 pm	2nd	Cancer
Feb 3, 9:15 am–Feb 5, 12:16 pm	3rd	Scorpio
Feb 12, 2:23 am–Feb 14, 10:54 am	1st	Pisces
Feb 21, 10:53 pm–Feb 24, 7:23 am	2nd	Cancer
Mar 2, 3:38 pm–Mar 4, 5:43 pm	3rd	Scorpio
Mar 4, 5:43 pm–Mar 6, 9:20 pm	3rd	Sagittarius
Mar 11, 9:44 am–Mar 13, 6:44 pm	4th	Pisces
Mar 21, 8:18 am–Mar 23, 5:56 pm	1st	Cancer
Mar 30, 1:33 am–Apr 1, 1:59 am	3rd	Scorpio
Apr 1, 1:59 am–Apr 3, 4:13 am	3rd	Sagittarius
Apr 7, 4:30 pm–Apr 10, 2:11 am	4th	Pisces
Apr 17, 3:25 pm–Apr 20, 2:11 am	1st	Cancer
Apr 26, 12:18 pm–Apr 28, 11:42 am	2nd	Scorpio
Apr 28, 11:42 am–Apr 30, 12:16 pm	3rd	Sagittarius
May 4, 10:09 pm–May 7, 7:52 am	4th	Pisces
May 14, 9:30 pm–May 17, 8:44 am	1st	Cancer
May 23, 11:00 pm–May 25, 10:39 pm	2nd	Scorpio
May 25, 10:39 pm–May 27, 10:23 pm	2nd	Sagittarius
Jun 1, 5:07 am–Jun 3, 1:59 pm	3rd	Pisces
Jun 11, 3:23 am–Jun 13, 2:22 pm	1st	Cancer
Jun 20, 7:58 am–Jun 22, 8:55 am	2nd	Scorpio
Jun 22, 8:55 am–Jun 24, 9:05 am	2nd	Sagittarius
Jun 28, 1:51 pm–Jun 30, 9:21 pm	3rd	Pisces
Jun 30, 9:21 pm–Jul 3, 8:28 am	3rd	Aries
Jul 8, 9:51 am–Jul 10, 8:21 pm	4th	Cancer
Jul 17, 2:38 pm–Jul 19, 5:08 pm	2nd	Scorpio
Jul 19, 5:08 pm–Jul 21, 6:36 pm	2nd	Sagittarius
Jul 25, 11:30 pm–Jul 28, 5:58 am	3rd	Pisces
Jul 28, 5:58 am–Jul 30, 4:08 pm	3rd	Aries
Aug 4, 5:17 pm–Aug 7, 3:31 am	4th	Cancer
Aug 13, 8:01 pm–Aug 15, 11:12 pm	1st	Scorpio
Aug 15, 11:12 pm–Aug 18, 1:58 am	2nd	Sagittarius
Aug 22, 8:43 am–Aug 24, 2:57 pm	3rd	Pisces
Aug 24, 2:57 pm–Aug 27, 12:27 am	3rd	Aries
Sep 1, 1:26 am–Sep 3, 11:58 am	4th	Cancer
Sep 10, 2:05 am–Sep 12, 4:34 am	1st	Scorpio
Sep 18, 4:22 pm–Sep 20, 11:13 pm	2nd	Pisces
Sep 20, 11:13 pm–Sep 23, 8:38 am	3rd	Aries
Sep 28, 9:34 am–Sep 30, 8:53 pm	3rd	Cancer
Oct 7, 10:22 am–Oct 9, 11:24 am	1st	Scorpio
Oct 15, 10:22 pm–Oct 18, 6:04 am	2nd	Pisces
Oct 18, 6:04 am–Oct 20, 3:59 pm	2nd	Aries
Oct 25, 5:00 pm–Oct 28, 5:07 am	3rd	Cancer
Nov 3, 8:52 pm–Nov 5, 8:52 pm	4th	Scorpio
Nov 12, 2:54 am–Nov 14, 10:48 am	2nd	Pisces
Nov 14, 10:48 am–Nov 16, 9:18 pm	2nd	Aries
Nov 21, 10:33 pm–Nov 24, 10:59 am	3rd	Cancer
Dec 1, 6:55 am–Dec 3, 7:13 am	4th	Scorpio
Dec 9, 9:53 am–Dec 11, 4:46 pm	1st	Pisces
Dec 11, 4:46 pm–Dec 14, 3:11 am	2nd	Aries
Dec 19, 4:42 am–Dec 21, 4:54 pm	3rd	Cancer
Dec 28, 4:16 pm–Dec 30, 6:08 pm	4th	Scorpio

Dates to Destroy Weeds and Pests

Date	Sign	Qtr.
Jan 9 6:15 am–Jan 11 8:30 am	Sagittarius	4th
Jan 28 2:16 pm–Jan 30 3:02 am	Leo	3rd
Jan 30 3:02 am–Feb 1 6:25 am	Virgo	3rd
Feb 5 12:16 pm–Feb 7 3:52 pm	Sagittarius	4th
Feb 9 8:20 pm–Feb 11 2:06 pm	Aquarius	4th
Feb 27 3:17 am–Feb 28 2:17 pm	Virgo	3rd
Mar 4 5:43 pm–Mar 5 8:30 pm	Sagittarius	3rd
Mar 5 8:30 pm–Mar 6 9:20 pm	Sagittarius	4th
Mar 9 2:41 am–Mar 11 9:44 am	Aquarius	4th
Apr 1 1:59 am–Apr 3 4:13 am	Sagittarius	3rd
Apr 5 9:04 am–Apr 7 4:30 pm	Aquarius	4th
Apr 10 2:11 am–Apr 11 10:31 pm	Aries	4th
Apr 28 11:42 am–Apr 30 12:16 pm	Sagittarius	3rd
May 2 3:31 pm–May 3 3:50 pm	Aquarius	3rd
May 3 3:50 pm–May 4 10:09 pm	Aquarius	4th
May 7 7:52 am–May 9 7:46 pm	Aries	4th
May 26 7:14 am–May 27 10:23 pm	Sagittarius	3rd
May 30 12:04 am–Jun 1 5:07 am	Aquarius	3rd
Jun 3 1:59 pm–Jun 6 1:46 am	Aries	4th
Jun 8 2:47 pm–Jun 10 6:53 am	Gemini	4th
Jun 26 10:09 am–Jun 28 1:51 pm	Aquarius	3rd
Jun 30 9:21 am–Jul 1 5:11 pm	Aries	3rd
Jul 1 5:11 pm–Jul 3 8:28 am	Aries	4th
Jul 5 9:24 pm–Jul 8 9:51 am	Gemini	4th
Jul 23 10:37 pm–Jul 25 11:30 pm	Aquarius	3rd
Jul 28 5:58 am–Jul 30 4:08 pm	Aries	3rd
Aug 2 4:46 am–Aug 4 5:17 pm	Gemini	4th
Aug 7 3:31 am–Aug 8 9:50 am	Leo	4th
Aug 22 8:02 am–Aug 22 8:43 am	Aquarius	3rd
Aug 24 2:57 pm–Aug 27 12:27 am	Aries	3rd
Aug 29 12:42 pm–Aug 30 3:13 am	Gemini	3rd
Aug 30 3:13 am–Sep 1 1:26 am	Gemini	4th
Sep 3 11:58 am–Sep 5 7:06 pm	Leo	4th
Sep 5 7:06 pm–Sep 6 8:52 pm	Virgo	4th
Sep 20 11:13 pm–Sep 23 8:38 am	Aries	3rd
Sep 25 8:36 pm–Sep 28 9:34 am	Gemini	3rd
Sep 30 8:53 pm–Oct 3 4:38 am	Leo	4th
Oct 3 4:38 am–Oct 5 8:41 am	Virgo	4th
Oct 20 10:57 am–Oct 20 3:59 pm	Aries	3rd
Oct 23 3:57 am–Oct 25 5:00 pm	Gemini	3rd
Oct 28 5:07 am–Oct 28 4:05 pm	Leo	3rd
Oct 28 4:05 pm–Oct 30 2:09 pm	Leo	4th
Oct 30 2:09 pm–Nov 1 7:11 pm	Virgo	4th
Nov 19 9:33 am–Nov 21 10:33 pm	Gemini	3rd
Nov 24 10:59 am–Nov 26 9:12 pm	Leo	3rd
Nov 26 9:12 pm–Nov 27 7:28 am	Virgo	3rd
Nov 27 7:28 am–Nov 29 3:55 am	Virgo	4th
Dec 3 7:13 am–Dec 4 2:43 am	Sagittarius	4th
Dec 18 11:36 pm–Dec 19 4:42 am	Gemini	3rd
Dec 21 4:54 pm–Dec 24 3:24 am	Leo	3rd
Dec 24 3:24 am–Dec 26 11:24 am	Virgo	3rd

Time Zone Map

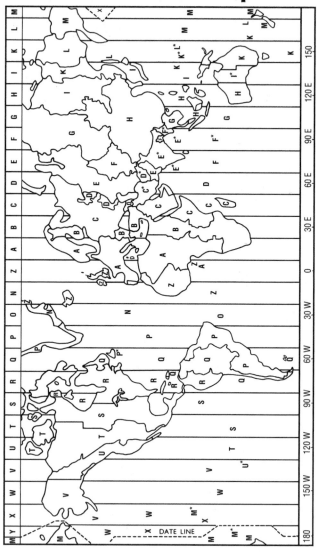

Time Zone Conversions

(R) EST—Used in book
(S) CST—Subtract 1 hour
(T) MST—Subtract 2 hours
(U) PST—Subtract 3 hours
(V) Subtract 4 hours
(V*) Subtract 4½ hours
(U*) Subtract 3½ hours
(W) Subtract 5 hours
(X) Subtract 6 hours
(Y) Subtract 7 hours
(Q) Add 1 hour
(P) Add 2 hours
(P*) Add 2½ hours
(O) Add 3 hours
(N) Add 4 hours
(Z) Add 5 hours
(A) Add 6 hours
(B) Add 7 hours
(C) Add 8 hours
(C*) Add 8½ hours

(D) Add 9 hours
(D*) Add 9½ hours
(E) Add 10 hours
(E*) Add 10½ hours
(F) Add 11 hours
(F*) Add 11½ hours
(G) Add 12 hours
(H) Add 13 hours
(I) Add 14 hours
(I*) Add 14½ hours
(K) Add 15 hours
(K*) Add 15½ hours
(L) Add 16 hours
(L*) Add 16½ hours
(M) Add 17 hours
(M*) Add 18 hours
(P*) Add 2½ hours

Important!

All times given in the *Moon Sign Book* are set in Eastern Time. The conversions shown here are for standard times only. Use the time zone conversions map and table to calculate the difference in your time zone. You must make the adjustment for your time zone and adjust for Daylight Saving Time where applicable.

Weather, Economic & Lunar Forecasts

Forecasting the Weather

by Kris Brandt Riske

Astrometeorology—astrological weather forecasting—reveals seasonal and weekly weather trends based on the cardinal ingresses (summer and winter solstices, and spring and autumn equinoxes) and the four monthly lunar phases. The planetary alignments and the longitudes and latitudes they influence have the strongest effect, but the zodiacal signs are also involved in creating weather conditions.

The components of a thunderstorm, for example, are heat, wind, and electricity. A Mars-Jupiter configuration generates the necessary heat and Mercury adds wind and electricity. A severe thunderstorm, and those that produce tornados, usually involve Mercury, Mars, Uranus, or Neptune. The zodiacal signs add their energy to the planetary mix to increase or decrease the chance for weather phenomena and their severity.

In general, the fire signs (Aries, Leo, Sagittarius) indicate heat and dryness, both of which peak when Mars, the planet with a similar nature, is in these signs. Water signs (Cancer, Scorpio, Pisces) are conducive to precipitation, and air signs (Gemini, Libra, Aquarius) are conducive to cool temperatures and wind. Earth signs (Taurus, Virgo, Capricorn) vary from wet to dry, heat to cold. The signs and their prevailing weather conditions are listed here:

Aries: Heat, dry, wind
Taurus: Moderate temperatures, precipitation
Gemini: Cool temperatures, wind, dry
Cancer: Cold, steady precipitation
Leo: Heat, dry, lightning
Virgo: Cold, dry, windy
Libra: Cool, windy, fair
Scorpio: Extreme temperatures, abundant precipitation
Sagittarius: Warm, fair, moderate wind
Capricorn: Cold, wet, damp
Aquarius: Cold, dry, high pressure, lightning
Pisces: Wet, cool, low pressure

Take note of the Moon's sign at each lunar phase. It reveals the prevailing weather conditions for the next six to seven days. The same is true of Mercury and Venus. These two influential weather planets transit the entire zodiac each year, unless retrograde patterns add their influence.

Planetary Influences

People relied on astrology to forecast weather for thousands of years. They were able to predict drought, floods, and temperature variations through interpreting planetary alignments. In recent years there has been a renewed interest in astrometeorology.

A weather forecast can be composed for any date—tomorrow, next week, or a thousand years in the future. According to astrometeorology, each planet governs certain weather phenomena. When certain planets are aligned with other planets, weather—precipitation, cloudy or clear skies, tornados, hurricanes, and other conditions—are generated.

Sun and Moon

The Sun governs the constitution of the weather and, like the Moon, it serves as a trigger for other planetary configurations that result in weather events. When the Sun is prominent in a cardinal ingress or lunar phase chart, the area is often warm and sunny. The Moon can bring or withhold moisture, depending upon its sign placement.

Mercury

Mercury is also a triggering planet, but its main influence is wind direction and velocity. In its stationary periods, Mercury reflects high winds, and its influence is always prominent in major weather events, such as hurricanes and tornadoes, when it tends to lower the temperature.

Venus

Venus governs moisture, clouds, and humidity. It brings warming trends that produce sunny, pleasant weather if in positive aspect to other planets. In some signs—Libra, Virgo, Gemini, Sagittarius—Venus is drier. It is at its wettest when placed in Cancer, Scorpio, Pisces, or Taurus.

Mars

Mars is associated with heat, drought, and wind, and can raise the temperature to record-setting levels when in a fire sign (Aries, Leo, Sagittarius). Mars is also the planet that provides the spark that generates thunderstorms and is prominent in tornado and hurricane configurations.

Jupiter

Jupiter, a fair-weather planet, tends toward higher temperatures when in Aries, Leo, or Sagittarius. It is associated with high-pressure systems and is a contributing factor at times to dryness. Storms are often amplified by Jupiter.

Saturn

Saturn is associated with low-pressure systems, cloudy to overcast skies, and excessive precipitation. Temperatures drop when Saturn is involved. Major winter storms always have a strong Saturn influence, as do storms that produce a slow, steady downpour for hours or days.

Uranus

Like Jupiter, Uranus indicates high-pressure systems. It reflects descending cold air and, when prominent, is responsible for a jet stream that extends far south. Uranus can bring drought in winter, and it is involved in thunderstorms, tornados, and hurricanes.

Neptune

Neptune is the wettest planet. It signals low-pressure systems and is dominant when hurricanes are in the forecast. When Neptune is strongly placed, flood danger is high. It's often associated with winter thaws. Temperatures, humidity, and cloudiness increase where Neptune influences weather.

Pluto

Pluto is associated with weather extremes, as well as unseasonably warm temperatures and drought. It reflects the high winds involved in major hurricanes, storms, and tornados.

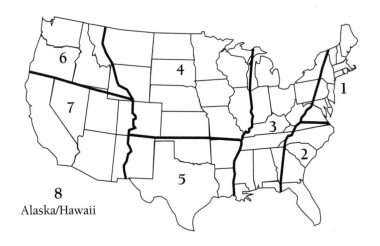

6

4

1

7

3

2

8
Alaska/Hawaii

5

Weather Forecast for 2021

by Kris Brandt Riske

Winter

Zone 1 can expect a winter with above-average precipitation and seasonal temperatures, while Zone 2, to the south, will see significant storms and chilly temperatures in coastal areas. Inland and throughout most of Florida, Zone 2 will be seasonal, but with periods of cold weather and potential for ice storms and freezing rain in the mid-Atlantic states. Temperatures in eastern and central areas of Zone 3 will be unseasonably cold with average moisture, and the northeastern part of the zone will be very cold.

Major weather systems will bring precipitation and cold temperatures to Zones 4 and 5. These will form and be centered in north-central areas of Zone 4, coming from Canada, and reach maximum intensity in the central areas of the plains states (southern Zone 4 and northern Zone 5) as storm fronts move through the region. Precipitation will be abundant at times.

The northwestern area of Zone 4, and eastern areas of Zones 6 and 7, will see significant precipitation from storms entering the continental United States from the northwest (western part of Zone 6, which will see significant storms and cold temperatures). Storm fronts will most often move southeast from central Zone 6 to eastern Zone 7 and western Zone 5. Western areas of Zone 7 will have temperatures above normal and below-average precipitation.

Alaska will be seasonal, with average precipitation, but western parts of the state will see abundant downfall. Temperatures will be colder in eastern areas and more seasonal in central regions. Hawaii's weather will be generally seasonal but with more cloudiness and precipitation in eastern areas.

Full Moon, December 29, 2020–January 5, 2021

Zone 1: The zone is windy and stormy with precipitation, and temperatures range from seasonal to below.

Zone 2: Cloudy and windy skies accompany temperatures seasonal to below with precipitation, some abundant.

Zone 3: The zone is mostly fair to partly cloudy, seasonal, and windy with precipitation, some abundant.

Zone 4: Skies are variably cloudy and very windy central and east, with seasonal temperatures.

Zone 5: The zone is partly cloudy to cloudy and windy east and central with a chance for strong thunderstorms with tornados.

Zone 6: Conditions are windy and wet as a front moves across much of the zone with strong winds in central and eastern areas.

Zone 7: Western areas see precipitation under mostly cloudy skies, and conditions are stormy south, cloudy west, partly cloudy east, and seasonal to below.

Zone 8: Alaska is cold under variably cloudy skies. Hawaii is seasonal and fair to partly cloudy with scattered precipitation.

4th Quarter Moon, January 6–12

Zone 1: Precipitation across the zone accompanies windy conditions, variably cloudy skies, and seasonal temperatures with potential for thunderstorms with snow or rain.

Zone 2: The zone sees thunderstorms under partly cloudy to cloudy skies and temperatures ranging from seasonal to above, with heavy precipitation in some locations triggering flooding.

Zone 3: Heavy precipitation could trigger flooding in central and eastern areas; skies are variably cloudy and windy with overcast central and east, and temperatures are seasonal to above.

Zone 4: Skies are windy and fair to partly cloudy, and temperatures are seasonal to above.

Zone 5: Temperatures range from seasonal to above, skies are partly cloudy and windy with scattered precipitation and thunderstorms in the central and eastern areas.

Zone 6: Most of the zone is cloudy with heavy precipitation central and east, and temperatures range from seasonal to below.

Zone 7: Western areas are windy with precipitation, the zone is variably cloudy and windy, temperatures are seasonal to below, and northern areas see precipitation.

Zone 8: Alaska sees scattered precipitation and wind with temperatures seasonal to below. Hawaii is seasonal and partly cloudy with precipitation later in the week.

New Moon, January 13–19

Zone 1: The zone is stormy, windy, and variably cloudy.

Zone 2: Skies are fair to partly cloudy with temperatures seasonal to above.

Zone 3: Precipitation central and south accompanies fair to partly cloudy skies, with northern areas mostly fair, and seasonal temperatures.

Zone 4: Eastern and central areas see precipitation with some abundant, skies are mostly cloudy, northern parts are very windy with abundant precipitation.

Zone 5: Areas south and east are mostly cloudy, northern and central areas are mostly fair and windy, and temperatures are seasonal to below.

Zone 6: The zone is windy with variable cloudiness and temperatures seasonal to below.

Zone 7: Skies are fair to partly cloudy west, windy central and east, with precipitation.

Zone 8: Cloudy skies yield precipitation across much of the state, and temperatures are seasonal to below. Hawaii is seasonal with variable cloudiness, scattered precipitation, seasonal temperatures, and wind.

2nd Quarter Moon, January 20–27

Zone 1: The zone is variably cloudy and cold with a chance for precipitation.

Zone 2: Skies are fair and temperatures are seasonal to above.

Zone 3: Much of the zone is cloudy and windy with precipitation, and temperatures are seasonal to below.

Zone 4: Western and southern parts of the zone see precipitation that moves into central areas of the eastern plains, and eastern areas see precipitation later in the week; temperatures are seasonal, but colder west.

Zone 5: Western and central areas are cloudy with precipitation, with the heaviest downfall in central parts of the zone. Temperatures are seasonal, and eastern areas are very windy later in the week.

Zone 6: Western areas are cloudy with precipitation, and other parts of the zone are mostly fair and windy with a chance for precipitation. Temperatures are seasonal to below, and northern coastal areas see increasing cloudiness and precipitation later in the week.

Zone 7: Skies are variably cloudy west and central, with a chance for precipitation east; temperatures are seasonal to below.

Zone 8: Central Alaska is cold and windy, and other areas are more seasonal, with precipitation east. Much of Hawaii is windy with temperatures seasonal to below, and there is a chance for precipitation in central parts of the state.

Full Moon, January 28–February 3

Zone 1: Much of the zone is windy and cloudy, with abundant precipitation north, and temperatures seasonal to below.

Zone 2: The zone is windy and cloudy with scattered precipitation, abundant downfall in the central and southern areas, and seasonal temperatures.

Zone 3: Scattered precipitation in some areas accompanies windy and cloudy skies and temperatures seasonal to below, with other areas receiving abundant downfall.

Zone 4: Northwestern areas are stormy, with winds moving across the zone to bring heavy precipitation to some locations, bringing clouds to eastern areas, and temperatures are seasonal to below.

Zone 5: The zone is windy with higher temperatures west, precipitation in the central and eastern areas, possibly with thunderstorms and tornados, and heavy precipitation east.

Zone 6: The zone is windy with high temperatures west, overcast skies, and precipitation central and east with potential for strong thunderstorms.

Zone 7: The zone is windy and cloudy, stormy in the western area with a front moving east, bringing heavy precipitation to some areas.

Zone 8: Alaska is windy, especially western and central areas, which see precipitation. Hawaii is windy, fair, and seasonal.

4th Quarter Moon, February 4–10

Zone 1: Windy with precipitation, which is heavy in the southern area, and much of the zone is cloudy and stormy with temperatures seasonal to below.

Zone 2: Central and southern areas are windy with thunderstorms, temperatures are seasonal to above, and clouds prevail.

Zone 3: Precipitation from the west extends into central and eastern areas with strong thunderstorms, abundant downfall, and seasonal temperatures

Zone 4: Northwestern parts of the zone are windy, especially at higher elevations, and into the western plains states, skies are cloudy, and temperatures are seasonal to below.

Zone 5: Skies are partly cloudy to cloudy with more cloudiness central and east along with precipitation, some heavy.

Zone 6: Temperatures are seasonal to below, skies are windy, and heavy downfall is possible in eastern areas.

Zone 7: Skies are fair to partly cloudy and windy, and temperatures are seasonal to above.

Zone 8: Western areas of Alaska are windy with scattered precipitation, and temperatures are seasonal. Hawaii sees fair to partly cloudy skies, showers, and seasonal temperatures.

New Moon, February 11–18

Zone 1: Skies are fair to partly cloudy, and the zone is seasonal with scattered precipitation.

Zone 2: Much of the zone is cloudy with precipitation, some heavy, and temperatures are seasonal to below.

Zone 3: Windy skies are fair to partly cloudy with scattered precipitation and temperatures seasonal to below.

Zone 4: Western areas are windy and stormy with scattered precipitation, some heavy, and temperatures are seasonal to below.

Zone 5: Thunderstorms are possible west, skies are fair to partly cloudy, but more cloudiness east, and temperatures are seasonal to below.

Zone 6: Central areas are stormy and cloudy with precipitation, some heavy, that moves into eastern areas.

Zone 7: Much of the zone is cloudy with precipitation, some heavy; western and central areas are stormy, eastern areas are windy, and temperatures are seasonal.

Zone 8: Alaska is windy and wet, western areas are partly cloudy to cloudy, and temperatures are seasonal to below. Hawaii sees variably cloudy skies with precipitation, some abundant.

2nd Quarter Moon, February 19–26

Zone 1: The zone is windy and partly cloudy with temperatures seasonal to below.

Zone 2: Skies are partly cloudy to cloudy across the zone and windy with precipitation east and south, some heavy with flood potential.

Zone 3: Skies are partly cloudy to cloudy with seasonal temperatures and precipitation across much of the zone; central areas are especially prone to flooding.

Zone 4: The zone is windy with temperatures seasonal to above, skies are partly cloudy east, with precipitation west.

Zone 5: Precipitation west moves into central and eastern areas under partly cloudy to cloudy skies, and temperatures are seasonal to above.

Zone 6: Western skies are cloudy and windy, central and eastern areas are fair to partly cloudy, and temperatures are seasonal.

Zone 7: Skies west and east are windy and cloudy, partly cloudy in the central and eastern areas, windy in the central area, and seasonal to below.

Zone 8: Alaskan temperatures are seasonal to below with wind and precipitation. Much of Hawaii is partly cloudy, windy, and seasonal with scattered precipitation.

Full Moon, February 27–March 4

Zone 1: Variable cloudiness and stormy conditions combine over much of the zone with temperatures seasonal to below.

Zone 2: The zone sees scattered precipitation with cloudy skies, heaviest in the south, and temperatures seasonal to below.

Zone 3: Much of the zone has variable clouds, and strong winds in the central and eastern areas, heavy precipitation in the west, and temperatures seasonal to below.

Zone 4: The zone sees heavy precipitation in the western area, windy skies, heavy precipitation in the eastern area, and variable clouds.

Zone 5: Windy west and into central areas under variable clouds, and temperatures are seasonal to above.

Zone 6: The zone is windy, central and east, and cloudy with precipitation east under cloudy to partly cloudy skies.

Zone 7: Western skies are windy with precipitation in coastal areas and central mountains, cloudy in the eastern area and windy, and temperatures seasonal to below.

Zone 8: Alaskan skies are overcast, cold, and windy west and central with precipitation, and temperatures are seasonal to below. Hawaii is cloudy with precipitation, some heavy, and seasonal temperatures.

4th Quarter Moon, March 5–12

Zone 1: Skies are fair to partly cloudy with scattered precipitation, some heavy, and seasonal temperatures.

Zone 2: Wind and thunderstorms bring precipitation to much of the zone, skies are partly cloudy, and temperatures are seasonal.

Zone 3: Much of the zone sees showers and thunderstorms under partly cloudy to cloudy skies, with precipitation heaviest in the western area, and seasonal temperatures.

Zone 4: Clouds and overcast skies west with precipitation that moves into central areas of the zone, with seasonal temperatures and strong thunderstorms.

Zone 5: Western and central areas see variable clouds, with showers and thunderstorms across the zone, and seasonal to above temperatures, with heavy downfall possible east.

Zone 6: The zone is windy with thunderstorms, temperatures are seasonal to above, and skies are fair to partly cloudy.

Zone 7: Skies are fair to partly cloudy with heavy precipitation in the central area, which moves into eastern areas, and temperatures are seasonal to above.

Zone 8: Much of Alaska sees precipitation, and temperatures are seasonal to below, with stormy conditions central. Hawaii is cloudy with heavy precipitation, and temperatures are seasonal to above.

New Moon, March 13–20

Zone 1: The zone is windy with precipitation and variably cloudy skies, with heavy precipitation north, and seasonal temperatures.

Zone 2: Temperatures are seasonal to above with strong winds central and south and possibly thunderstorms with tornados.

Zone 3: Western skies are cloudy, eastern and central areas are windy with scattered clouds, and temperatures are seasonal to below.

Zone 4: Skies are fair to partly cloudy, central and eastern areas are very windy, and temperatures are seasonal to above.

Zone 5: Skies are fair to partly cloudy but overcast and windy with scattered thunderstorms; temperatures are seasonal to below.

Zone 6: Eastern and central areas see precipitation under cloudy skies, western areas are mostly fair, and temperatures are seasonal.

Zone 7: Western skies are windy with precipitation that moves into central and eastern areas, some heavy; much of the zone is cloudy or overcast, and temperatures are seasonal to below.

Zone 8: Alaska is cloudy with abundant precipitation central, eastern areas are windy, and temperatures are seasonal to below. Much of Hawaii sees showers, some heavy, and temperatures are seasonal to below.

Spring

Wind and cold weather are dominant weather features in Zone 1, with southern areas also seeing above-normal precipitation. Coastal areas of Zone 2 are also windy with above-normal precipitation, cool temperatures, and increased potential for tornadoes. To the west in Zone 3, precipitation will be abundant in states from Ohio south, while most of the zone is at high risk for tornadoes and increased precipitation in western parts of the zone.

The plains states of western and central Zones 4 and 5 also have above-normal potential for strong thunderstorms with high winds and tornadoes, and states from Montana south to Texas will see abundant precipitation at times. The more northern areas of Zone 4 will be unseasonably cold at times.

Central areas of Zones 6 and 7 will see abundant precipitation, primarily at higher elevations, and windy, cold conditions. Precipitation will in general be normal to above in both of these zones. But the southern coastal areas will have periods of high temperatures, with more dryness than in other parts of Zone 7.

Eastern Alaska can expect significant precipitation this spring with flood potential, and most areas of the state will have average precipitation and temperatures seasonal to below. Hawaii will be seasonal and windy, with some areas receiving below-normal precipitation.

2nd Quarter Moon, March 21–27

Zone 1: The zone is windy, cloudy, and stormy with temperatures seasonal to below.

Zone 2: Fair to partly cloudy skies yield precipitation in the central area, scattered precipitation with partly cloudy skies south, and seasonal temperatures.

Zone 3: Cloudy and overcast skies dominate with strong thunderstorms and precipitation, and temperatures seasonal to below.

Zone 4: The zone sees strong thunderstorms and heavy precipitation, with variable cloudiness with tornado potential, and temperatures are seasonal to above.

Zone 5: Strong thunderstorms dominate much of the zone, eastern areas are windy, and temperatures are seasonal to above.

Zone 6: Western and central areas are windy and fair to partly cloudy with precipitation moving from west to central, and temperatures are seasonal.

Zone 7: The zone is variably cloudy, mostly fair in central and eastern areas, and temperatures are seasonal.

Zone 8: Alaska is windy in the western area, mostly fair to partly cloudy with scattered precipitation, and seasonal. Hawaii is windy and seasonal and variably cloudy with scattered precipitation.

Full Moon, March 28–April 3

Zone 1: Much of the zone sees precipitation, which will be heaviest in the north, windy skies, and temperatures seasonal to below.

Zone 2: Skies are cloudy to partly cloudy and windy with precipitation across northern and central areas, with scattered precipitation south and temperatures seasonal to below.

Zone 3: Windy conditions accompany cloudy skies, precipitation, some heavy, thunderstorms, possibly with tornados, and temperatures seasonal to below.

Zone 4: Precipitation, some abundant, moves from the west into central areas, windy and partly cloudy to cloudy skies, and temperatures seasonal to below.

Zone 5: Skies are fair to partly cloudy with more cloudiness in the central area, and thunderstorms with potential for tornados along with temperatures seasonal to above.

Zone 6: The zone is windy, partly cloudy to cloudy, and seasonal, with precipitation west and central.

Zone 7: The zone is windy west and central, skies are partly cloudy to cloudy, central areas see precipitation, some heavy in the west, and temperatures seasonal to above.

Zone 8: Central Alaska is cloudy with precipitation, some heavy, and eastern and western areas see scattered precipitation, with seasonal temperatures. Hawaii—Much of the state is partly cloudy to cloudy, central areas are mostly cloudy, and temperatures are seasonal to below.

4th Quarter Moon, April 4–10

Zone 1: The zone is windy with scattered precipitation, partly cloudy to cloudy skies, and temperatures seasonal to below,

Zone 2: The zone is windy with strong thunderstorms and tornados in south and central areas, partly cloudy to cloudy, and temperatures seasonal to above.

Zone 3: Skies are partly cloudy to cloudy and windy with thunderstorms and tornados, and temperatures are seasonal to above.

Zone 4: Precipitation west and central, partly cloudy to cloudy, and thunderstorms with tornados east and central.

Zone 5: Abundant downfall possible in the western area accompanied by partly cloudy to cloudy skies and temperatures seasonal to above.

Zone 6: Western and central areas see precipitation, some abundant, and seasonal temperatures.

Zone 7: Much of the zone is windy with partly cloudy to cloudy skies and scattered precipitation.

Zone 8: Alaska is fair to partly cloudy with heavy precipitation east, windy skies in the central area, and seasonal temperatures. Hawaii is variably cloudy and windy with temperatures seasonal to above.

New Moon, April 11–19

Zone 1: The zone is partly cloudy to cloudy and windy with precipitation, some heavy, with temperatures seasonal to below.

Zone 2: Much of the zone is windy with precipitation and partly cloudy to cloudy skies with temperatures seasonal to above.

Zone 3: The zone is windy with scattered precipitation, partly cloudy to cloudy, and seasonal.

Zone 4: Skies are windy and cloudy and overcast with precipitation, some heavy, and stormy with temperatures seasonal to below.

Zone 5: Cloudy and overcast skies west and central accompany partly cloudy skies east and temperatures seasonal to below.

Zone 6: The zone is windy with strong winds in the central area, precipitation, and temperatures seasonal to below.

Zone 7: West and central areas see precipitation, eastern areas are windy and partly cloudy, and temperatures are seasonal to below.

Zone 8: Alaska is windy and cloudy with precipitation, some heavy, and temperatures are seasonal to below. Hawaii is windy and seasonal with scattered precipitation.

2nd Quarter Moon, April 20–25

Zone 1: The zone is overcast and windy, with precipitation in the southern area, some abundant.

Zone 2: The zone is cloudy and windy with precipitation, skies are overcast, and southern areas see thunderstorms and possibly tornados, with seasonal temperatures.

Zone 3: There are thunderstorms with tornado potential across much of the zone with high winds and seasonal to below temperatures.

Zone 4: Variable clouds accompany thunderstorms with tornado potential and seasonal temperatures, with precipitation across much of the zone.

Zone 5: Precipitation, some heavy, variable cloudiness, and seasonal temperatures accompany high winds in western areas.

Zone 6: Skies are fair to partly cloudy with scattered precipitation and thunderstorms east.

Zone 7: Western areas see thunderstorms and showers with seasonal temperatures.

Zone 8: Alaska is fair to partly cloudy, temperatures are seasonal to below, and eastern areas see precipitation. Hawaii is seasonal and partly cloudy with scattered precipitation.

Full Moon, April 26–May 2

Zone 1: The zone sees precipitation, some heavy, skies are cloudy, some areas are stormy, and temperatures are seasonal.

Zone 2: Temperatures are seasonal, skies are fair to partly cloudy, and heavy precipitation could trigger flooding.

Zone 3: Partly cloudy skies yield scattered precipitation and heavier downfall east, skies are windy and stormy central and east with possible flooding.

Zone 4: The zone is seasonal under partly cloudy skies with precipitation, some heavy, with possible flooding in the eastern area.

Zone 5: Skies are partly cloudy to cloudy in the central area with heavy precipitation and thunderstorms, and temperatures are seasonal.

Zone 6: The zone is partly cloudy to cloudy and windy with precipitation and temperatures seasonal to above.

Zone 7: Areas west are windy and cloudy with precipitation, and temperatures are seasonal to above.

Zone 8: Alaska is variably cloudy with scattered precipitation and seasonal temperatures. Hawaii is seasonal with fair to partly cloudy skies and scattered precipitation.

4th Quarter Moon, May 3–10

Zone 1: Cloudy skies yield precipitation, some heavy in the southern area, and temperatures seasonal to below.

Zone 2: Abundant precipitation possible in the north and coastal areas with partly cloudy to cloudy skies, storm conditions, and seasonal temperatures.

Zone 3: Much of the zone is cloudy with abundant downfall, western areas are stormy, and temperatures are seasonal.

Zone 4: The zone is windy with precipitation west under partly cloudy to cloudy skies, seasonal temperatures, and mostly fair skies east.

Zone 5: Western areas see precipitation and seasonal temperatures under partly cloudy skies, western and central areas are windy, and heavy downfall is possible west.

Zone 6: Skies are fair to partly cloudy and seasonal with more cloudiness in the central and eastern areas, windy conditions central and east, and precipitation east.

Zone 7: The zone is windy and stormy; skies are mostly overcast with precipitation across much of the zone and seasonal to below temperatures.

Zone 8: Central Alaska is windy with precipitation, western areas see heavy downfall, and temperatures are seasonal. Hawaii is windy with partly cloudy skies and showers.

New Moon, May 11–18

Zone 1: The zone is windy with variable cloudiness, scattered precipitation, and seasonal temperatures.

Zone 2: Weather patterns in Zone 1 prevail in this zone, with precipitation, seasonal temperatures, and variable cloudiness.

Zone 3: Windy skies bring precipitation, including strong thunderstorms, and temperatures are seasonal.

Zone 4: Scattered showers and thunderstorms accompany windy conditions and temperatures seasonal to above.

Zone 5: The zone is variably cloudy and windy with scattered precipitation and temperatures seasonal to above.

Zone 6: Much of the zone is windy, central and eastern areas are stormy, and temperatures range from seasonal to below.

Zone 7: Eastern and central areas are cloudy, and conditions are stormy throughout the zone with temperatures ranging from seasonal to below.

Zone 8: Alaska is seasonal and windy with scattered precipitation. Much of Hawaii sees showers, and temperatures are seasonal to above.

2nd Quarter Moon, May 19–25

Zone 1: Northern skies are mostly fair, southern areas are partly cloudy with scattered precipitation, and temperatures are seasonal to below.

Zone 2: Much of the zone is cloudy and windy with precipitation, heavy in the south with thunderstorms and tornados, and temperatures seasonal to below.

Zone 3: Cloudy and windy skies prevail with precipitation and temperatures seasonal to below, with overcast skies east.

Zone 4: The zone is fair to partly cloudy with precipitation, some heavy, thunderstorms and tornados in central areas, and temperatures seasonal to above.

Zone 5: Cloudy skies yield precipitation, some abundant, and wind, with temperatures seasonal to above, and thunderstorms and tornados.

Zone 6: Western skies are overcast, central skies are variably cloudy with precipitation and wind, and temperatures are seasonal to below.

Zone 7: Temperatures ranging from seasonal to above, wind, and variable clouds trigger thunderstorms.

Zone 8: Alaska is seasonal to below and windy with scattered precipitation. In Hawaii, skies are variably cloudy with showers and thunderstorms, and temperatures are seasonal.

Full Moon, May 26–June 1

Zone 1: Northern areas are windy, seasonal, and cold with precipitation and possible strong thunderstorms.

Zone 2: Temperatures are seasonal to above, sparking strong thunderstorms and tornados.

Zone 3: Thunderstorms and tornados, some strong, bring precipitation to much of the zone with variable cloudiness and temperatures seasonal to above.

Zone 4: The zone is windy, cloudy, and seasonal with thunderstorms and possible tornados, and the heaviest precipitation will fall in the eastern area.

Zone 5: Western areas are variably cloudy and windy with scattered precipitation, thunderstorms with possible tornados, and seasonal temperatures.

Zone 7: Conditions are windy, variably cloudy with more cloudiness west and central, thunderstorms east, humid, and temperatures are seasonal to above.

Zone 8: Alaska is windy and cloudy with precipitation in the central and eastern areas, and seasonal temperatures. Hawaii is windy and cloudy with precipitation central and east.

4th Quarter Moon, June 2–9

Zone 1: Windy with temperatures seasonal to above, scattered showers and thunderstorms, and more cloudiness north.

Zone 2: The zone is windy with temperatures seasonal to above and strong thunderstorms, some severe.

Zone 3: Much of the zone sees showers and strong thunderstorms, with high winds in the east along with possible tornados and abundant precipitation, and temperatures are seasonal to above.

Zone 4: The zone is cloudy and humid and precipitation could be heavy with flooding from thunderstorms and tornados; temperatures are seasonal to above.

Zone 5: The zone is variably cloudy with more cloudiness east, along with showers and thunderstorms, some strong, tied to flooding, and wind and humidity.

Zone 6: Much of the zone is windy and variably cloudy, central and eastern areas are overcast with strong thunderstorms, and temperatures are seasonal.

Zone 7: The zone is mostly fair to partly cloudy, temperatures are seasonal to above; heavy precipitation could occur in some areas along with strong thunderstorms.

Zone 8: Alaska is windy and mostly fair with scattered precipitation. Hawaii is windy with temperatures seasonal to above and thunderstorms.

New Moon, June 10–16

Zone 1: Showers and thunderstorms across the zone pair with windy skies and temperatures that are seasonal to above.

Zone 2: The zone is windy, seasonal to above, variably cloudy, and humid, with scattered showers and thunderstorms.

Zone 3: Temperatures are seasonal to above, the zone sees scattered showers and thunderstorms, variable cloudiness, windy skies, and strong thunderstorms with tornado potential.

Zone 4: The zone is variably cloudy and humid, with temperatures seasonal to above, showers west and central, and a possibility of strong thunderstorms with tornado potential.

Zone 5: The zone is windy and variably cloudy, with showers and thunderstorms and temperatures seasonal to above.

Zone 6: Skies are windy, temperatures are seasonal to above, and the zone sees showers and thunderstorms.

Zone 7: Much of the zone is windy and variably cloudy with showers west and central, thunderstorms east, and temperatures seasonal to above.

Zone 8: Alaska is windy, cloudy, and seasonal. Hawaii is humid with showers, windy, variably cloudy, and temperatures are seasonal to above.

2nd Quarter Moon, June 17–23

Zone 1: Southern areas are windy with strong scattered thunderstorms, and northern areas see showers and thunderstorms; temperatures are seasonal.

Zone 2: Temperatures are seasonal to above with strong thunderstorms, some with tornado potential, across the zone.

Zone 3: Cloudy skies bring scattered showers and thunderstorms to western areas, while other parts of the zone, especially those to the east, see thunderstorms, some severe with high winds; temperatures are seasonal to above.

Zone 4: Western and eastern skies are mostly fair, while central areas of the zone are cloudy with scattered precipitation; temperatures are seasonal.

Zone 5: Skies are mostly fair in west and central areas, with some cloudiness and scattered precipitation in central northern areas. Cloudy skies prevail to the east with scattered showers and thunderstorms; temperatures are seasonal to above.

Zone 6: Western areas see partly cloudy skies and scattered precipitation, while central and eastern areas are windy and cloudy with some abundant precipitation as a front moves through the zone.

Zone 7: Desert areas are hot and dry, central areas see heavy precipitation, and western and northeastern parts of the zone are variably cloudy with scattered precipitation; temperatures are seasonal to above.

Zone 8: Alaska is mostly fair and seasonal with scattered precipitation east. Hawaii is fair and seasonal with scattered precipitation west.

Summer

Zone 1 will be prone to severe storms—including hurricanes—this summer as well as unseasonably cool temperatures and wind. Temperatures will range higher in Zone 2, along with below-average precipitation. Temperatures in Zone 3 will be about average but with periods of excessive heat, which will trigger thunderstorms followed by cooler temperatures.

The central plains states in Zones 4 and 5 will experience periods of abundant precipitation, as will the eastern parts of Zone 5 and the Mississippi River Valley. Western areas of these zones can expect normal precipitation levels and temperatures from seasonal to cool. Northwestern areas of Zone 4 will also be prone to strong storms.

Precipitation will range from normal to slightly below in Zone 6, and temperatures will be seasonal to above. Although western and central parts of Zone 7 will see precipitation, these areas can also expect periods of high temperatures. Eastern areas of Zone 7 can expect significant monsoon storms with high winds and seasonal temperatures.

Central Alaska will be cooler than normal with periodic major storms, while western parts of the state will be seasonal with average precipitation, and western areas will see more cloudiness and windy conditions along with cooler temperatures. Summer in Hawaii will be generally seasonal but with potential for strong thunderstorms and locally heavy precipitation.

Full Moon, June 24–30
Zone 1: The zone is humid with precipitation, some heavy, winds are strong, temperatures are seasonal to below, and skies are cloudy.
Zone 2: Showers and strong thunderstorms with some heavy precipitation visit the zone, along with variable cloudiness and seasonal temperatures.
Zone 3: Western areas see showers, central and eastern areas see thunderstorms, skies are variably cloudy, and temperatures are seasonal to above.
Zone 4: Western areas see precipitation, much of the zone is fair to partly cloudy and windy, temperatures are seasonal to above, thunderstorms with tornados are prevalent.

Zone 5: Strong thunderstorms with tornados are possible, temperatures are seasonal to above, skies are variably cloudy, and much of the zone sees precipitation, with more cloudiness west.

Zone 6: The zone is windy with variable clouds, thunderstorms in central and eastern areas, and temperatures are seasonal.

Zone 7: The zone sees precipitation west and into central mountains with thunderstorms, some with heavy downfall, variably cloudy skies, and temperatures seasonal to above.

Zone 8: Alaska is mainly fair to partly cloudy with more cloudiness central, and temperatures are seasonal. Hawaii is windy with variable cloudiness, temperatures seasonal to above, strong thunderstorms with precipitation and potential for flooding.

4th Quarter Moon, July 1–8

Zone 1: The zone is windy and variably cloudy with scattered thunderstorms and abundant precipitation, and temperatures are seasonal to below.

Zone 2: The zone is variably cloudy with temperatures seasonal to above and scattered showers and thunderstorms.

Zone 3: Temperatures are seasonal to above and skies are fair to partly cloudy.

Zone 4: Much of the zone is cloudy, eastern areas are partly cloudy, western parts of the zone see thunderstorms, some strong, with tornados, and the zone is windy and seasonal to above.

Zone 5: Skies are cloudy west and central with precipitation that moves into central areas with strong thunderstorms and tornados, and temperatures are seasonal to above.

Zone 6: The zone is windy with precipitation in the central area, some heavy, high winds, seasonal temperatures, cloudy in the east, and scattered precipitation.

Zone 7: Central areas see precipitation, some heavy, and high winds with scattered precipitation east, and seasonal temperatures.

Zone 8: Alaska is variably cloudy, windy, and seasonal with precipitation, some abundant. Hawaii is windy, temperatures are seasonal to above, and central and eastern areas see strong thunderstorms.

New Moon, July 9–16

Zone 1: The zone is fair to partly cloudy with temperatures seasonal to above.

Zone 2: From windy conditions come strong thunderstorms with tornado potential in the south and central areas, and there will be fair to partly cloudy skies.

Zone 3: Much of the zone is overcast and windy with scattered precipitation and seasonal temperatures.

Zone 4: Variable clouds produce showers and thunderstorms, some severe, seasonal temperatures, and more cloudiness east.

Zone 5: The zone is windy with strong scattered thunderstorms and showers, more cloudiness east with some abundant precipitation, and temperatures ranging from seasonal to above.

Zone 6: Seasonal temperatures accompany skies fair to partly cloudy, with more cloudiness east and scattered precipitation.

Zone 7: The zone is variably cloudy with scattered precipitation and thunderstorms, some abundant in the central and eastern areas, and temperatures seasonal to above.

Zone 8: Alaska is windy in the western area with precipitation, scattered showers are in the central and east, it is cloudy in the west, and temperatures are mostly seasonal. Hawaii is fair to partly cloudy and seasonal to above.

2nd Quarter Moon, July 17–22

Zone 1: Skies are fair to partly cloudy and windy in the southern area with seasonal temperatures and scattered precipitation north.

Zone 2: The zone is windy with showers and thunderstorms, and temperatures are seasonal to above.

Zone 3: Windy conditions accompany showers and thunderstorms with heavy precipitation east, and temperatures are seasonal to above.

Zone 4: Much of the zone sees showers; there will be isolated thunderstorms and precipitation east with flood potential, variable cloudiness, humidity, and seasonal temperatures.

Zone 5: Eastern areas are windy with precipitation, some heavy, variable cloudiness, and seasonal temperatures.

Zone 6: Western areas see showers into central parts of the zone, skies are fair east, partly cloudy to cloudy west and central, seasonal and windy.

Zone 7: Showers west and into central areas accompany partly cloudy to cloudy skies, precipitation in central and eastern areas, some heavy, and high winds possible east.

Zone 8: Alaska is windy east and seasonal under fair to partly cloudy skies. In Hawaii, skies are partly cloudy and windy, and the state is humid with temperatures seasonal to above.

Full Moon, July 23–29

Zone 1: Skies are windy and cloudy with strong thunderstorms, abundant precipitation with flood potential, seasonal temperatures, and possibly a tropical storm or hurricane.

Zone 2: Heavy precipitation could trigger flooding across the zone, possibly a tropical storm or hurricane, seasonal temperatures, and variable cloudiness.

Zone 3: Abundant precipitation could trigger flooding east as a result of a tropical storm or hurricane in central and eastern areas, with showers west and central, and windy and mostly cloudy skies.

Zone 4: Thunderstorms, some strong with tornado potential, high winds in some locations, seasonal to above temperatures, and partly cloudy to cloudy skies.

Zone 5: Strong thunderstorms can produce high winds, temperatures are seasonal to above, precipitation heavy in some locations, and skies are partly cloudy to cloudy.

Zone 6: Variably cloudy skies are windy with seasonal temperatures and overcast in western areas.

Zone 7: The zone is overcast west, fair to partly cloudy east and central, windy, and seasonal to above.

Zone 8: Alaska sees precipitation west and into central, some heavy, partly cloudy to cloudy skies, and seasonal temperatures. Hawaii is seasonal with showers and thunderstorms, some heavy with flood potential.

4th Quarter Moon, July 31–August 7

Zone 1: Northern and central areas see heavy precipitation that could result in flooding, skies are mostly cloudy, and conditions are seasonal and humid.

Zone 2: Precipitation across much of the zone with showers and thunderstorms and a possible hurricane; there will also be variably cloudy and windy skies with temperatures seasonal to above.

Zone 3: Skies are windy and cloudy with precipitation, possibly from a tropical storm or hurricane, and temperatures are seasonal.

Zone 4: The zone is windy with thunderstorms, some strong with heavy precipitation, and temperatures are seasonal to above.

Zone 5: Much of the zone sees showers and thunderstorms with windy skies and temperatures seasonal to above.

Zone 6: Western and central areas are cloudy with showers and thunderstorms; there will be wind and seasonal temperatures.

Zone 7: The zone is windy with showers and thunderstorms, variable cloudiness, and temperatures seasonal to above.

Zone 8: Western and central Alaska see precipitation, some heavy, under windy skies, with possible flooding, and seasonal temperatures. Hawaii sees showers and thunderstorms, some heavy, and seasonal temperatures.

New Moon, August 8–14

Zone 1: Heavy precipitation across much of the zone could produce flooding under mostly cloudy skies, and temperatures are seasonal.

Zone 2: Showers and thunderstorms, along with potential for a tropical storm or hurricane, and temperatures seasonal to above under variably cloudy skies.

Zone 3: Cloudy skies accompany precipitation, wind, and seasonal temperatures.

Zone 4: The zone is windy with strong thunderstorms, some yielding heavy downfall, with temperatures seasonal to above.

Zone 5: Much of the zone sees showers and thunderstorms under windy skies with temperatures seasonal to below.

Zone 6: Western and central areas are windy and cloudy with showers and thunderstorms.

Zone 7: The zone is windy with showers and thunderstorms, variably cloudy, and seasonal to above.

Zone 8: Alaska sees precipitation west and central, with flood potential, and is also windy and seasonal. Seasonal temperatures in Hawaii accompany showers and thunderstorms, some strong.

2nd Quarter Moon, August 15–21

Zone 1: The zone is windy with strong precipitation, wind, and temperatures seasonal to below.

Zone 2: Thunderstorms with tornado potential accompany humidity, variable cloudiness, and temperatures seasonal to above.

Zone 3: Skies are fair to partly cloudy with tornado-producing thunderstorms and high winds in the eastern area, and temperatures are seasonal to above.

Zone 4: Thunderstorms with strong tornado potential produce abundant downfall west and central under windy and variably cloudy skies.

Zone 5: The zone sees precipitation, some abundant, cloudy skies, and temperatures seasonal to above.

Zone 6: The zone is windy and mostly cloudy with strong thunderstorms in the eastern area; temperatures are seasonal to above.

Zone 7: Scattered precipitation east with thunderstorms accompanies temperatures seasonal to above.

Zone 8: Central areas of Alaska are stormy with variable cloudiness, precipitation west, and temperatures seasonal to below. Much of Hawaii is cloudy and stormy with temperatures seasonal to below.

Full Moon, August 22–29

Zone 1: Much of the zone sees heavy precipitation under cloudy skies and temperatures seasonal to below, possibly indicators of a tropical storm or hurricane.

Zone 2: The zone is windy and stormy with strong winds, and temperatures are seasonal to above.

Zone 3: The zone is variably cloudy with high winds and temperatures seasonal to below.

Zone 4: Precipitation west and central, some heavy, variable cloudiness and temperatures seasonal to below.

Zone 5: Showers in the western area and mostly fair in the central and east with seasonal temperatures.

Zone 6: Much of the zone is cloudy and windy with precipitation and temperatures seasonal to below.

Zone 7: The zone sees strong thunderstorms, variably cloudy skies, wind, and temperatures seasonal to above.

Zone 8: Western and central Alaska see heavy precipitation with temperatures seasonal to below. Much of Hawaii sees showers and partly cloudy to cloudy skies.

4th Quarter Moon, August 30–September 5

Zone 1: The zone sees precipitation from windy and partly cloudy to cloudy skies, and temperatures are seasonal to above.

Zone 2: The zone is seasonal, windy, and variably cloudy with thunderstorms and tornados.

Zone 3: Skies are fair to partly cloudy and windy with strong thunderstorms with tornado potential.

Zone 4: The zone is variably cloudy and windy with showers and thunderstorms, some strong.

Zone 5: The zone is windy, humid, and variably cloudy with strong thunderstorms, possibly with heavy precipitation.

Zone 6: Skies are fair to partly cloudy with scattered precipitation, showers and thunderstorms.

Zone 7: The zone is fair to partly cloudy, and seasonal to above, with precipitation in the eastern area.

Zone 8: Western areas of Alaska see showers, the state is windy, and temperatures are seasonal. Much of Hawaii sees showers and wind with temperatures seasonal to above.

New Moon, September 6–12

Zone 1: Skies are windy in the southern area with showers and thunderstorms, partly cloudy to cloudy skies, and seasonal temperatures.

Zone 2: The zone sees showers and strong thunderstorms in central and southern areas, with variable cloudiness and seasonal temperatures.

Zone 3: Windy skies accompany showers, strong thunderstorms, and seasonal temperatures.

Zone 4: Skies are fair to partly cloudy and humid with scattered thunderstorms and temperatures seasonal to above.

Zone 5: Much of the zone sees scattered showers; eastern areas see strong thunderstorms and variably cloudy skies with heavy precipitation.

Zone 6: Temperatures are seasonal to above, and the zone sees fair to partly cloudy skies.

Zone 7: The zone is windy with strong thunderstorms east, skies are fair to partly cloudy, northern coastal areas see showers, and temperatures are seasonal to above.

Zone 8: Alaska sees showers west and central, temperatures are seasonal, and skies are partly cloudy to cloudy. Central areas of Hawaii see showers and high winds, and temperatures are seasonal to above.

2nd Quarter Moon, September 13–19

Zone 1: The zone is fair to partly cloudy and windy with scattered precipitation and temperatures seasonal to above.

Zone 2: Windy conditions, humidity, and scattered thunderstorms accompany seasonal temperatures.

Zone 3: Strong thunderstorms, precipitation, variably cloudy skies, heavy downfall east, and humidity accompany temperatures seasonal to below.

Zone 4: Much of the zone sees thunderstorms and showers with cloudy skies central and east, abundant downfall and seasonal temperatures.

Zone 5: Scattered precipitation, showers and thunderstorms, and seasonal temperatures move across the zone.

Zone 6: Temperatures are seasonal to above with scattered thunderstorms.

Zone 7: Western and central areas see precipitation under variably cloudy skies, eastern areas are mostly fair; temperatures are seasonal to above with strong thunderstorms.

Zone 8: Alaska is mostly cloudy in the western and central areas and seasonal. Hawaii is seasonal to above with variable cloudiness.

Autumn

Coastal areas of Zones 1 and 2 can expect precipitation to range from average to above, with higher levels and hurricane potential in northern areas of Zone 1. These zones will also be prone to an increased level of severe thunderstorms, with tornado potential in early autumn and winter storms later in the season. Northeastern areas of Zone 3 will experience much the same weather, and western and central parts of this zone will also see abundant precipitation and strong thunderstorms with tornado potential at times. Temperatures will dip quite low at times in Zone 3 and central areas of Zone 2.

The plains states of Zones 4 and 5, as well as northeastern areas of Zone 4, will at times see abundant precipitation, strong low pressure systems, and cool temperatures. A southerly flow of moisture will elevate temperatures and humidity, aiding in the development of storm systems. These areas can also expect periods of colder than average temperatures, as can the western plains, which will also see abundant precipitation as a result of low pressure systems. Heaviest downfall throughout these zones is likely to occur in the central parts of the zones.

To the west, the northwestern, coastal part of Zone 6 will experience cold temperatures and abundant precipitation, while central and eastern areas will be more seasonal. Temperatures will tend to be above normal in western parts of Zone 7, and this area will also be prone to high winds, which could equate to severe fire weather. Central areas of Zone 7 will see more cloudiness and precipitation, and temperatures in eastern parts of this zone will be above normal, especially in desert areas.

Central Alaska can expect an increased number of cloudy and windy days with average precipitation and temperatures from seasonal to below. Western Alaska will see abundant precipitation at times, and temperatures will be seasonal, while eastern parts of the state will be generally seasonal. Hawaii will be generally seasonal, although precipitation may be below average.

Full Moon, September 20–27

Zone 1: The zone is cloudy, overcast, and windy with precipitation and temperatures seasonal to below.

Zone 2: Temperatures are seasonal to above, skies are windy and partly cloudy, and the zone sees scattered showers and thunderstorms.

Zone 3: The zone is windy and humid with variable cloudiness and temperatures seasonal to above, along with strong thunderstorms.

Zone 4: Much of the zone is humid and windy with thunderstorms that have tornado potential; it will also include some heavy precipitation and temperatures seasonal to above.

Zone 5: The zone is windy with showers and thunderstorms, some with heavy downfall in the east, humidity, and temperatures seasonal to above.

Zone 6: Scattered showers and thunderstorms accompany partly cloudy and windy skies with seasonal temperatures.

Zone 7: Temperatures are seasonal to above, and skies are windy and partly cloudy with scattered precipitation.

Zone 8: Alaska is windy with precipitation, and temperatures are seasonal to above. Hawaii is windy with temperatures seasonal to above and scattered showers.

4th Quarter Moon, September 28–October 5

Zone 1: The zone is windy, partly cloudy, cold, and damp with precipitation.

Zone 2: Temperatures are seasonal and the zone is windy with precipitation.

Zone 3: The zone is windy with precipitation and clouds and is seasonal to below.

Zone 4: Skies are cloudy and the zone sees precipitation with wind and seasonal temperatures.

Zone 5: The zone sees precipitation and showers under cloudy skies with wind.

Zone 6: Conditions are windy and cloudy with showers throughout much of the zone, and temperatures are seasonal to above.

Zone 7: The zone sees windy skies, showers, and temperatures seasonal to above.

Zone 8: Alaska is seasonal, humid, windy, and partly cloudy with showers. Hawaii is humid with showers and clouds and seasonal temperatures.

New Moon, October 6–11

Zone 1: The zone is windy with precipitation and seasonal to below.

Zone 2: Western areas are windy with precipitation, much of the zone is cloudy, and temperatures are seasonal to below.

Zone 3: The zone is overcast and windy with precipitation, and temperatures are seasonal to below.

Zone 4: Cloudy, windy skies yield abundant downfall, and temperatures are seasonal to below.

Zone 5: Much of the zone is cloudy with precipitation, which is heavy in central areas, and there may be a tropical storm or hurricane with strong thunderstorms, humidity, and seasonal temperatures.

Zone 6: Skies are variably cloudy with temperatures seasonal to above and windy; there will be abundant downfall in the western area and heavy cloud cover in mountainous areas.

Zone 7: Skies are windy and variably cloudy with scattered precipitation that is abundant in some areas.

Zone 8: In Alaska, skies are fair to partly cloudy with precipitation in the western areas and scattered showers central and east. Hawaii is fair to partly cloudy with scattered showers and temperatures seasonal to above.

2nd Quarter Moon, October 12–19

Zone 1: Skies are windy with precipitation, and temperatures are seasonal to below.

Zone 2: The zone is windy and cloudy with scattered precipitation and temperatures seasonal to above.

Zone 3: Precipitation, some heavy in the eastern area, accompanies windy conditions and temperatures seasonal to below.

Zone 4: Eastern areas see scattered precipitation, central and western areas see heavy precipitation and wind; along with temperatures seasonal to below, a major winter storm is possible.

Zone 5: Skies are fair to partly cloudy with showers and thunderstorms, some strong, and seasonal temperatures.

Zone 6: Precipitation from the west moves across much of the zone, conditions are windy, temperatures seasonal to above, western skies cloudy, and skies fair to partly cloudy.

Zone 7: The zone is windy with precipitation in coastal areas and across the zone, and showers and thunderstorms are active.

Zone 8: Alaska sees showers with some abundant downfall, cloudy skies, and temperatures seasonal to below. Much of Hawaii sees scattered precipitation, skies are partly cloudy to cloudy, and temperatures are seasonal.

Full Moon, October 20–27

Zone 1: Scattered precipitation accompanies windy and fair to partly cloudy skies and seasonal temperatures.

Zone 2: The zone sees variable cloudiness, scattered showers in the south, and seasonal temperatures and precipitation, some heavy.

Zone 3: Cloudy skies across much of the zone are accompanied by temperatures seasonal to below, and abundant downfall in the eastern area.

Zone 4: Temperatures are seasonal to below, and the zone sees precipitation, thunderstorms, and partly cloudy skies.

Zone 5: Much of the zone is cloudy and windy with precipitation in the central area, some of which is abundant, and overcast skies.

Zone 6: Cloudy skies and temperatures seasonal to below accompany scattered precipitation and wind.

Zone 7: Western areas are overcast with precipitation, strong thunderstorms central and east, with temperatures seasonal to above.

Zone 8: Alaska is cloudy and windy with precipitation east and temperatures seasonal to below. Hawaii is partly cloudy to cloudy and seasonal with scattered precipitation.

4th Quarter Moon, October 28–November 3

Zone 1: The zone is seasonal to below and stormy with abundant precipitation possible in the southern area.

Zone 2: Northern areas are windy and stormy with heavy precipitation and seasonal to below temperatures, all possibly the result of a hurricane or tropical storm.

Zone 3: Abundant precipitation is possible along with temperatures seasonal to below and cloudy, windy conditions.

Zone 4: Temperatures range from seasonal to below, and skies are windy and cloudy with precipitation.

Zone 5: Skies are partly cloudy to cloudy and windy with seasonal temperatures and scattered precipitation.

Zone 6: Much of the zone is cloudy with precipitation in the east and temperatures seasonal to below.

Zone 7: Western areas see precipitation, as do northern coastal areas and into central parts of the zone under cloudy skies, and temperatures are seasonal to above in eastern areas with scattered precipitation.

Zone 8: Western parts of Alaska and some central areas are windy and partly cloudy to cloudy with seasonal temperatures. Hawaii sees scattered showers, some heavy, in the western and central areas, variably cloudy skies, and seasonal temperatures.

New Moon, November 4–10

Zone 1: Southern areas are mostly fair, and northern parts of the zone are cloudy with scattered precipitation; temperatures are seasonal.

Zone 2: The zone is partly cloudy in the south and central areas, fair in the north, and seasonal.

Zone 3: The zone is generally fair to partly cloudy and seasonal with a chance for precipitation in the west.

Zone 4: Variably cloudy skies accompany temperatures seasonal to above; western areas see scattered precipitation later in the week.

Zone 5: Western and central areas see scattered precipitation, and the zone is seasonal.

Zone 6: Temperatures are seasonal to above, and skies are fair to partly cloudy with a chance for precipitation in central areas.

Zone 7: Southern coastal and central areas of the zone see precipitation, eastern areas are fair and windy, and the northern coast is windy with a chance for precipitation; temperatures are seasonal to above.

Zone 8: Central Alaska is stormy, and eastern and western parts of the zone are mostly fair and seasonal. Hawaii is mostly fair and seasonal; eastern areas see showers and thunderstorms.

2nd Quarter Moon, November 11–18

Zone 1: The zone is seasonal, northern areas are windy, and southern areas see scattered precipitation.

Zone 2: Weather is seasonal under variably cloudy skies.

Zone 3: Eastern areas see scattered precipitation, and the zone is seasonal and fair to partly cloudy.

Zone 4: Precipitation centers northwest, eastern areas are cloudy with scattered precipitation, and temperatures range from seasonal to below.

Zone 5: Temperatures are seasonal to below, and the zone is mostly fair with some cloudiness in the east.

Zone 6: Western skies are partly cloudy, while central parts of the zone are mostly fair; eastern areas are very windy with precipitation followed by cooler temperatures.

Zone 7: Northern coastal areas have a chance for showers, but western and central skies are mostly fair, while eastern areas see precipitation.

Zone 8: Alaska is windy and seasonal with fair to partly cloudy skies. Hawaii is fair to partly cloudy, windy, and seasonal.

Full Moon, November 19–26

Zone 1: The zone is fair and seasonal.

Zone 2: Northern areas are fair, and central and southern areas see scattered precipitation; temperatures are seasonal.

Zone 3: Temperatures are seasonal to above and the zone is fair to partly cloudy.

Zone 4: Variable cloudiness prevails across the zone with a chance for precipitation west; temperatures are seasonal to below but warmer east.

Zone 5: The zone is fair to partly cloudy and seasonal with a chance for precipitation in the western area.

Zone 6: Temperatures range from seasonal to below under variably cloudy skies with precipitation in the west part of the zone.

Zone 7: Northern coastal and eastern areas of the zone see precipitation, and skies are variably cloudy with temperatures seasonal to below.

Zone 8: Central Alaska is stormy, eastern areas are cloudy with precipitation, and western parts of the zone are cold. Hawaii is cool and windy with precipitation.

4th Quarter Moon, November 27–December 3

Zone 1: The zone is windy and seasonal with precipitation.

Zone 2: Northern areas see precipitation, and central and southern areas are fair to partly cloudy; temperatures are seasonal to below.

Zone 3: Temperatures are seasonal, and the zone is windy under fair to partly cloudy skies.

Zone 4: Western areas are stormy, the plains see scattered precipitation, eastern areas are partly cloudy, and temperatures are seasonal to below.

Zone 5: Much of the zone sees precipitation, some abundant, under very windy, cloudy skies, with temperatures seasonal to below.

Zone 6: The zone is variably cloudy with precipitation west and central, some abundant, and eastern areas are windy; temperatures range from seasonal to below.

Zone 7: Western and central areas see precipitation, and eastern areas are partly cloudy and warmer than the rest of the zone.

Zone 8: Central and western Alaska are stormy, and eastern areas are mostly fair and windy. Hawaii is cool and cloudy with showers.

New Moon, December 4–9

Zone 1: Temperatures are seasonal to below with fair skies north and precipitation south.

Zone 2: The zone is windy with precipitation and temperatures are seasonal to below.

Zone 3: Western and central areas have a chance for precipitation, and some eastern areas see abundant downfall; temperatures are seasonal to below.

Zone 4: Western parts of the zone are cloudy and windy with precipitation, the plains are fair to partly cloudy, and eastern areas see scattered precipitation; temperatures are seasonal.

Zone 5: Eastern and western areas are fair to partly cloudy, and western parts of the zone are cloudy with precipitation; temperatures are seasonal.

Zone 6: Temperatures are seasonal to below, with stormy conditions east, mostly fair skies central, and windy west with precipitation.

Zone 7: The zone is fair to partly cloudy, and windy in the east, with temperatures seasonal to below; northern coastal areas see scattered precipitation.

Zone 8: Western Alaska sees precipitation, and central and eastern areas are variably cloudy; temperatures are seasonal. Much of Hawaii is windy with precipitation, but eastern areas are mostly fair; temperatures are seasonal.

2nd Quarter Moon, December 10–17

Zone 1: The zone is windy and seasonal with precipitation.

Zone 2: Northern areas see precipitation, and central and southern areas are fair to partly cloudy, with temperatures seasonal to below.

Zone 3: Temperatures are seasonal and the zone is windy under fair to partly cloudy skies.

Zone 4: Western areas are stormy, central areas see scattered precipitation, eastern areas are partly cloudy, and temperatures are seasonal to below.

Zone 5: Much of the zone sees precipitation, some abundant, under very windy, cloudy skies, with temperatures seasonal to below.

Zone 6: The zone is variably cloudy with precipitation west and central, some abundant, and eastern areas are windy; temperatures range from seasonal to below.

Zone 7: Western and central areas see precipitation, and eastern areas are partly cloudy and warmer than the rest of the zone.

Zone 8: Central and western Alaska are stormy, and eastern areas are mostly fair and windy. Hawaii is cool and cloudy with showers.

Full Moon, December 18–25

Zone 1: Northern areas are cold with precipitation and high winds, and southern areas are more seasonal with precipitation.

Zone 2: Southern and central areas are very windy with precipitation, and northern parts of the zone are partly cloudy; temperatures are seasonal to below.

Zone 3: Western skies are partly cloudy, central areas are cloudy and windy with precipitation, and eastern parts of the zone are fair to partly cloudy; temperatures are seasonal to below.

Zone 4: The plains are partly cloudy with precipitation, eastern areas are fair to partly cloudy, and western parts of the zone are cloudy with precipitation; temperatures are seasonal.

Zone 5: Western and central areas are variably cloudy, eastern skies are mostly fair, and temperatures are seasonal to below.

Zone 6: Eastern parts of the zone are windy with precipitation, and central and western areas are fair to partly cloudy; temperatures range from seasonal to below.

Zone 7: Central and eastern areas see precipitation, some abundant, and western parts of the zone are variably cloudy with a chance for precipitation.

Zone 8: Eastern and central Alaska are stormy; western areas are mostly fair, and temperatures are seasonal. Hawaii is very windy and cool with precipitation.

4th Quarter Moon, December 26, 2021–January 1, 2022

Zone 1: The zone is windy with precipitation, and temperatures are seasonal to below.

Zone 2: Northern areas are cloudy with precipitation, central and southern areas are windy with variable cloudiness and thunderstorms, and temperatures are seasonal.

Zone 3: Western areas see more cloudiness, and much of the zone is windy with precipitation; temperatures are seasonal.

Zone 4: The zone is variably cloudy, with temperatures seasonal to below, and precipitation in eastern areas.

Zone 5: Temperatures are seasonal, and the zone is variably cloudy, with more cloudiness central and east with precipitation, some abundant.

Zone 6: Much of the zone sees precipitation, and temperatures are seasonal to below.

Zone 7: The zone is cloudy with precipitation, there are high winds in eastern areas, and temperatures are seasonal to below.

Zone 8: Alaska is variably cloudy with precipitation in western and central areas, and temperatures are seasonal to below. Hawaii is windy and cool with showers and thunderstorms, some strong.

Economic Forecast for 2021

by Christeen Skinner

Economists have long recognized a twenty-year business cycle. It is not, of course, exact but does have a close correlation with the twenty-year Jupiter-Saturn cycle whose conjunction in December 2020 is actually termed a Grand Mutation, as it is the first of a series of conjunctions in the Air element for the next 240 years. Yes, there was a conjunction in the Air sign Libra in 1981. As we shall see, this, the penultimate in that series, offered clues as to how this complete series in 2020 would unfold. The most recent conjunction in May 2000 was the last in the Earth series. The twenty-year business cycle is also close in length to the nodal cycle of 18.6 years.

Writing in the first half of the twentieth century, the financial astrologer Louise McWhirter noted that as the lunar nodes moved toward Aquarius—the lunar nodes move backward through the zodiac—there was a marked decline in growth reflected in falling indices. This shows most strongly as the nodes pass through the quarter of the zodiac from Taurus to Aquarius. In December 2021 the nodal cycle begins this last phase of its cycle—reaching Aquarius in 2026 or 2027 when a recession is to be expected. McWhirter would have drawn the conclusion that from late 2021 there would be decided downturn in economic activity. Being aware of this pending downturn is important for both investors and entrepreneurs starting out on new commercial adventures: the latter will be doing so "against a tide."

In contrast, another type of business cycle is indicated from December 2020 when Jupiter and Saturn begin their new cycle. The juxtaposition of just these two cycles—and there are many more to consider—poses clear difficulties. However exciting the new business opportunities are from late 2020, achieving the level of support required to develop a new business project will not be easy. Those starting enterprises in the first half of 2021 especially will need to be sure that they are cushioned by good cash reserve. Operating on a shoestring budget against prevailing financial crosswinds is sure to bring early collapse.

It is not just the pending downturn indicated by the nodal position that threatens commercial pressure: The forty-five-year synodic cycle of Saturn and Uranus reaches its last quarter phase in 2021. Throughout the last 120 years, it can be shown that the key aspects (0, 90, and 180 degrees especially) between these two planets have coincided with falling indices and political—leading to economic—tension. That these two planets reach this phase ahead of the indicated lunar downturn suggests that well-established (saturnine) companies will be faced with serious challenges and that their ability to give support to young enterprises (Uranus) will be limited.

In recent years, as banks have put in place tough lending criteria, funding circles have gone some way toward filling the gap. Peer-to-peer lending has gained momentum. From 2024, these schemes should become commonplace. However, it is probable that through much of 2021, even these alternative lending sources will dry up as individuals find that they have less cash available to support others. Instead, loan seekers will need to reach into their reserves to sustain their own businesses.

Solar Cycles

We must also consider solar cycles. Though the Sun does not have an exact rhythm, analysis shows correlation between the sunspot cycle and business activity. Solar cycle 25 was due to begin around 2019 or 2020, with maxima due to be reached in 2025 or 2026. Forecasters are already suggesting that this cycle will be highly unusual with few sunspots recorded. In some years (as in 2000) there can be as many as over 200 in one day. A cycle with minimal spots suggests a "slow Sun," in turn coinciding with slow business activity. Even the best and most experienced of entrepreneurs will surely find it challenging to access zeal and initiative under these conditions.

Yet, no year is ever all bad, and growth can be found somewhere. Jupiter's position by sign yields clues as to which sectors should expect to see growth. For much of 2021, Jupiter moves through Aquarius—the sign associated with cutting-edge technology. We should expect companies linked to the space age to go against the prevailing trend and make headway. Though it takes Jupiter 11.88 years to travel through all twelve signs of the zodiac, it does not spend an equal amount of time in each sign. In 2021, Jupiter begins the year in Aquarius, crosses into Pisces (from the geocentric perspective), and then returns to Aquarius before making its final Pisces ingress late in the year.

The Aquarius market sector covers all new technology, artificial intelligence, and space exploration. The sectors covered by Pisces include oil, pharmaceuticals, media, alcoholic drinks, and—vitally—water. Given Jupiter's relationship with other

outer planets through this time, those companies offering water security and water purification (covering both Aquarius and Pisces) should do very well indeed.

Thus the promise for 2021 is that a few green shoots of enterprise will thrive against the background of challenging conditions. Where then to start with our overview of 2021? We should perhaps begin by considering the special New and Full Moons, whose alignment with the lunar nodes create the phenomena known as eclipses.

Eclipses

Eclipses make trails or patterns through the zodiac. Each solar eclipse is part of a thread whose length varies. It is not enough to examine only the eclipses for the year in question but to understand where these eclipses lie within those threads and, importantly, over which part of the Earth they will be seen—or not seen. Though we may stand in awe as so many did in 2017 to witness the Great American Eclipse, every eclipse has an impact across the world, although focus tends to be on its viewable path.

We should note too that there can be as many as five solar eclipses in any given year and that a solar eclipse does not have to be accompanied by a lunar eclipse. Accompanying lunar eclipses fall two weeks on either side of the main solar event. These eclipse "windows," i.e., the period between a solar and lunar or lunar and solar, bring changes to the geomagnetic sphere and have been known to coincide with movement in the Earth's crust leading to volcanic activity, earthquake, or tsunami. The probability of such events appears increased if either the solar or lunar eclipse takes place when the Moon is at perigee (i.e., closest to Earth).

The solar eclipses of 2021 are in the mutable signs of Gemini and Sagittarius. The first takes place in June at 19° Gemini and will be visible across the northeast areas of the USA and Canada, into Greenland, and on into the far east of Russia. This is a highly unusual eclipse in that its path crosses the North Pole. It is part of Saros Cycle 147, a series of 80 solar eclipses, and this is the twenty-third of that cycle. Most eclipses move from west to east, making this eclipse unusual in that it follows a reverse path (something only possible in the pole areas of Earth).

The initial eclipse in Saros Cycle 147 took place on October 12, 1624, at 19° Libra, and the last will not occur until 3049. A review of the first eclipse of the series and the closest midpoint to the eclipse itself, places it at the exact midpoint of Uranus and Chiron. The mix of advanced thinking (Uranus) and Chiron (healing) perhaps says something about this series marking significant progress in the development of the healing arts (medicine). We should certainly not discount the possibility of breakthroughs in this area—perhaps linked to the kidney area of the body (Libra's domain). This is perhaps one area that might be considered for investment prior to the eclipse.

The second solar eclipse of 2021 occurs on December 4 at 12° Sagittarius and will only be visible in the South Atlantic. What the two eclipse paths of 2021 have in common is that they both promise much in terms of mineral wealth, even whilst being inhospitable areas of the world. Trade disputes involving both regions will likely lead to territorial dispute.

The December 4 eclipse belongs to Saros Cycle 152 and will be number thirteen in a total of 70 for that series. Cruises offering spectacular views of the Antarctic peninsula have been on offer for some years, and yes, this promises an amazing visual adventure.

The first eclipse in series 152 was on July 26, 1805. Echoes of the horoscope for this event will be heard throughout the entire series. Within that chart there is an exact conjunction of Chiron with the lunar node whilst the eclipse is on the Venus/node midpoint. This again draws attention to health and, with Venus involved (who rules both Taurus and Libra), the kidney area of the human body. Might new forms of dialysis be made available?

In a search for promising areas of investment, the health industry must surely rate highly in 2021.

Before making further consideration, however, we should return to the nodal cycle and its dovetailing with the business cycle. As the node moves from the mutable Gemini/Sagittarius axis to the fixed Taurus/Scorpio axis, as noted by McWhirter, the business trend is said to relax or decline from high activity, reducing to "normal." It is perhaps noteworthy that the lunar eclipse at the end of November is in one of the "financial" signs of the zodiac and likely to be the precursor to economic difficulties appearing before the end of the year.

McWhirter lived prior to the computer age and was unable to test theories as we can today. With data from the Dow Jones index available for over a hundred years, and large amounts of data of other indices available too, we can see how markets have reacted to the passage of the lunar north node through the same zodiacal space in the past. The results are interesting:

On its nineteen-year journey through the zodiac, the lunar north node moved through Gemini between October 2001 and May 2003 when the Dow Jones index (DJI) rose from approximately 9,500 at the start of that transit to 10,600, fell back to 7,200, and concluded its stay in that sign at 8,700. Of course, it is to be expected that during an eighteen-month period an index will fluctuate. The degree of fluctuation and the position at the end of that node's transit through a sign is of interest, however. From the moves in 2001–2003, we might expect that by the time the lunar node moves into Taurus in November 2021, the Dow Jones index will be lower than its position at the start of this transit in May 2020.

This though is an examination of just one cycle. It is essential to look back at each Gemini nodal period of the twentieth century. In 1984, the DJI rose from 1108 to 1203, whilst between late 1964 and 1966, the DJI went from 841 to 966. In 1946 it fell from 190 to 182, but from 1926 to 1928, it rose from 170 to 299. Clearly analysis of the nodal cycle against this one index does not give us sufficient information on which to trade. We must then check to see which other cycles dovetail these earlier years and determine from this the probability of a fall or rise in index value. It is more than a little interesting that the years in which there were marked losses (2002 and 1946), Saturn and Uranus reached major aspect—as they will do in 2021.

The nodal position is never irrelevant. Eclipses are important cosmic punctuation marks. Whether solar or lunar, they each give clues as to probable trading conditions—which are obviously a human activity and dependent on human behavior and reaction. What we know is that even minor changes in the geomagnetic sphere bring activity that can appear unusual and is therefore eventful—at times giving rise to major moves in indices. Marking eclipses in your trading diary and being aware that the period between them often brings volatility is a useful exercise. The dates in 2021 are: lunar eclipse on May 26, solar eclipse on June 10, another lunar eclipse on November 19, and another solar eclipse on December 4.

The lunar eclipse of November 2021 at 27° Taurus marks exactly the same degree as a lunar eclipse on November 20, 2002. That lunar eclipse was followed—as will be the case in 2021—by a solar eclipse in early December. The S&P index rose between the two dates.

However, between the solar eclipses in June and December of 2002, the S&P index fell from approximately 1030 to 940, with key dates in that fall definitely resonating with the position of the planets in the eclipse charts. In 2021, it might not be just the echoes of eclipse planetary positions that coincide with sharp moves but also the square aspect between Saturn and Uranus.

End of Year

It is not uncommon for financial astrologers to be asked to assess the end of year position for the various indices, and it is notable that although Wall Street may react in one way, every country's index will react differently. A full forecast would require study of each country and index. This article focuses on Wall Street. Please note that any dates given use the EST time zone.

In 2021 there are three dominating factors, which together seem to indicate that the Dow Jones index (DJI), Standard and Poor (S&P) and NASDAQ will likely close the year lower than at its start. The lunar node moving from Gemini to Taurus is one factor indicating the potential for lower values at year end. Another is Venus's cycle: Venus goes retrograde on December 19, two days before, but very close to, the solstice. Venus's retrograde in the past has sent indices lower. At a recent Venus retrograde (in Scorpio in 2018) indices fell dramatically. Prior to that, a Venus retrograde in Capricorn also saw indices fall. It is quite possible that a similar fate will befall the market in the last trading week of 2021.

Capricorn is the sign associated with banking and with large corporations—as well as governments. This could prove a difficult time for associated bonds and may be the determining factor in indices closing lower.

To turn back to the opening of the year: the chart for the December solstice preceding the New Year offers a tantalizing view of the year ahead. As we have noted, in 2020 the solstice coincides with the Grand Mutation. Though Jupiter and Saturn align approximately every two decades, these events take place at different degrees of the zodiac. Over approximately a quarter of a millennium, the conjunctions occur in element sequence: either Fire, Earth, Air, or Water. A curious fact is that the penultimate conjunction in the last (Earth) series was in 1981 in the Air sign Libra. The following decade has been described as the "yuppie"

era. It is also the decade when many of the now-termed "financial weapons of mass destruction," which ultimately led to the global financial crisis, were developed. Air is, after all, an "ideas" area— not necessarily workable or practical! Hopefully lessons from the previous debacle will have been learnt and any new concept subjected to intense scrutiny before being put into practice.

As always, it is useful to look back. There was a similar Grand Mutation in 1226—far predating the banking and economic systems in use today! The thirteenth century was a period of rapid European prosperity as trade routes running both east to west and north to south flourished, in part due to expanding infrastructure that made the passage of trade easier and safer. By the end of that century, and with new banking systems and coinage in place, trading routes were well established. The coinage aspect of this is noteworthy. In 2021, rather than expanding use of specific florins as happened in the thirteenth century, we may see specific cryptocurrencies entering the mainstream. In fact, this particular Jupiter-Saturn conjunction could be the trigger needed for an entire appraisal of currency systems and the rapid development of blockchain currencies.

First Quarter

For thousands of years, astrologers have watched the planets and nodes make apparent formations in the sky with some planetary patterns, such as a perfect isosceles triangle being deemed "fortunate" and others, such as a T-square, being seen as potentially eventful, stressful, and difficult.

Notwithstanding the promise of the Aquarius Jupiter-Saturn business cycle at the solstice in December 2020, that year concludes with a Grand Cross (four planetary bodies or important points in space, such as the nodes at right angles to one another) dominating. The nodal axis dominates the charts for each New and Full Moon in the early months of 2021. At right angles to the nodes, and in opposition to one another, are the trading asteroid

Vesta and the planet Neptune. Together this paints a picture of decidedly treacherous trading conditions.

This will likely be felt most acutely on Wall Street. There is a horoscope for the New York Stock Exchange. Though there is some dispute as to the actual time of day to be used, it is generally agreed that the key date is May 17, 1792. In this chart Mars holds position at 18° Virgo. In recent decades, the passage of planets over this degree has coincided with volatility.

It seems reasonable to assume that with Neptune opposing this degree, there will be loss of energy and drifting. True, most markets should rise in the first few days of January. From January 10, however, a downward trend seems more likely than not. Vesta's role here is not to be underestimated. A strong possibility is that currency wars will have major impact, with trade apparently "frozen" in the process. This possibility is supported by the right angle between Saturn and Uranus in February and which in the past has coincided with limitation on trade through revised rules and regulation.

Where then to invest in the first two months of 2021? The answer must surely be in those companies linked to Aquarius industries (as per the new Jupiter-Saturn business cycle). These include genetic engineering, space travel, and computer programming. Also to be considered are rare earth metals: their mining and application. True, it could be some years before profit is realized, but shares in these companies may be at an excellent price at the start of the cycle.

There is a military theme at work in the chart of the Full Moon on January 28. The Sun and Jupiter are conjoined and both square a Mars-Uranus conjunction in Taurus. The latter could express itself through sudden land upheaval. We should not discount the possibility of an earthquake—especially since this is a Full Moon (a not uncommon feature during this time). Yet the whole planetary picture also suggests the display of military might. Since the planetoid Chiron is moving through Aries and crosses a highly sensitive degree (8° Aries) in March 2021, it may be that some nations feel that military action is their only option. Certainly we should expect the demand for military hardware to increase under this configuration. Those inclined to invest in this area could move in at the start of the year.

Mars conjoins with Sedna at 27° Taurus at the February Full Moon. This will be the penultimate of conjunctions in this sign for thousands of years. It is fascinating that the Sabian symbol for this degree is of "an old Indian woman selling beads and trinkets." Given that currency mayhem is a strong possibility, the value of precious metals and jewels seem set to dominate the business pages of the newspapers.

Investors and traders alike should give considerable attention to the next Full Moon on March 28. This lunation occurs on a Sunday when Western markets are closed. However, the effect of this could be felt at the end of the previous working week when Mercury opposes that critical degree in the NYSE chart. The volume of trade may be considerable—and to the downside.

That this late March Full Moon lies across the 8° Aries-Libra axis, with an exact conjunction of both Venus at 8° Aries and Chiron at the same degree, suggests that this could be a day of awesome accounting. It is highly likely that shares across the world will move sharply when markets open on Monday, March 29. Traders should, of course, synchronize this forecast with their technical analysis before taking action.

Second Quarter

The economic focus this quarter is on Aries: the "Tarzan" of the zodiac. There is a stellium (group) of planets in that sign at the April New Moon. Yes, this may be indicative of military action but also indicates the promise of young, green shoots. Perhaps because they are despairing of the antics of large corporations, an increase in the number of start-ups seems likely. Obviously it is vital that these new enterprises have sufficient capital to sustain them through the early years. Yet the sheer courage and bravado of those launching during this period may be enough to get them noticed and to attract support. If you are born under Aries, then this might be your time—though you might be well advised to read manuals as to how best to finish what you start!

The chart for the Full Moon on April 26, when the Sun and Uranus (both in Taurus) oppose the Moon whilst Saturn takes up position midway between them, suggests a slamming on of the financial brakes. This could prove a tough week in the markets—perhaps led by government restrictions and yes, again, the challenge of currency devaluation and manipulation.

Coinage and currency valuation in general are features of the chart for the May New Moon. This could be expressed in a myriad of ways, with bartering becoming more commonplace as many reject systems they consider no longer useful or viable. This period could also see a rise in the value of precious metals, with silver especially gaining strength. An upsurge in these prices could continue through the lunar eclipse on May 26 given Neptune's conjunction with Pallas and both in trine to Mars, which is then moving through Cancer.

Many people will surely show a preference for tangible currencies rather than the cryptocurrencies, which are likely to fall out of favor—albeit temporarily.

Mercury turns retrograde on May 29 at 24° Gemini, which is one of the important degrees in its orbit and likely to indicate an exaggerated turning point. It will still be in retrograde position at the solar eclipse on June 10. Whilst retrograde periods often get apparently well-deserved bad press for communication errors, misunderstandings, and so on, this is not always the case—but could be so in this instance. Mercury will be travelling through a sign it is said to "rule." So yes, commercial instability is probable with wildly fluctuating share values. This may have particular effect on travel and media stock prices.

Though Mercury is stationary direct at the solstice, it would be wise for those initiating new enterprises to wait until early July before launching. Mercury returns to its retrograde station on July 7. From then on, the business flow should ease, with fewer challenges to distribution and networking departments.

Mention has already been made of the possibilities of break-throughs in medicine. The aforementioned Neptune-Pallas-Mars combination may be indicative of the application of drugs based on DNA profiling. Paying attention to companies working in this field and when these are brought to market could yet prove an interesting area for research and investment.

Third Quarter

The commercial winds are set to change direction halfway through this quarter, which begins with Jupiter having moved into Pisces, where related sectors should flourish. That said, at the July 9 New Moon, difficult aspects involving Mars, Saturn, and Uranus indicate considerable tension, with rules and regulations being fiercely applied. This planetary picture could also indicate strife. The question is, "On which stage will this occur?" Will it be actual military warfare, trade, or currency war? And yes, all three could be involved.

Focusing on currencies: a critical date might be the July 9 New Moon. This favors the US dollar against a basket of currencies as well as sterling (British Pound). That said, the exchange rate between the two may be marked at this New Moon, with the high probability of sterling gaining strength.

Jupiter enters into Pisces on May 13, bringing focus to the sectors associated with that sign: the media, pharmaceuticals, drinks industries, ocean engineering, and ocean management—such as shipping and even luxury cruising. As Jupiter returns to Aquarius

for a short time, it may be that July proves a good time to buy—before those "Pisces" prices really move forward when Jupiter reaches Pisces fully on December 28.

The focus moves from ocean voyage to potential space travel by the next New Moon on August 8. By then Jupiter will have returned to Aquarius (July 28) and will be in very loose opposition to the Sun. The Sun–Jupiter annual opposition is often a time when people over-reach. A boost to shares in companies linked to exploration—and space travel especially—is probable. This same aspect could coincide with movement in precious metal markets. In some cultures, major aspects between the Sun and Jupiter are chosen for celebrations and festivities. The gift of gold and other valuables around this time often see their prices move forward, only to fall in the weeks following.

By the Full Moon on August 22, the tension of previous weeks gives way to different energies. If there is war, then it may be that new and powerful alliances are then forged. At the economic level, prices should stabilize. At this Full Moon, Mars and Uranus are in near exact 120° (trine) to one another. It would not be abnormal for prices to rise into this aspect and then subside.

Markets experience anniversaries when repeats of past highs and lows often occur. A clear example of this could be apparent at the New Moon on September 6. In this chart, the Sun, Moon, and Mars conjoin in Virgo. A strong possibility is that the value of sterling (British Pound) will fall that month. This might not be the only value to turn downward: indices in general could experience a downturn whilst precious metals—especially silver—could reach a high as they did in September 2019.

The charts of some of the giants of the computer industry (Google, Microsoft, etc.) share similar degrees. That these are all highlighted at the Full Moon on September 20 (just slightly ahead of the equinox) suggests that these share prices might be vulnerable around this date. Given the apparent right angle between Saturn and Uranus still in operation, this may be linked to new rules and regulations reaching across boundaries and being ratified in international courts.

Fourth Quarter

The last quarter of the year is usually commercially busy and often volatile. The Wall Street crash, the October 1987 crash, and more recently, the global financial crash which accelerated in the last quarter of 2007, have all taken place during these months. This is perhaps understandable from the zodiacal perspective, in that this quarter includes the Sun's passage through Libra—the sign of the scales and arguably the optimum time for "balancing the books."

The first date of some significance is the Full Moon on October 20. In recent years, Pluto has played a pivotal role at this particular lunation. Positioned, apparently, halfway between the Sun and Moon and moving through Capricorn, this has coincided with major, usually government-determined, decisions, which then affect the trading mood. That in 2021 this lunation coincides with an opposition of Vesta to Uranus suggests that market reaction will be driven by pressure in the currency and precious metal markets. Might it be that a government decrees a change in regulations? Restrictions as to how much can be owned or transported is a distinct possibility.

Another feature of this quarter—and often coinciding with major moves in equity markets—is the entry of Mercury, Venus, or Mars into Scorpio. This has occasionally brought a "day of reckoning" when indices adjust (usually to the downside). While Mercury and Venus make this passage annually, Mars doesn't necessarily pass through Scorpio during this three-month period but will in 2021. Venus will have made Scorpio ingress on September 10, perhaps leaving hints as to what is to come. The fact that this date, too, is so close to the anniversary of the collapse of Lehman Brothers suggests downward action. Mars then makes Scorpio ingress on October 30 and is followed into that sign by Mercury on November 5.

October 30 is very close to several key financial anniversaries when indices have turned negative. Should there be an echo of those earlier times, and disappointing as this may be for many, this might also signal buying opportunities (though it is of course important to discuss proposed action with your financial advisor). The week between October 30 and November 5 could bring buying opportunities.

A different kind of seismic—likely political shock, though it could also be a natural disaster—could affect markets around the New Moon on November 4. That this coincides with Mercury's arrival in Scorpio again suggests events that prompt traders to take profits. Currency traders especially should be prepared for further major moves. Of course, what appears negative in one area is often a positive elsewhere. Rapid developments in blockchain could find many people attracted to the idea of owning one of these currencies but fearful perhaps that they're too late to join this market.

This, though, could mark the start of another slippery start for cryptos. The alignment of Vesta with the lunar south node does not augur well for forex trading generally. Coinciding with the nodal transition from the Gemini/Sagittarius axis to Taurus/Scorpio, profound developments in the way these markets operate are to be anticipated in 2022, but they will begin in November 2021.

Burgeoning wealth in companies working in the field of artificial intelligence is indicated in the chart for the Full Moon on November 19, suggesting that it will bring reward to investors who moved into this sector in 2019. This might, however, be the moment to consider taking profits, as there is the high probability of another downturn in December.

The New Moon on December 4 includes a stellium in Sagittarius favoring travel stocks. That month brings the last of the three Saturn-Uranus hard aspects, Chiron's station at 8° Aries (a degree area often prominent at the time of eventfulness), and Venus's retrograde station on December 19—just ahead of the solstice. Volatility could come via Asian markets. Note too that the Full Moon on December 18 coincides with Venus's retrograde station and is within orb of the Galactic Center—arguably promising high drama.

In summary, there could be an unhappy ending to 2021. Discussing this possibility with your financial advisor and taking steps to secure assets is always wise. Readers might like to set up meetings for the last quarter of 2021 to discuss investment opportunities for 2022 that will take advantage of the very considerable medical advances likely to have been made during the previous year.

References

Cox, Jeff. "The Value of What Buffett Called 'Financial Weapons of Mass Destruction' Is Plunging." CNBC. Updated May 4, 2018. https://www.cnbc.com/2018/05/04/the-value-of -financial-weapons-of-mass-destruction-is-plunging.html.

Hill, Lynda. "Mars on Taurus 27: Selling Beads and Trinkets." Sabian Symbols. May 6, 2015. https://sabiansymbols.com/mars-on -taurus-27-selling-beads-and-trinkets/.

McWhirter, Louise. *Astrology and Stock Market Forecasting*. New York: ASI Publishers, 1977.

New and Full Moon Forecasts for 2021

by Sally Cragin

You'd have to go to Greenland or one of the poles to have a completely unobstructed view of the moving constellations, but even city dwellers can see the moving Moon making her journey over the skyscrapers. Earth's little sister satellite presides over a complex system of tides and earthly rhythms. Can you "tell" when the Moon is full? Or when it's new? Do you find that people in your environment go through mood swings at certain times of the month? Or that you do?

I teach classes in astrology, tarot, palmistry, and related folk traditions in New England and find that females are much more "tuned in" to the idea that the Moon makes a difference in our lives. Until menopause, women have that monthly reminder in the form of menstrual cycles, which can have an enormous influence on their life in terms of how much high or low energy they have. For linguists out there, both "Moon," "menstrual," and "menses" come from the Latin word "mensis," which means month, which is drawn from the Greek word "mene" (Moon). In short, living your life by the phases of the Moon has a long and firm history in human culture.

So what does that mean? When I teach, folks always fasten onto the notion that the Full Moon is a time when "everyone's crazy," but the rhythms are more complex than that. Think of the lunar phases as a four-act play: the New Moon, when everything begins; the first quarter, when patterns are established; the Full Moon, when action comes to a climax; and the last quarter, which provides an opportunity to review or adjust projects right up to the next New Moon.

If you have a pet at home, particularly a dog or cat, you may find they are more active in the evening during the days leading up to the Full Moon. This phase brings more outside light into your home, and even if the blinds are closed, animals are very aware of these rhythms. (For a long time we kept hermit crabs in an elaborate "crabitat," and during the evenings of the Full Moon their clanking shells against the glass walls sounded like a crazy tea party with clinking cups.)

The New Moon Through First Quarter
That New Moon brings second chances, new opportunities, and new people into your life. When you look into the night sky and see a capital-letter *D* shape, the shadow of the Earth will be diminishing as the Moon gains light on the right.

The First Quarter Through Waxing Gibbous Moon
That first quarter indicates a "turning point" in a project that may have begun the week before at the New Moon. The day of the first quarter may be useful to chart in terms of what complications

emerge or arise as a result of outside individuals. This is a three- to four-day phase.

Waxing Gibbous Moon Through Full Moon

The party is on, and the vehicle is in fourth or fifth gear. This three- to four-day period brings opportunities (or crises) forward that you may not have foreseen. Courage may be required—also the courage not to speak when others are sputtering. Think of a train chugging slowly up a hill, cresting at the full Moon, and hurtling down after.

Full Moon Through Waning Gibbous Moon

I know many artists who find this a helpful and useful period. The party (or madness) continues. This three- to four-day period may bring further clarity on a situation which may have gotten overly complex during the waxing Moon. This is an excellent time for a social gathering.

Waxing Gibbous Moon Through Last Quarter

Folks who need a lot of excitement in their lives may find this cycle makes them anxious or feel disempowered to speak up for themselves or others. Simplification is the keyword: evaluate current projects and relationships and see if they are getting less complex (someone comes home from the hospital, or a final piece of the puzzle falls into place).

Last Quarter Through New Moon

A time of potential emotional fragility. Starting projects not advised until after the New Moon. Everything that "doesn't fit" may go away, and you won't even miss it. However, the day before the New Moon, also known as "the dark of the Moon," can be a time when one is unexpectedly accident prone. I've found that decisions made on this day tend not to stick after the Moon begins waxing again. Wait until after the New Moon to make decisions that will have a long-term impact on your life.

Wednesday, January 13, New Moon in Capricorn

With Capricorn, Venus, and Mars in Taurus harmonizing with the Moon, your practical yet beauty-loving side steps forward. An elegant solution is possible for a question revolving around home decoration or structure. Capricorn: frankness with loved ones pays off, and if this makes you uncomfortable, think about a reward for your courage. A project you start now could reach fruition around June 24, during the Capricorn Full Moon. Libra, Aries, Cancer, Leo, and Gemini: take your time and be patient with folks who strike you as "slothful." Virgo, Taurus, Aquarius, Pisces, Scorpio, and Sagittarius: parts fit into place.

Thursday, January 28, Full Moon in Leo

The "Wolf Moon." Jupiter and Saturn in Aquarius oppose this Full Moon, which means work methods that have been "tried 'n' true" might be less successful. Plus, Full Moon in Leo is about socializing, not snout-to-grindstone. Find your most amusing companions and go play through the weekend. Be cautious about communication during this time as Mercury retrogrades (January

30 through February 20). Leo (especially July lions): frustration could come easily, particularly with folks who have been less than reliable. Enlarge your circle. Taurus, Aquarius, Scorpio, Capricorn, and Pisces: if you pride yourself on being steady, a comeuppance could be in store. Aries, Sagittarius, Cancer, Gemini, Libra, and Virgo: you have to see the funny side of things. It's there and more pleasant than more teeth grinding.

Thursday, February 11, New Moon in Aquarius

Mercury retrograde (since January 30) compromises conversation, and exaggeration comes easily to all. After February 21, when Mercury moves forward, consider upgrading technology. Humanitarian impulses are widespread, and even the most shrinking violet will want to take a spin on the dance floor. Aquarius: the planets are giving you contradictory information. Fly high and conserve energy. Try new things but stick to old habits. This New Moon is an eye opener for you as to what you truly want. What you plan now could pay off around July 23, during the Aquarius Full Moon. Taurus, Leo, Scorpio, Virgo, and Cancer: keep the lid on, especially if folks who enjoy antagonizing are in your orbit. Libra, Gemini, Pisces, Aries, Capricorn, and Sagittarius: the sky's the limit.

Saturday, February 27, Full Moon in Virgo

The "Snow Moon" is a highly productive time, particularly when it comes to reviewing your health. The days continue to lengthen, and with Mars in compatible Taurus, extraordinary endurance is a theme. Now's the time to increase your efforts at the gym for example. Virgo: no one can turn you down, but you may also have your arms full helping others. Indulge in some self-care, even if you have to lock the door behind you. Libra, Gemini, and Aquarius could be irked by slow processes (or slowpokes). Aries, Leo, Sagittarius: take your time—this lunar phase doesn't favor the "rush job." Capricorn, Taurus, Scorpio, Cancer, and Pisces: your "fine-tuning" instincts will be at high rev. Take pleasure in precision.

Saturday, March 13, New Moon in Pisces

Enormously romantic weekend in store, particularly for folks with a lot of water in their charts (and those who love them). Making art or improving the appearance of an area that's mostly hidden (bed sheets?) brings pleasure, particularly for the homebodies. Pisces: be forceful, and no second-guessing yourself during this New Moon. Follow your heart and treat yourself well. Projects and personalities arriving now could become more important during the Pisces Full Moon on September 20. Sagittarius, Virgo, and Gemini: a turn—or reverse—in direction is the right move. Scorpio, Cancer, Aries, and Aquarius: your instinct to "go to the dark side" will amuse you. But probably not others. Capricorn, Taurus, Libra, and Leo: someone with a "poor me" complex could wander into your orbit and take up time. A lot of time.

Sunday, March 28, Full Moon in Libra

Welcome to the "Worm Moon," when the invertebrates sleeping beneath our feet begin to awaken. This Full Moon favors all kinds of partnerships, and if you've been looking for a collaboration (roommate, business partner, spouse), this Moon favors those connections. Mars and the Moon make beautiful music together (in Gemini and Libra), so conversations are more enjoyable than usual. Libra: if you are the kind of person who keeps adding items on both sides of the scales, this Full Moon period will tempt you to take on even more! Aries, Capricorn, Cancer, Taurus, Pisces: you may be hearing just half the story. It's the opposite for Aquarius, Gemini, Scorpio, Sagittarius, Virgo, and Leo who may see a side of a friend that was hitherto hidden.

Sunday, April 11, New Moon in Aries

Nothing old will suit as well as something new; Aries's energy is excellent for expansion and innovation. This Moon is harmoniously tucked between Mars and Jupiter (in thoughtful Gemini and Aquarius), and it's full speed ahead for doing things differently.

Aries may have amusing new workmates or the opportunity to be flattered. All good stuff, but use this phase for bold changes. What can you put together that reaches fruition around October 20 during the Aries Full Moon? Libra, Capricorn, Cancer, Scorpio, and Virgo: you may be short tempered, particularly if others are less than reliable. Sagittarius, Leo, Taurus, Pisces, Gemini, and Aquarius: move quickly even if it's not your preferred mode.

Monday, April 26, Full Moon in Scorpio

The "Pink Moon" is also an eye-popping "Supermoon." Talk about romantic! This Full Moon brings an appreciation of the beautiful, and even those with no taste at all will develop an aesthetic and find their gaze lingering on something (or someone!) that delights. However, this Moon is at odds with Jupiter and Saturn, so some folks may bring the Monday morning blues to work with them. Scorpio: if you're feeling emotionally on edge, you're in tune with the Moon. Throttle back for your own emotional health. Capricorn, Virgo, Gemini, Cancer, Aries, and Pisces: money matters beckon. Straighten out your spending. Taurus, Sagittarius, Libra, Leo, and Aquarius: you may want to set limits on others versus yourself.

Tuesday, May 11, New Moon in Taurus

Excellent for planting—what can you start that you can harvest in three or four months? (It doesn't have to be something filled with chlorophyll.) Taurus Moons help us be more thorough and painstaking about simple tasks and also help sharpen our taste when it comes to diet or home décor. Taurus: your charm is noticed by others. Do you see them noticing you? What can you plan or put together that makes a splash around November 19 during the Taurus Full Moon? Scorpio, Leo, Aquarius, Sagittarius, and Libra: if conservative thinking makes you crazy, walk away from those who do it. Capricorn, Virgo, Gemini, Pisces, Aries, and Cancer:

you may feel like being stubborn, which is a good thing, but one that gets remarked upon by others. Don't mind them.

Wednesday, May 26, Full Moon in Sagittarius

The "Flower Moon" finds the world in bloom—and preparing to bloom even more. Sagittarius Moons focus our attention on higher education and a grand sense of fairness. Since Jupiter is now in Pisces (as of May 14), finishing a twelve-year zodiacal cycle, a sense of generosity towards those who suffer emotionally will become a theme for the rest of the year. For now, Sagittarius may have to resist that "ride to the rescue" impulse (that we love, let's be fair). Instead, archers should focus on their own pleasures and needs. Aries, Leo, Scorpio, Libra, Capricorn, and Aquarius: stick with the folks who make you laugh and feel good. Pisces, Gemini, Virgo, Cancer, and Taurus could be accident prone. Wear sensible shoes!

Thursday, June 10, New Moon in Gemini

Superb day for talking and writing except for a pesky Mercury retrograde (May 29 through June 21), which may compromise precision. Gemini Moons encourage a lot of chatter, and your task is sifting the silly from the serious. The slowness or indecisiveness of others could rankle Gemini whose leadership skills are in the ascendant today. As much as you enjoy being in "the moment" ask yourself what you can plan that can pay off around December 18 during the Gemini Full Moon. Sagittarius, Virgo, Scorpio, Pisces, and Capricorn: you're not seeing the full picture—hold back your response. Libra, Aquarius, Taurus, Aries, Cancer, and Leo: partnership themes are emphasized. Don't "phone it in" with a partner.

Thursday, June 24, Full Moon in Capricorn

The "Strawberry Moon" brings sweetness, and we all have enormous potential for organization. Mars in Leo urges everyone to move quickly, but don't be fooled. Slow and steady wins this race, although some folks (Libra, Aries, Cancer, Leo, and Gemini) could be passive aggressive. Capricorn: look back to January 13, or that week, and assess how far you've come. Taurus, Virgo, Scorpio, Sagittarius, Aquarius, and Pisces: take the test, make the decision, and trust your instincts.

Friday, July 9, New Moon in Cancer

Family life is emphasized during this New Moon as is cooking or working with your hands. Fishing, gardening, or relaxing with loved ones will bring joy, but some folks may have a short fuse. Defensiveness is a danger with a Cancer Moon, especially for crabs. Cancer: you are not responsible for the choices (or comfort) of others. Today, indulge yourself, but see what you can begin that could pay off around late January 2022, when the Moon is full in Cancer. Taurus, Gemini, Leo, Virgo, Scorpio, and Pisces: comfort counts, and if someone's irritability puts you on edge, find a hidey-hole (or a hammock). Sagittarius, Libra, Aries, Capricorn, and Aquarius: others' sensitivity could bug you big-time. But these folks may be making a useful point you need to hear.

Friday, July 23, Full Moon in Aquarius

The "Buck Moon" could find some folks all too willing to lock antlers, so if social skirmishing is not your thing, consider spending the night in. New ideas are exploding everywhere and eccentrics will seek you out. If you're the eccentric in question, this is your time to shine. Also excellent for home décor. Aquarius: take the chances, buy the lottery ticket, say your piece. Sagittarius, Pisces, Gemini, Libra, Capricorn, and Aries: your creativity shines, and faraway friends want to hear from you. Taurus, Leo, Scorpio, Virgo, and Cancer: give the folks who are unreliable a wide berth during this Full Moon. You could be caught up in their next never-to-be-completed project.

Sunday, August 8, New Moon in Leo

Leo: the universe has plenty of good stuff in store for you, but you may be feeling it's hard to get to it (Jupiter and Saturn in Aquarius). This Full Moon is useful for borrowing money and cultivating plants. Do you want to break a habit? New Year's is not the only time for a resolution. Leo: celebration is called for—reach out to your nearest and dearest. And have some fun with your appearance. What changes can you make in your social life that can bring you to a new level of delight in mid-February when the Moon is full in your sign? Aries, Sagittarius, Cancer, Gemini, Virgo, and Libra: if you need to ask a favor, the planets are with you. Aquarius, Taurus, Scorpio, Capricorn, and Pisces: being short tempered could come easily, and you could surprise yourself by how outspoken you are about something you didn't think was bugging you.

Sunday, August 22, Full Moon in Aquarius

The "Sturgeon Moon" brings out acquisitiveness, and your tech-savvy friends may be jazzed up about the latest device. Speaking of eccentrics, they may need to seek you out and share exotic trivia about their obsessions. Aquarius: look back to February and think about a project or relationship that began that could be enlarged or improved. Sagittarius, Gemini, Capricorn, Pisces, Aries, and Libra: tech innovations beckon and you could have insights into your devices that makes life easier. This is where you want to stay close to the folks who love that sort of thing! Taurus, Scorpio, Virgo, Leo, and Cancer: folks who don't take things as seriously as you do, or who don't feel responsible for others, could put you on edge. How can you avoid their (otherwise delightful) company?

Monday, September 6, New Moon in Virgo

These Moons are superb for cleaning and decluttering or reviewing your financial statement. Do you need to switch a health-care practitioner or start a training program? The Moon is on your side, particularly for self-improvement practices that focus on digestion and diet. Virgo: from now through March 18, 2022 (the next Virgo Full Moon), you need to focus on keeping yourself further challenged. Virgo is the original "lifelong learner," and this New Moon is throwing a lot of new ideas your way. Cancer, Taurus, Leo, Libra, Scorpio, and Capricorn: your work ethic is being nudged. Who do you want to impress? Are they worth it? Pisces, Aquarius, Aries, Gemini, and Sagittarius: you could invest a lot of time or money into a go-nowhere scheme.

Monday, September 20, Full Moon in Pisces

The "Corn Moon." Pisces Moons prompt curiosity—and can bring out your dark, goth side. (Feel like listening to trancey emo music?) This Moon favors acts of daring, particularly having to do with speaking up for those who don't have a voice. Pisces: hidden places (in your subconscious? Or one of those "escape rooms") preoccupy you. You may have some friends who are momentarily hypervigilant about your mood. They'll diagnose depression when all you need is a "time out." Look back at the last week of March when the Moon was new in your sign. What opportunities or challenges arose then? Resolve them now. Capricorn, Aquarius, Aries, Taurus, Cancer, and Scorpio: art and music bring much joy—as does shoe shopping! Gemini, Virgo, Sagittarius, Libra, and Leo: exaggeration comes easily and could get you into hot water.

Wednesday, October 6, New Moon in Libra

"On the one hand . . ." Seeing two sides of a situation comes easily, as does holding off on an important decision because data keeps flowing in (plus, caution is advised since Mercury is retrograde). Libra Moons are excellent for painting houses or renewing relationships, as well as purchasing items that come in pairs (shoes, earbuds). Libra: the Sun, Moon, and Mars are on your side, and everyone else might decide to play "follow the leader" with you out in front. Start a project that reaches fulfillment around April 16, 2022, the time of the next Libra Full Moon. Cancer, Capricorn, Aries, Pisces, and Taurus: don't force an issue with a partner, you could easily be misheard right now. Aquarius, Leo, Gemini, Scorpio, Sagittarius, and Virgo: you've got great taste and style right now—improve your look.

Wednesday, October 20, Full Moon in Aries

The "Hunter Moon." It's easy to make quick decisions during this Full Moon as well as to be intemperate. Rush-rush-rush is the mode, especially as Mercury is no longer retrograde. Purchases relating to barbeque equipment, spices, and headwear could "spark joy" as they say. Aries: look back to April 11, or thereabouts. What project could use some adjustment? Cancer, Capricorn, Libra, Virgo, and Scorpio: you could feel discouraged for no darn good reason. Have you overbooked? Sagittarius, Leo, Taurus, Gemini, Aquarius, and Pisces: you can finish projects quickly and efficiently—really!

Thursday, November 4, New Moon in Scorpio

With the Moon in alignment with Mars (also in Scorpio), sex, lies, and finance become hot topics. Time to binge watch the latest nighttime drama or talk to your friend who has the most insights into motivation. Scorpio shines a light on dark places, so if you're squeamish, stay home. Scorpio: for the next six weeks, the world is your oyster. Decide if you want to let it stew slowly or be gobbled down at the raw bar. Few can say "no" to you now. What are you working on that could come to a climax around Mother's Day next year? Taurus, Leo, Aquarius, Aries, and Gemini: unexpected rudeness or frankness could come your way. Or come from you, bringing perplexed and hurt gazes. Mind your manners. Cancer, Pisces, Libra, Virgo, Sagittarius, and Capricorn: sensual pleasures await and abound—enjoy.

Friday, November 19, Full Moon in Taurus

Taurus is preoccupied with security, finance, and life at home. This is an excellent period for getting a beauty treatment or making or upcycling clothing. Taurus Moons are also helpful if you need to "stick to your guns." Taurus: others are looking to you to make big decisions or to improve upon a project you began back in May. However, Mars is saying your deepest convictions may be disregarded by others. Scorpio, Leo, Aquarius, Sagittarius, Libra: misspeaking comes easily, and you may find yourself offering to complete a task that you have no interest in. (But you'll look fabulous doing it with this Moon!) Capricorn, Virgo, Gemini, Cancer, Aries, and Pisces: invest in the long term. Now is the time to buy items that will last.

Saturday, December 4, New Moon in Sagittarius

Travel and education are critical, and this is a fine time to have a family discussion about possibly taking a big trip together instead of a mountain of mall-bought presents. Humor is emphasized during this Moon. Consider indulging in a weekend of comedies or getting together with your drollest friends. Sagittarius: what can you take apart in order to make it more functional or multipurpose? Your practical side launches, and with Mars in your Sun sign (December 13 through January 24), the sky's the limit. Plan a project that culminates around Father's Day 2022. Pisces, Gemini, Virgo, Taurus, and Cancer: watch your step. Awkwardness comes easily for you. Aquarius, Capricorn, Scorpio, Libra, Leo, and Aries: give in to your generous side; you have great ideas about how to improve your local community.

Saturday, December 18, Full Moon in Gemini

The "Cold Moon." Gemini Moons bring great new ideas and lightheartedness as well as an emphasis on partnership and items that come in twos. Advertising your talents is a great idea, as is putting together a group for brainstorming. If you've been wanting a canine companion, the Moon is in your favor. Gemini: look back to mid-June and see what personalities played a big role in your life. Have things changed for the better? Virgo, Sagittarius, Pisces, Capricorn, and Scorpio: you may not be hearing the "whole truth," which could make you antagonistic towards folks who aren't always reliable. Libra, Aquarius, Taurus, Aries, Cancer, and Leo: frankness matters. Put yourself forward and spend time with a wider variety of acquaintances. Folks want to hear what you have to say.

2021
Moon Sign Book
Articles

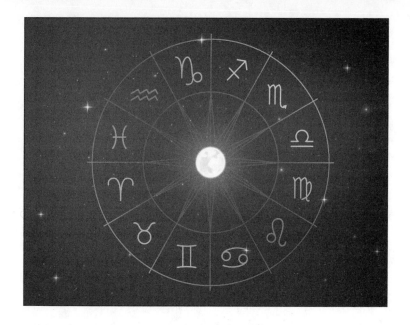

Complete Guide to Your Natal Moon

by Charlie Rainbow Wolf

You've probably heard people talking about their Sun sign, and there's a good chance you know what your Sun sign is. Each of the twelve signs lends certain personality traits and characteristics to people born during that time of year. The Sun moves through all twelve signs every year, starting with Aries at the spring equinox. The other equinoxes and solstices not only mark the beginnings of the different seasons, but they are also times of year when the Sun moves into its next sign. On the calendar, Aries begins spring, Cancer begins summer, Libra begins autumn, and Capricorn begins winter.

But as well as having a Sun sign, you also have a Moon sign. In fact, every planet—as well as other asteroids, lights, and fixed points—in our solar system was in a particular sign of the zodiac when you were born. Examining their positions and their angles to each other is how astrologers interpret your birth chart. Your Sun sign is indicative of your personality traits, and your Moon sign—the sign the Moon was passing through when you were born—reveals a lot about your feelings and your emotional responses.

Finding your Moon sign means more than just picking up a book and looking at the calendar. Because the Moon takes less than a month to make a full cycle through the zodiac, it changes signs approximately every sixty hours. If you were born on a day when the Moon was changing signs, you need to know the time and place of your birth in order to accurately calculate your Moon sign.

Knowing your Moon sign is valuable because it helps you to understand yourself. We all do the best with what we know, but as Maya Angelou said, when we know better we can do better. When you have greater insight into your emotions, you can better understand what you need in order to feel whole and comfortable with your authentic self.

In this technological era it is easy to find your natal Moon sign. Look for free natal astrology sites on the computer and type in your date, time, and place of birth. If you don't know the time, guesstimate. For example, perhaps you know you were born in the morning, or maybe someone remembers it happening between lunch and supper. Unless the Moon is very close to changing signs, a rough idea will work—but the precise time is better, and might be obtainable from your birth records. My favorite resources are alabe.com, which will calculate your natal birth chart, and lunarium.co.uk, which will reveal the Moon's sign (GMT) for any given date back to 1900.

Moon Phases

As the Moon passes through the signs of the zodiac, it is also changing phases. You may share the same natal Moon sign as someone else, but the various phases will influence you in different ways. The Moon cycles through eight phases every lunar month, each one lasting just over three days.

The New Moon is when the Moon is dark, because it rises and sets with the Sun. It's a time to contemplate new beginnings. People born under this phase are filled with a childlike wonder about their lives and are naturally curious.

The first crescent Moon is a time of growth and seeking understanding. People born under this phase often need to seek new means of dealing with old issues. They frequently have to find a way to overcome opposition from others in order to achieve their goals.

The first quarter Moon brings both energy and concentration, often needed in order to get something accomplished. Those born under this Moon don't have any hesitation to tear down what is not working and rebuild it in a better way, but need to make sure they don't come across as argumentative or difficult in the process.

The gibbous Moon can often look full at this time, but that's just atmospherics. There's an urgency to get things completed here, and people born at this time may seem to be on a quest to better understand themselves. They might be gullible, but they're sincere enough, and with patience and time they will find their fulfillment and maturity.

The Full Moon is when everything comes to fruition. People often want to get together in a positive way at this time, seeking amiable conclusions to their goals. Those born during this phase will be intuitive and creative, and need to find a practical way to express themselves, lest they succumb to fears and insecurities.

The disseminating Moon is when energies may feel scattered. You could feel out of sorts, or find it hard to concentrate. People born at this time are the teachers and the revolutionaries, if they can just find a way to bring their desires into harmony with the needs of others.

The last quarter Moon is when the energy raised during the first quarter has reached fruition and is now abating. Those born under this Moon are usually sympathetic and understanding, although they may be prone to stubbornness. They need to guard against too much nostalgia, as it is easy for them to get melancholy and despondent.

The balsamic Moon is the perfect period for releasing what has not come to pass, in order to make room for new ideas and projects. People who are born at this time are introspective, perhaps reserved, with a strong intuition about their future. They are likely to see many changes in their lives, and need to develop the integrity to go with the natural flow of their evolution.

This completes the lunar month, and the cycle starts again with the next phase, the next New Moon. There are many online resources where you can calculate the Moon's phase; my favorites are stardate.org and—once again—lunarium.co.uk. Lunarium provides the phases of the New, first quarter, Full, and last quarter Moon, as well as the time that it enters the phases and when the Moon changes signs.

Moon Signs

Aries Moon: Aries is a cardinal fire sign. These people are enthusiastic and passionate about what interests them. They're fairly fearless when it comes to trying something new, but they can't stand indecision in any form. Their no-nonsense approach is often tactless, and they need to remember to consider the feelings of others. They should strive to keep their minds busy, for they have a tendency to become rather unpleasant when they get bored!

They have a lot of energy to start things, but they're easily distracted by what could be happening next. Delegating the more mundane tasks will help them to get things finished. They do best in managerial roles, often preferring to work alone rather than as part of a team. They're quite competitive, with the potential to excel in everything they attempt. They're not afraid to take calculated risks, which will help them lay the foundation for an exciting and successful life.

Taurus Moon: Taurus is a fixed earth sign. They're reliable and have a strong sense of responsibility. Practical and pragmatic, but maybe a bit lazy at times, they have no hesitation to pursue their desires with the focus of the proverbial bull in a china shop! Security is important to them, and that includes feeling comfortable and confident in their relationships as well as their environment.

They're very sensual, experiencing life through the five senses, and would rather be doing than thinking. They appreciate the finer things and have an eye for beauty. They don't adapt easily to change, and need to adjust to any transformation in a slow and methodical manner. They must ensure they don't hang onto things from the past that need to be laid to rest. Their natural charm will draw people toward them and help them to make the connections needed for them to feel self-assured about their lives.

Gemini Moon: Gemini is a mutable air sign. These folks are moody and changeable and cannot stand to be bored. While this can be confounding for their loved ones, they're never down in the dumps for long—and that's a good thing! They know just how to work an audience to get what they need from those around them, but need to be careful that this does not turn into a manipulative tactic. No one likes to think that they're being used.

Gemini Moons have a keen intellect that needs constant stimulation, or it might turn into nervous energy and anxiety. They're witty and intelligent and amusing, and people enjoy their company. They're naturally curious about life and all it has to offer, eagerly moving on from one event to the next, but effort is needed when it comes to getting them to fulfill their obligations and commitments. Remaining adaptable and versatile will get them where they want to go.

Cancer Moon: Cancer is a cardinal water sign. They're naturally nurturing and sensitive to the needs of others, but perhaps over-sensitive when things don't go the way they'd planned. It's important that insecurities are faced so they don't become defensive when met with challenges. They need to work on not taking what everyone else says or thinks quite so much to heart. For the opinions of other people are just that; they are not facts.

For Cancer Moons, home really is where the heart is, and it is important that there's a safe haven to retreat to at the end of the day. They treasure their loved ones and will go out of their way to ensure that their needs are met, but they may overlook their own needs in the process. They're intuitive and insightful, and the Moon is this sign's astrological ruler. They'll learn a lot about themselves by tapping into the natural ebb and flow of the lunar energy.

Leo Moon: Leo is a fixed fire sign. They do nothing by halves and their emotional response is to go big, with grandiose expressions of love and devotion. They're generous to a fault, but need

to make sure they're being generous and kind because it is the right thing to do, and not because they're seeking some kind of recognition or reward for their actions. They love to be the center of attention, and most people don't mind giving it to them, since they're so gregarious and amiable.

It takes a lot to bring them down, for their mood is naturally sunny. They've got natural leadership skills and the ambition to be successful in whatever they attempt. They might struggle to share the spotlight with others at times, but can learn to overcome this when they understand that letting others have the recognition is also a gift that can be given. Leo Moons are most happy when they're throwing themselves into something new and living life to the fullest.

Virgo Moon: Virgo is a mutable earth sign. They keep their emotions quite cool on the whole, and tend to feel things by thinking them through as opposed to just having a gut reaction. They worry more than is good for them, and should find a creative outlet to help them escape this habit of overthinking things. Very often the things worrying them are the things that don't manifest in the end, and then they've spent all that time and energy working themselves up over nothing!

Virgo Moons have a strong mind and a quick wit, but in their endeavor to help people there's a tendency to perhaps come off as bossy or critical, which is usually not the case. It's hard for others to fool them, for they have a knack for seeing through the fluff and getting right to the heart of the matter. Keeping things orderly and settling into some kind of a routine will help them to take control of that nervous energy and channel it in a positive and constructive manner.

Libra Moon: Libra is a cardinal air sign. They're so charming, and it's easy to enjoy their company. They're a natural mediator, making sure everyone is included and treated fairly, and when this doesn't happen they then become the diplomat, trying to understand both sides of the story and heal any rift that has been created. They need beauty in their lives and will make a conscious effort to seek it out and draw it close.

Like the scales that represent Libra, they're always weighing their feelings, trying to determine what is best or where they belong, and this has a tendency to make them indecisive. They want the best for everyone concerned, and frequently struggle with that resolution. Discord of any kind upsets them, and it is vital that they find a way of learning how to take the rough with the smooth so they can achieve internal harmony no matter what is happening around them.

Scorpio Moon: Scorpio is a fixed water sign. They love a mystery, and need to sense at least a little bit of excitement in all areas of life to feel truly alive. They don't do anything by halves, and while they may not reveal their emotions immediately, they're the proverbial still waters that run deep. If they've been bottling things up, they take others by surprise when all those emotions suddenly burst forth.

Scorpio Moons' need to control their emotional responses is a reflection of them needing to feel in control of any situation, and when they don't, they start to feel uncomfortable and anxious. Focusing on one thing at a time rather than trying to cope with the entire issue will help them. They have tremendous integrity, and their mystery and charm will carry them toward the best life has to offer if they can just learn to lighten up a bit.

Sagittarius Moon: Sagittarius is a mutable fire sign. They're warm and open and friendly, but they do have a knack for saying exactly how they feel, and that bluntness may not always go down well. They see the bigger picture rather than getting bogged down by minutiae, and have a zest for life and an optimistic outlook. They do tend to act on their gut feelings rather than thinking things through at times, and capriciousness isn't always a good thing!

This Moon is independent and fun-loving, but woe betide anyone who tries to make them conform or tries to tame their spirit. They love to learn and have a childlike wonder about life that is endearing and infectious. Adaptability is one of their main strengths, but if left undisciplined, this can turn into restlessness. A philosophical angle is the best approach for dealing with their ever-changing feelings.

Capricorn Moon: Capricorn is a cardinal earth sign. They're naturally cautious and reserved and keep a close guard on their feelings. They have a strong sense of responsibility and when they say they'll do something, they do their very best to keep their word. It takes them a long time to make up their mind about something—or someone—not because they're indecisive, but because they hate to be wrong.

Those who don't know them well might accuse them of being cold or distant, which they're not; they just don't have any use for superficial relationships. They want sincerity and maturity, and when they get it, they'll go the distance and be completely devoted to those in their inner circle. They simply want to be appreciated, and one of their lessons in life is to learn to appreciate themselves and love themselves, for others might not always be there.

Aquarius Moon: Aquarius is a fixed air sign. They're humanitarian and sincere, but they frequently struggle to get in touch with their true feelings. They spend a lot of time in their heads, seeking new solutions to old problems and contemplating better ways of doing things. They need a purpose in order to feel whole; when they don't have a goal they tend to drift, and that may get them into some sticky situations.

They're original and maybe even a bit eccentric, and even when they go out of their way not to be the center of attention, somehow there they are! It's because no matter how they try to disguise it, there's something unique and enticing about them that people want to get to know. Their successes come not in spite of their intense feelings, but because of them. Their challenge is to learn to get in touch with and express their emotions.

Pisces Moon: Pisces is a mutable water sign. Gentle and sympathetic by nature, this Moon sign abhors aggression of any kind, and finds the world can sometimes be too harsh for their delicate souls. They have a natural and strong sense of empathy, but have to learn to distinguish their own feelings from what they are picking up from others. Romantic and dreamy, they are often intuitive and more than a bit psychic.

Their strength lies in being able to take whatever they're feeling at the moment and channel it into something creative. This is a healthy means of escape for it helps them to purge their feelings away from their own energy and into something tangible. They may even find they touch other people who relate to this self-expression because they are going through something similar themselves.

In Conclusion

Learning your natal Moon sign, and how that sign expresses itself through the phase of the Moon when you were born, is a great start when it comes to getting to know yourself better. An astrologer will take this even further, looking at the way the Moon interacts with the other planets through the aspect ratios and midpoints. The one thing to remember, though, is whatever your Moon sign and whatever the stars advise, this is only a map, a blueprint, a guide. You are the architect of your life, and you alone are in control of manifesting your destiny and creating the reality in which you want to live. May it be a long and happy one!

References

Angelo, Megan. "16 Unforgettable Things Maya Angelou Wrote and Said." Glamour. Condé Nast. May 28, 2014. https://www.glamour.com/story/maya-angelou-quotes.

Restorative Yoga for Full Moon Time

by Robin Ivy Payton

When the Moon becomes Full, the force is strong. The power of the Full Moon has been recognized and celebrated widely through beliefs, stories, and traditions from countless cultures. Buddhists regard the Full Moon with a reverence directly related to the Buddha, who is said to have been born, enlightened, and transitioned out of earthly life during Full Moons. In India and Nepal, one Full Moon each year is known as the Guru Purnima, a time to honor one's spiritual teachers with festivals, gifts, fasting, or prayer, depending on cultural beliefs. Full Moon is regarded as an auspicious and mystical time in other traditions as well. Native American tribes named the monthly Moons for their unique qualities and seasonal attributes. For example, the cycle springing the earth into life is recognized as the Flower Moon, and harvest season includes the Corn Moon.

Our bodies and minds feel the power of Full Moon just as the earth and waters do. From a yoga perspective, *prana vayu*, an upward moving energy, increases with Full Moon. The winds of life force become strong, increasing internal fluids and physical energy, which can also result in overstimulation and excess. Potentially, these upward rising forces may feel ungrounding to the physical body and disorienting or distracting to the mind. Some downward leaning energy, known as *apana*, may be called for at these peak times to balance out the strong upward flows. Think of a tree when the winds are high, considering how sometimes the roots can be pulled right out of the ground. As humans, we can be like the trees as Full Moon acts like the winds.

Emotionally, our moods also become full and feelings intensify. The Full Moon stimulates enhanced experiences of romance, excitement, gratitude, grief, despair, restlessness, and more. Even during a peak of happiness or elation, our bodies and minds benefit from harmony and balance, a respite from the extremes of any feeling that temporarily alters the responses of our nervous system. Grounding, rooting, and earthing, we feel more stable and secure. Our parasympathetic nervous system induces calm when we feel physically safe and mentally clear. Restorative practices of yoga and meditation activate the parasympathetic response.

Full Moon bestows light on the earth and represents illumination and awakening to what may have been hidden or sleeping. Restorative yoga practices open doors to what may be dormant or repressed within you. Your inner realm holds answers, memories, and limitless potential. Often the wisdom one seeks has been there inside all along, waiting for the space and quietness from which to arise. The climax of the lunar cycle syncs well with restorative yoga, a practice of getting close to the earth, releasing tension or stress, and reconnecting gently with oneself.

As you withdraw external senses, diminish the effects of mental stories and clutter, and release long exhales, internal fog or storms may clear. Inner light grows to match the Moon's radiance.

The bliss state that yoga moves you toward reflects lunar energy. It is not heated or fiery like the Sun, so much as it is cool and content. Restorative yoga postures and sequences help to reduce the charge of constant activity and interaction that leads to stress, fatigue, anxiety, or even excitement. Supporting the body with blankets, pillows, or other props comforts the physical body, while breathing consciously or being guided in meditation simultaneously helps rest the mind, ideally creating more ease and bringing one closer to contentment. You can practice restorative yoga at home anytime, and particularly when you're feeling the upward rising tide for a few days before and a day or so after Full Moon. Ahead is a restorative series designed for home practice, using regular blankets and pillows. If you own yoga props like blocks or a bolster, you can substitute them in any way that makes sense.

To prepare, gather some blankets you can fold or roll up and some pillows from the bed or couch. Couch cushions can also work well. An ottoman, chair, couch or empty wall may be of value for some postures too. Once you are ready, turn off devices that could beep or ring. For sound, choose quiet music or simply rest in silence. Crystal bowl sounds, flutes, or binaural beats assist in relaxing the nervous system, and you may find an online album or collection to listen to during yoga.

To begin, take a comfortable seat or lie down on your back and form the hand posture of wholeness, also known as a mudra, by joining the backs of your right fingers with the palm side of your left fingers. Then bring the thumbs together to create the circular seal. This is a mudra of emotional balance and wholeness. Center in your breath as you enter the energy of things that come full circle. You do not need to conjure specific situations and can simplify by noticing where the inhale begins and the exhale ends, a circle of breath that is constantly with you. Let your eyes rest and your breath deepen so your abdomen and ribs move with your inhales and exhales. A mantra to repeat to yourself can be useful during your practice. The Moon relates to emotions, the heart center, and the word *love*; phrases like "I am love" or "I am loved" are examples to try out. You may choose any mantra that suits you and state it to yourself in the most kind and encouraging way. Closure, successful completion, and abundance are also intentions that may arise near Full Moon. Spend five minutes or more centering to open your restorative sequence.

Since Full Moons are high energy, your next posture can be a downward facing position, which reduces external stimulus and brings the heart toward the earth. Such postures signify turning inward and protecting the soft front side of the body. Choose here from child posture or downward facing rest on the stomach. For child posture, come to your shins and bend your knees so the hips and seat move to the heels, or come close to the heels. You can place a blanket between the calves and thighs and behind the knees for more comfort. Your head will come down to the earth or you can place a rolled blanket under the forehead for ease. Allow the neck to relax as the head touches down. Find a place where your arms rest naturally either forward on the forearms or back with hands on the feet and upper arms on your thighs. Rock your forehead side to side to soothe the brow bones and the center known as the third eye. This may help calm the mind.

As an alternate posture, for example if the knees or ankles feel overstretched, lie on your stomach with arms or hands stacked under your head. You can turn your head to the side or rest with your forehead down. A blanket positioned from the hip bones up may ease the lower back and provide a gentle place for the belly and chest to rest. Adding a rolled blanket or a pillow between the ankles and the floor may also support the back. Whichever of these forward-facing postures you choose, give yourself plenty of time here (ten to fifteen minutes recommended), and follow your breath or your mantra to keep the mind from wandering. When the mind drifts to tasks or problem-solving, replace those thoughts with the present moment again and again. Remember this is a practice and it takes time. You are engaging in self-care. Finally, you can move from child to downward facing rest, splitting up your time in any manner, knowing that your priorities are comfort and ease.

The next posture will be a contrast to the downward facing posture. For this one, roll or fold a blanket about two or three inches wide and as long as your whole back, from head to tailbone, and maybe slightly longer. Think of this as mimicking your spine. If you begin by opening a blanket and folding it in half or fourths, then folding or rolling it into a narrower width, that's all you need to do. Sit on the earth, mat, or floor and place the blanket under the center of your back. The top of the blanket can tuck under your neck and head until you have the right support. Allow your shoulders to drift off each side of the blanket onto the floor. Your seat and legs will be a little bit lower than your back as the blanket runs the length of your spine. Adjust until you feel just right.

An alternate could be a deeper backbend with a pillow under your head and a blanket folded evenly and rolled up into a 3–6-inch high bolster that runs across the shoulder blade area of your back. In this shape, your head may tip back slightly, but make sure it's

not much of a stretch since restorative yoga is meant to open you gently and with complete support for your joints, in this case the neck. In this posture you might also place a blanket or pillow under the backs of your knees so there is no tug on the lower back as you extend your legs. Any comfortable leg position will do. The feet should hold no tension here as you let them drop open to each side and neither point nor flex the ankles. Arms open next to the side of your body with palms facing either down or up. Otherwise, you can rest your hands on your ribs or stomach and feel the movement of your breath. If you feel at ease, spend another ten to fifteen minutes here. If you need something to occupy your mind, count back from 108 and restart each time you lose count or reach 1 again. Your breath and mantra are also there to return to anytime.

Following your upward facing posture or backbend, remove the blankets and lie down on your back for a gentle spinal twist to each side. You may place a blanket under your whole body and have a pillow or rolled blanket to rest under or between the legs. Your arms can spread out like wings, and if a blanket under one shoulder feels good, place it there. This generally will be the shoulder opposite the knees, as it may lift when you twist the mid body. Allow five minutes or more with both knees to the right, and then both knees to the left, with pillows or blankets for the legs and hips, place as you like.

To finish your restorative session, take your feet up. Either gently lower yourself onto your back and lift the legs and feet up a wall or lie in front of an ottoman or couch and let your legs rest there with the knees bending. Another option is to stack your pillows and blankets and swing your legs up onto them with your back resting on the floor. Make sure your knees feel comfortable and that the back of the knee joint rests on the props you've chosen. A blanket that meets the shoulder line supports your head and neck. Pull another blanket over your body for a cozy feeling in this posture or in every posture throughout your practice. In this final posture, let go of everything and let your breath be natural and soft. Give yourself enough time here for an optional yoga nap, should that arise. When you awaken or choose to release your resting posture, sense any way or any place in the body you feel centered and secure. Place your fingertips in the center of your forehead and smooth in both directions: over the eyebrows, down the temples, around the back of the ears, and under the occipital bones until your fingertips meet at the back of your head. Give your neck muscles a gentle massage and mindfully move into the rest of your evening or day, replenished.

Wildlife Rehabilitation in Your Own Neighborhood

by Mireille Blacke, MA, LADC, RD, CD-N

Purchasing and renovating a Queen Anne Victorian home brings significant challenges, unexpected benefits, and a number of surprises, many of which I've shared with Llewellyn readers over the years. Some of my greatest learning experiences in undertaking such a long-term project involved the house only indirectly, since the diverse ecological landscaping, gardening, and overall maintenance of this property was as unfamiliar to me in practice as daily living a century ago would be. But due to my fondness for modern living, and my regular tendency to poke fun at myself, you should know that a drive-through barista prepares my morning brew far better than I do, and I whine about mosquito bites, ants, and creepy-crawly things more than any petulant toddler you've ever met.

I did more than whine during "the bat incident" last year.

At that time, the house was busy inside and out with renovations, as well as the usual frenzy involved with "owning" two active, healthy, quite mischievous, and easily bored adult male Bengal cats. Racing up and down the quarter-turn staircases like howling, thundering stallions is a common choice activity for Cayenne and Cajun, especially in the early morning hours. Impressive high-jumps and kamikaze wrestling antics are the norm for these two, but my heart stopped when Cayenne, ever the modern hunter, paused during play-fighting with his brother *on the grand staircase* to effortlessly grab a *live bat* out of the air, a creature that swooped down upon us seemingly out of nowhere.

While the term "bats in the belfry" was familiar to me, I'd always associated the phrase with campy, haunted houses in dated black-and-white horror films from old Hollywood, or something I'd hear about in a joke on *The Munsters* when I was a kid. I'd never seen a bat up close in real life and never planned on it.

Even without an actual "belfry" (bell tower), older homes with eaves and attic crawl spaces may eventually house a lost or misdirected "creature of the night" or two. Considering that habitat loss and disease threaten the bat population, it's important for uninformed humans to react appropriately and not panic or resort to lethal measures if these creatures end up in such unexpected places. But more on that later…

Roles in the Ecosystem

Each species plays a specific role in its ecosystem, which in turn allows the whole ecosystem to work. This includes prey animals like rabbits, squirrels, and opossum, as well as raptors and birds of prey (hawks, owls, vultures, etc.), and yes, bats! Bats, the only mammals that can both flap their wings and fly, also pollinate our crops and control insect populations in our neighborhoods. According to the Humane Society's website, "A single brown bat can catch 600 mosquitoes or more in an hour!" ("Bats"). Okay, now that's impressive and extremely useful!

Urbanization has led to more wildlife seeking refuge in our backyards, gardens, and neighborhoods. Situations may then arise in which these animals are injured, orphaned, or abandoned on these properties (or nearby areas). Many of us would not know whether to provide aid or who to call for assistance if we stumbled across one of these creatures; some people may respond in an unsafe manner, leading to harm for the responder, or improper care for or death of the animal. Baby wild animals might *seem* like they need our help, but unless the animal is truly orphaned or injured, there is no need to rescue them. Whether an animal is orphaned and needs your help depends on their age, species, and behavior. Babies of some species are left alone all day and rely on camouflage for protection, while others are closely supervised by their parents. For example, wild rabbits and deer frequently leave their young for long periods of time, while raccoons and skunks rarely do.

Wow, that's complicated!

According to the Humane Society's website, the following are definite signs that "a wild animal needs your help:

- The animal is brought to you by a cat or dog.
- There's evidence of bleeding.
- The animal has an apparent or obvious broken limb.
- A bird is featherless or nearly featherless and on the ground.
- The animal is shivering.
- There's a dead parent nearby.
- The animal is crying and wandering all day long."

Translation: Find help for the animal if you see any of those signs. If necessary, you should "safely capture and transport them to the appropriate place for treatment" ("Found an Oprhaned or Injured Baby Wild Animal?").

I can barely get my cats into a carrier for a veterinarian appointment, and I hide under the dining room table when a bat shows up. I'm quite sure the "capture and transport" of a wild animal is outside of my comfort zone. Enter wildlife rehabilitation centers and licensed wildlife rehabilitators.

Wildlife Rehabilitation Centers

The goals of wildlife rehabilitation centers are to temporarily care for recuperating wild animals and release them, when viable, back into the wild. Again, though licensed by the state, rehabilitators' efforts are fully voluntary. Licensed Wildlife Rehabilitators (LWRs) are neither paid nor reimbursed for their expenses or time. Veterinarians who assist these rehabilitation centers usually donate their time and services as well.

For individuals interested in volunteering for this demanding but rewarding work, many wildlife rehabilitation centers offer rescue/transport seminars to show people how to properly and safely rescue injured, orphaned, or sick animals and secure them for safe transport. Such educational programs typically have fees because these centers are not funded by state or federal governments, and rely on grants, donations, and supporters for supplies, time, and money.

For the same situations listed above, call a licensed wildlife rehabilitator (LWR) for assistance. (See the Resources section of this article to find a local LWR in your area or online.) If you're unable to locate an LWR, try contacting an animal shelter, humane society, animal control agency, nature center, state wildlife agency, or veterinarian.

Species-Specific Tips

I recommend wearing thick gloves for any wild animal contact (find "animal handling gloves" locally or on Amazon).

Bats

It's not too hard to figure out common points of entry for bats within old homes: gaps and tiny openings that lead to attics, eaves, cellars, etc. Nooks and cracks aplenty! Bats will usually roost somewhere in your house and inadvertently wind up in the home's living space. Just inspect your whole house thoroughly and seal *every single potential interior entrance*, right? I don't know about you, but I think most reasonable people would risk a bat or two!

Unlike in myths and movies, bats don't want to suck your blood or nest in your hair! Their dramatic, swooping flight patterns are how they stay airborne in small spaces. They're not actually flying at you, and it's not too tough to help them back outside. You just need to remain calm enough to do it!

Usually opening a window on each end of the floor the bat is flying on will allow the bat to show itself out; in my case, it took more creativity. As I hid under the dining room table and the Bengals were shut away for safety, my husband cleverly opened our enormous windows and the front door while blasting bat communication sounds on his phone from outside the house. Considering how dark it was and the large hedges we have, this terrified the neighbors who walked by, but (a) the bat eventually flew out toward the sounds, and (b) trick-or-treaters are getting some serious surround sound entertainment this year!

Birds

This is an immense category that could comprise an entire book, so please refer to the References and Resources section for additional direction.

Birds are most commonly injured by flying into windows or being hit by motor vehicles. Other methods of injury reported by rehabilitation centers include ingesting rat poison or lawn chemicals, becoming entangled in garbage, or getting hit when trees are cut down. Birds are sometimes so severely injured they cannot be returned to the wild, and rehab centers will care for them for life.

With baby birds that are clearly injured or in imminent danger, contact an LWR. If featherless or nearly featherless baby birds have fallen from their nest but appear unharmed, put them back in the nest (wearing your gloves!) if you can do so without danger to yourself.

Please note that it's a myth that birds will abandon their young if a person touches them. However, it is true that *birds are best raised by birds*, so try to reunite them with their parents before calling an LWR.

Fledglings are adolescent birds that have left the nest. It's normal for them to hop on the ground, unable to fly, supervised and fed by their parents several times per hour, before they learn to fly. The presence of white-gray fecal material indicates the fledglings are being cared for, as birds defecate after being fed. Keep cats indoors and dogs leashed until the fledglings are old enough to fly. If you're positive the parents aren't returning to feed the babies, contact an LWR.

Note: It's illegal to have wild birds as pets, and nearly always fatal to the bird should it ever return to the wild. Once a wild bird imprints on a human, its likelihood of surviving in the wild decreases by 98 percent.

Deer

Yes, we're in Bambi territory: motherless fawns (baby deer). Do not assume that a fawn alone is orphaned. If a fawn is lying down peacefully, its mother is nearby and all is well. A doe only visits to nurse its fawn several times per day to avoid attracting predators.

Unless you're certain its mother is dead, you may leave the fawn on its own.

Mother deer want their babies back even if humans have handled them. The fawn should be returned to the exact spot from which it was taken (or found), and you should vacate the area, as the mother will not show herself until you leave.

If you noticed the fawn lying on its side, wandering, or crying all day, contact an LWR. (And avoid animated Disney movies for a while.)

Now, on to Thumper…

Rabbits

Young rabbits that are at least four inches long, with erect ears and open eyes, and that hop well, should be considered safely independent from their mothers, and do not need assistance. Leave uninjured baby rabbits in an intact nest alone. As with deer, mothers will avoid visiting their offspring frequently during the day to avoid attracting predators. We should not confuse this for abandonment by the mother. If you notice the nest has been disturbed, avoid touching the baby rabbits. *In this case, unfamiliar scents will cause the mother rabbit to abandon her offspring.* Lightly cover the disturbed nest with natural materials you've found around it (grass, leaves, etc.). Use yarn or string to make a "tic-tac-toe" pattern over the nest to monitor the mother rabbit's return over the next twenty-four hours. Keep pets and children out of the area. If the yarn or string was moved, but the nest is still covered, assume the mother rabbit has returned to care for her babies. If the pattern is undisturbed after twenty-four hours, contact an LWR.

Squirrels

A squirrel that has a full and fluffy tail; can run, jump, and climb; and is nearly full-sized does not need your assistance. However, contact an LWR if you notice a young squirrel that frequently follows or approaches humans, as it needs care. Intervention is also needed if you see a baby squirrel has fallen from a nest, a nest has fallen from a tree, or an intact nest remains from a fallen tree. If the tree has fallen in the last day, the mother squirrel may yet return to relocate her young to a new nest. If the baby squirrel(s) are uninjured, leave them and the area, and do your best to keep humans and other animals away while you provide surveillance from a safe distance.

If the baby squirrels are not reclaimed by dusk, *wearing thick gloves*, gather the offspring and place them inside a thick, soft cloth (like a fleece scarf or hat). If possible, insert a hot water bottle or heating pad with a cover, on the lowest setting. Place the baby squirrels, cloth, and warmer/bottle inside a small box or carrier, and call an LWR.

Opossums

Baby opossums nurse in their mother's pouch for about two months, and are not likely to be seen. They'll ride on mom's back at three to four inches long, and sometimes fall off without much notice. An opossum can survive on its own if it's seven inches long (including its tail). Call an LWR if you find an opossum less than seven inches on its own, as it's likely to be an orphan.

Raccoons

Mother raccoons are in frequent contact with their young, so if a baby raccoon is unattended for more than a few hours, it may be orphaned. Using a plastic, inverted laundry basket (with lattice sides) can assist the mother in finding her missing baby if she returns at night to search. Wearing your gloves, place the inverted basket over the baby, with a light weight on top. Monitor any activity, and expect a possible late night arrival, as raccoons are nocturnal. If the mother does not return, contact an LWR.

Unfortunately, in warmer months, some people set traps in a misguided effort to redirect garbage pilfering and other "nuisance" issues, which leads to trapped and killed mother raccoons that leave their starving babies behind. If anyone in your neighborhood is setting traps, please persuade them to use more humane and effective methods instead.

Skunks

Nose-to-tail baby skunks in a line without a mother in sight could be orphaned. The reason for this may be poor eyesight; babies can lose sight of their mother if she runs off to avoid a predator, and then may struggle to find her again.

As with the baby raccoon scenario, monitoring for the mother skunk's return is mostly a matter of corralling the young into one place and waiting for her to rejoin them. Put on your gloves and slowly place a plastic, inverted laundry basket (with lattice sides) over the babies to keep them in one spot and make it easier for the mother to find them. In this case, do not weigh down the laundry basket.

If the mother skunk returns to her young, she will flip up the basket and get them. You may assist if she has trouble. *Keep in mind that skunks are near-sighted and that fast movements may startle*

them into spraying. Be sure to move slowly and speak softly to reduce your chances of being sprayed. *An alarmed skunk will stamp its front feet to warn a potential predator,* so if the mother doesn't do this, consider yourself safe to proceed. If the mother doesn't come to reclaim her young by dawn, contact an LWR.

Safety on Both Sides

No matter the species, it's safety first at all times! Use extreme caution if you approach an injured, sick, or orphaned animal, even if you've already contacted a rehabilitator.

It's best to contact an LWR before attempting to handle an adult animal; animals of all sizes can cause injuries! Once you've made contact with a wildlife professional, you will be asked to describe the animal and its physical condition. Be as accurate and detailed as possible; consider texting a photo if you're able.

Unless you're told otherwise, there are ways to comfort an animal before transport or while you're waiting for assistance. Again, always wear thick gloves! You'll also need a safe, well-ventilated, escape-proof container. A cardboard box, lined with soft cloth, with holes punched from the inside out would be fine in most cases, depending on the size of the animal.

While wearing your gloves, cover the animal with a towel, old t-shirt, or pillowcase and gently scoop up and place the animal in the container or box.

Do not give the wild animal food or water. This can lead to choking, serious illness or digestive problems, aspiration, pneumonia, or death from force-feeding.

After you contact an LWR, place the container in a warm, dark, quiet place, removed from loud noises (including television, radio, loud conversation), pets, and children, until transport is possible. Avoid direct sunlight or air conditioning. Following these suggestions will help to lower the animal's stress levels significantly.

Transport the animal for treatment as soon as possible.

From Batsh*t Crazy to Educated and Informed

So, what became of my "bats in the belfry?" Well, there have been more bats in my house since that first one. I initially hid under the dining room table upon seeing that low-swooping flight pattern, but the safety of my two Bengal boys forced me to learn more about the situation, and wildlife rescue and rehabilitation in general. Also, I learned to appreciate a mosquito-free existence!

Sealing off every tiny nook and cranny of an old Victorian house is impractical and unlikely, so I expect other nocturnal swooping visitors to make their presence known to me in the main house again someday. One might make me jump once again by simply hanging upside down from the "rafters" in the dining room and having a snooze (yes, they really sleep like that). Though I may still have a human, visceral response to a bat's presence in the house, I'm more informed now. I made the choice to educate myself about my own role in all of this, as well as about the wildlife, and became less "batty" as a result.

Like I said, I have no problem taking shots at myself. Sometimes Mother Nature's impressive creatures help me out in that department, tossing in some irony with the life lessons.

One evening shortly after the first "bat incident," I felt the familiar pinch of a mosquito bite, and immediately smiled at the thought of my former houseguest elegantly dancing across the night sky as he freely soared, swooped extra low, and rejoiced.

References and Resources

"A Place Called Hope." A Place Called Hope. Accessed April 7, 2020. www.aplacecalledhoperaptors.com.

"Bats." Humane Society of the United States. Accessed April 7, 2020. https://www.humanesociety.org/animals/bats.

"Found an Orphaned or Injured Baby Wild Animal?" Humane Society of the United States. Accessed April 7, 2020. https://www .humanesociety.org/resources/found-orphaned-or-injured-baby -wild-animal.

"Welcome to the National Wildlife Rehabilitators Association." National Wildlife Rehabilitators Association (NWRA). Accessed April 7, 2020. www.nwrawildlife.org.

"How to Find a Wildlife Rehabilitator." Humane Society of the United States. Accessed April 7, 2020. www.humanesociety.org/resources /how-find-wildlife-rehabilitator.

"Step-by-Step." Connecticut Wildlife Rehabilitators Association (CWRA). Accessed April 7, 2020. www.cwrawildlife.org.

"Welcome to the National Wildlife Rehabilitators Association." National Wildlife Rehabilitators Association (NWRA). Accessed April 7, 2020. www.nwrawildlife.org.

How Your Moon Works with Feng Shui in Home-Buying Ventures

by Alice DeVille

Harmony complements house hunting. Did you know the Moon plays an important role in real estate purchases? The Moon is the natural ruler of the fourth house—home—the emotional driver that influences your choice in living quarters. Even though your natal Moon may not fall in the fourth house in your astrology chart, it is important to know both its sign and location, as well as the sign on the cusp (door) to your fourth house. That sign provides descriptive insight into the qualities and characteristics that will ultimately guide you in your quest for a home. Along with personal preferences, the ancient Chinese practice of Feng Shui (the art of placement) blends well with astrology and focuses on location, so that you find accommodations that make you feel prosperous, happy, and healthy at home. Many real estate contracts in today's market contain a contingency clause that reads "subject to Feng Shui inspection." The Feng Shui-savvy buyer initiates the action at the time of signing the contract purchase, inserting this contingency clause, and then usually hires, at their own expense, a Feng Shui practitioner to analyze the house. If it does not pass a Feng Shui inspection, just like with a home inspection, the buyer is under no obligation to buy.

Home shoppers flock to the internet, looking at the inventory of homes and desired features in their optimal price range. Before you connect with a realtor and begin a serious search, check your credit scores, meet with mortgage lenders offering competitive rates, and proceed to line up pre-approved financing. Many factors enter into your decision to buy a home: how much money you have to spend; where you want to live; the type and size of home that suits your needs; and curb appeal, the external layout or Feng Shui factor that attracts you to specific properties. This article aims to help you facilitate smooth real estate decisions by understanding how your Moon's qualities interact with sound Feng Shui principles to lead you to the perfect home.

Feng Shui and Real Estate

I was a realtor in the Commonwealth of Virginia for twenty-two years before moving to Florida in 2014. Many of my clients knew I was also an astrologer who could help them synchronize their charts to select dates for signing contracts and scheduling settlements, as well as examine potential properties from a Feng Shui perspective, another of my areas of expertise. I developed Feng Shui courses for public consumption and presented workshops to realtors wishing to know more about the emerging interests of sophisticated buyers looking for prime properties. If you are unfamiliar with Feng Shui, the following tips may help.

Feng Shui (pronounced "fung schway") is the key to environmental harmony. It creates flow that enhances the quality of your life; shows you how to arrange your outer world to balance your inner world; helps you attract positive business and personal relationships; and acknowledges your attitude, goals, and feelings. Feng Shui means wind and water; the art of living in harmony with earth; promotion of wellness, happiness, and contentment; and spiritual abundance. Terms of importance in home buying include Chi or dragon's breath—the universal life force found in every living thing—and Shar, or poison arrows, which are negative energies that travel in long straight lines or stabbing movements. A Shar is negative energy caused by the arrangement of specific features of the home, such as the contours. The Chinese believe everything was created from five basic elements: wood, fire, earth, metal, and water. Every home benefits from incorporating these elements to create Chi.

Avoid looking at properties that have an unkempt or cluttered look. Clutter is stagnant Chi and when you find it in a home it creates unsettled conditions and problems for buyers. As you tour a home, look at everything—kitchen, bedroom, living rooms, bathrooms, and garage; examine closets, drawers, décor, shelves, household maintenance in general, and the whole outdoor space, including the car. Clutter confuses home seekers and suggests unfinished business exists in the home. It may also contribute to ill health. Unkempt properties suggest sellers may have a poverty consciousness and it affects how principals (buyers and sellers) think and act. Unless you are in the market for a serious fixer-upper, look for a property that represents your idea of the perfect residence and radiates positive Chi.

Feng Shui Conventions

Very few houses are perfect. When looking at homes, pay attention to the shape and style. Square or oblong houses are more desirable than unusual shapes. Don't worry though, Feng Shui remedies exist for those odd shapes, especially if you are willing to square off or make the lot line rectangular using landscaping and contouring techniques. Look for properties with attractive, well-kept landscaping, plus fresh mulch and flowers that enhance curb appeal. Be sure you can see the front door as you approach the house; if a "blocker" tree diminishes the view, it creates a Shar, or negative flow of energy, that poisons the energy and may prevent prosperity from entering the home. You may notice blemishes such as uneven walls or floors when you tour a property, but plants help Chi to circulate and hide defects in walls and room shapes. Use of natural, artificial, or silk plants enhances Chi, but never use dried flowers (dead). Strong potpourri scents may be masking toxic odors and creating poor air quality. Split-level homes confuse Chi direction; in fact, so do any homes that require you to enter on a higher level than the rest of the house. This feature diminishes prosperity and resale power. Going "downstairs" to the rest of the house signifies a demotion or loss of status.

Moon Signs and Feng Shui

Your Moon sign drives the emotional attachment you have to your home. It governs personal preferences and those "gotta have" features you desire when you search for a residence. Use the following information to validate your choices and also to identify the sign on the cusp (front door) of your fourth house of home and foundation. These Feng Shui conventions apply to every sign.

Aries Moon: Homes represent personality and individuality. A unique exterior style begins at the front door with an entryway that features the five Feng Shui elements—a wood door painted red (fire) with a portico or porch painted a pale blue (water). Your foyer is likely to house collectibles displayed in étagères, on walls, or on shelves, designed to reveal your interests. If entry space cannot accommodate displays, look for a home with a hobby room, workshop, or den. Driving is one of your passions and you like ample parking space, preferring a double or triple garage to keep diverse vehicles—car, RV, scooter, or motorcycle—in pristine shape. You're good with tools and enjoy a space to build or repair equipment.

Taurus Moon: The value you derive from material things contributes to your peace of mind as you choose well-made furniture and accessories reflective of your refined style. Impressive landscaping that surrounds your home directs visitors to your large front door (double doors are preferred) and allows positive Chi to enter your home and circulate the wealth throughout every room. Never buy a home that has a large tree or unruly shrub blocking the view of your front door. Brick facades, walkways, and fireplaces highlight the earth element. Your flair for gardening transforms space with beautiful flowers, cheerful plants, and regal shrubs.

Gemini Moon: Location matters. Many Gemini Moons dislike yardwork and prefer residences that demand very little of it. Whether you are on a quest for a sleek condo, a towering highrise, or a classic two-story residence, pay attention to the surrounding energy. A home's roofline fascinates you more than most signs. To maximize positive Chi, never buy space at the bottom or the top of a high-rise or live in the basement of a condo. If you buy a single family residence, be sure it is not on a dead-end street. An avid communicator, you are naturally attracted to homes with built-in shelves and abundant storage to accommodate your collection of books, materials, and media equipment. If you opt for a library, select a room in the quiet part of the home. You're known for buying two of everything to balance energy—two candles, two lamps, two sets of shelves, and two computers.

Cancer Moon: "Nothing says lovin' like something in the oven," and you are the sign that wants a kitchen equipped with state-of-the-art double ovens, convection ovens, broilers, and grills to turn out your famous recipes. In Feng Shui, the kitchen is the heart of the home and controls the pulse, so select a home with a kitchen that is not visible from the front door. Centrally located kitchens emanate prosperity, while a front kitchen is conducive to eating out a lot. Never place the range in the space below a bathroom located on the floor above (plumbing leaks). Don't place it below a window either; it's not safe since winds may ignite a fire. Do choose stainless steel appliances with metal accessories and hardware to accelerate positive Chi. Eat-in kitchens are a must.

Leo Moon: Regal Leo loves to make a sweeping entrance to the home via a large foyer with curving staircase and dramatic chandelier. Look for stairs that angle gracefully away from a straight line up from the front door. The Leo Moon's housing choice reflects their desire for one-of-a-kind properties that look expensive. Avoid purchasing a home on a corner lot thinking your home's value will accelerate and you'll have more privacy. You'll pay more for it, yet the exact opposite occurs since traffic patterns hit in at least two directions, bringing huge distractions to the home's energy via those poison arrows or Shars. Enjoy decorative columns, marble floors, and space-doubling mirrors in a perpendicular line from the front door.

Virgo Moon: You prefer a nice backyard that gives you space to plant flowers, vegetables, and vining plants like tomatoes and squash. Balance yin and yang in the garden with a variety of light and dark shrubs planted along curving paths and walkways. Known for your organizational flair, you desire a laundry room with its own sink and efficiency-oriented washers and dryers, built-in folding tables, and ironing boards. Virgo Moons have a special interest in food preparation, nutrition, serving stations, and kitchen appliances. Round or oval tables are ideal for dining. A balanced meal includes both raw (yin) and cooked (yang) foods. Use candles, too.

Libra Moon: When house-shopping, check out the rooms that provide entertaining space: front porches, family rooms, sunrooms, outdoor decks, media lounges with theatre-type seating, or playrooms. A dining room is a must-have accommodation to showcase your talent for presenting celebratory meals. Add-ons include a butler's pantry or snack bar. Be sure to use chairs with backs, especially if your room has a number of windows (a Feng Shui protection convention for your back). Mirrors make the room look larger. Decorate with touches of red for abundance, good appetites, and festivity.

Scorpio Moon: You're one of the signs that examines the layout of the master bedroom for comfortable sleeping amenities and an en suite bathroom. If this bathroom is in the front of your home over the entrance door, keep looking for a better floorplan. Bathrooms expel waste, which flows out of the house and prevents prosperity from entering. Be sure your home inspection includes a thorough look at the plumbing system. Even if the master bathroom is located elsewhere, don't place the headboard next to the wall that houses the toilet or sleep will be disrupted from the sound of those negative "flushing" Shars. Square or rectangular bedrooms are the ideal shape and work best if you position your bed so you can see the door. Place your bed against a solid wall, never in front of a window, and don't install fans above the bed. Then buy those sexy, luxurious satin sheets and enjoy a restful night's sleep.

Sagittarius Moon: Your sign is adventurous when it comes to home buying. You tend to select vintage homes or those that need redecorating to meet your standards. Be wary of property owners (aka packrats) who leave garages, spare rooms, and basements filled with years of accumulated papers, records, and collectibles. The clutter amasses stagnant Chi and represents buried issues. It can be expensive to pay for removal. Negotiate with the seller to remove everything before settlement. Multistory homes are your preferred style, especially if you can turn attic space into a hobby room, study, or library. Remove confining walls and create an open space concept in family areas that can also display your treasured wood cabinetry and stone fireplace. After investing considerable cash to remodel and customize rooms to reflect your taste, make the outdoor space your next project. Sagittarius Moons often buy and flip homes when the market is ripe for these transactions, turning the profit into a new acquisition.

Capricorn Moon: Your observant Moon likes homes that make a great first impression with a "magazine" look and the Mr. Clean touch. You prefer homes with easily defined space and elegant dining rooms. Known for your workaholic tendencies in this telecommuting world, your "must have" home luxury is a custom office with privacy doors, built-in bookcases, a well-equipped computer workstation, and glass cabinets to showcase awards, citations, and collections. Minimize distractions by arranging your workspace so that you don't look out onto a hall or face stairs, closets, storage areas, or a window with significant traffic distractions that disturb concentration. Add a fountain in the northwest corner of your room to create soothing sounds. Decorate with favorite colors and use an inviting round or oval worktable with guest chairs for visitors.

Aquarius Moon: Mid-century modern and contemporary homes speak to you. Look at homes on streets where houses are relatively the same height so that a large McMansion does not block the light that energizes your uniquely laid out one-story home. Sometimes you like a minimalist or monochromatic approach to decorating. Be sure you have no bare walls. Musical instruments or photos of them create positive Chi. Use paintings, tapestries, and metal wall sculptures to add harmony and balance to your rooms. Plants revitalize corners and give a completed look to a room or foyer. Huge mirrors are a must to create an illusion of space, but make sure they are not comprised of mirrored tiles or that you face a mirror as soon as you open the front door, as this allows prosperity to rush right out the door.

Pisces Moon: You favor a home that is all on one floor, whether it is a sprawling ranch, a stylish condo, or a delightful duplex. Don't purchase a home on a T intersection or at the end of a cul-de-sac. Shars from oncoming traffic head straight to the front doors or windows, disturbing tranquility. Headlights from oncoming cars disrupt sleep. A home that includes a private loft is perfect for your desire to meditate, practice yoga, read, write, or work on hobbies. Another preference is a sumptuous master suite with a private bath that offers separate his and hers vanities, huge walk-in closets with built-ins, especially those that house your substantial shoe collection. Your shy nature prefers a private door to the water closet and a restful color scheme that includes your favorite aqua, sea green, or lavender tones.

References

Hale, Gill. *The Practical Encyclopedia of Feng Shui*. London: Lorenz, 1999

Webster, Richard. *Feng Shui for Beginners*. St. Paul, MN: Llewellyn Publications, 2003.

What Would Earth Be Like Without Its Moon?

by Bruce Scofield

On a clear night when the Moon is new (conjunct the Sun), the night sky is filled with stars—and maybe a few planets. When their orbits bring them close to Earth, Venus, Mars, or Jupiter will shine very brightly. But none hold a candle to the powerful presence of our only Moon. Its size in the sky alone is the same as that of the Sun, and when the Moon is full it can illuminate the night to make colors visible. Earth's Moon is so big and bright that it is like a second Sun, the "lesser luminary," as the ancient astrologers called it. Animals use the Full Moon for nocturnal navigation, and so did the ancient Maya, who built long, raised roads surfaced with reflective white gravel that made pedestrian travel possible in the cool of night. Today some winter lovers cross-country ski during the Full Moon when the snow amplifies moonlight. The Moon follows us as we walk or drive at night, the seas move to its rhythms, and poets marvel and sing through their words of its magic and mystery. The Moon is very much a companion to Earth and its inhabitants. Life wouldn't be the same without it.

How the Moon came to be has long been a science question, and several theories have been proposed. We do know that it originated shortly after Earth formed. Today most astronomers favor the idea that a large body, a planetoid perhaps as big as Mars (which has been named Theia), slammed into Earth, ejecting debris that first settled into an orbit, like Saturn's rings, and then coalesced into a large round body, becoming the Moon. When astronauts visited the Moon they found some evidence that supports this collision theory: the Moon is made of early Earth rock.

When our Moon was young, some four billion years ago, it was in a close orbit around Earth and would have appeared massive to an observer, maybe twenty times larger than today. Over time, the orbit of the Moon has evolved and is today receding from Earth at a rate of about 1.5 inches every year. While this amount is minuscule in the context of an average distance from Earth of roughly a quarter million miles, the Moon will eventually recede far enough that total eclipses will no longer be possible. Annular eclipses, when the Moon passes over the solar disk but doesn't obscure it, will continue, however. And don't worry, this won't happen for another six hundred million years or so. In that amount of time *Homo sapiens* will no longer exist and will have long been replaced by some other organism that may or may not have the ability to appreciate such a phenomenon.

One big thing the Moon does is pull the Earth. I'm talking about gravitational tides—powerful effects that have produced the world we know. Even though the Sun is far more massive than the Moon, solar tides are weaker because the Sun is more distant from Earth. The nearby Moon with its stronger gravitational effect lifts the oceans that (as Earth rotates) face it and simultaneously pulls Earth closer to it, causing tides on the opposite side of Earth. Importantly, tides cause mixing in the seas. The mixing of warm equatorial water with cold polar water is what moderates climate. Without this mixing, temperature differences would be more extreme between equator and pole, and the weather between these regions more violent. Over time this mixing prevents rapid climate change, giving life some time to adjust to the very long cycles of ice ages. It's not just ocean tides that are driven by the Moon. There are also atmospheric tides that move the atmosphere up and down twice a day, mixing and reducing temperature differences between air masses. Although the Sun contributes to oceanic and atmospheric tides, it is mostly the Moon's gravity that is stirring the fluids of our planet and neutralizing potential problems that would make the surface environment more challenging and even dangerous to life.

There are other things that lunar tides do and other possible effects with enormous consequences. As the Moon pulls on the oceans and atmosphere, it is also pulling on the surface of Earth, producing what are called Earth tides or crustal tides. Yes, the surface does move a foot or so twice a day, though we don't notice it. This movement of the crust has consequences. There is some evidence that the stronger tides at the Full or New Moon (when the gravity of Sun and Moon combine) may trigger earthquakes in regions prone to them. On a longer time scale, the Moon's gravity pulling on Earth for billions of years has slowed down its rotation, making the day steadily grow in length and also slowing down the violent winds of the rapidly-spinning early Earth. It has even been suggested that long ago, the Moon, orbiting much closer to Earth with extreme tidal forces, may have had a role in starting plate tectonics, the very slow motion of continents in the crust. Other planets, like Mars and Venus, don't have plate tectonics; the surfaces there are locked in place. If this were so, then the Moon would have to be credited with playing an even greater role in the recycling of elements, something that keeps life on the planet going strong.

There is another crucial thing that the Moon provides for Earth: axial stability. What this means is that Earth's axis, which is tilted by about 23 degrees from vertical (relative to the orbital plane of Earth around the Sun), stays pretty much in that position, moving only a degree or two over a forty-thousand-year cycle. During this period, the poles tip slightly toward or away from the Sun, which results in gradual climate change from cooler to warmer periods. This limited tilt of the axis, which is caused by the pull of the Moon on Earth's equatorial bulge, prevents extreme climate changes that would make life on Earth very difficult. Compare this situation to that on Mars. Orbited by only two puny moons, Mars has an axis cycle that tips the planet by as much as 60 degrees or more over time. This means that the cold poles can shift from northern latitudes, like they are on Earth, to near the equator. This wide wobble produces huge climate swings on the surface, making for conditions that work against the establishment of a viable biosphere. Imagine an organism adapting to the tropics and having to adapt to the arctic not long after!

When it comes to the origin of life on planet Earth, there are two leading theories. The early Earth was mostly water with only a few flat continents. With the Moon orbiting so close and producing very high tides, large areas of land would be regularly flooded with water, some of it trapped in basins to bake in the powerful solar radiation. As evaporation occurred, these pools would thicken with organic molecules and salts, but then another tide would dilute the water. This "stirring of the pot" resulted in what has been called the "primordial soup," a broth in which chemical processes were accelerated, eventually forming the first living cells. If this scenario is right, then the Moon probably played a major role in the origin of life. The other leading theory is that life originated deep in the seas near volcanic vents. There the tides would not be noticed, but tidal mixing above may have contributed to the distribution of vital elements in the seas.

Life, as bacteria, first evolved in water and stayed there for a couple billion years. Among the earliest life forms were the cyanobacteria, mistakenly called blue-green algae. These tiny cells did something very different from other organisms that were living off chemical reactions. Cyanobacteria evolved the ability to harness the Sun's light and make their own food out of carbon dioxide and water. The byproduct of this chemical reaction, called photosynthesis (inherited by algae and plants), is oxygen, and oxygen is necessary for life to grow beyond microscopic sizes. When enough oxygen had been produced and mixed into the oceans by the lunar tides and swirling winds, the first animals, mostly sponges and worms, appeared. Not much later, tides played a role. Changing shorelines between tides caused some animals to be temporarily stranded. Those that survived and adapted began

to colonize the land. It could be said that the Moon helped life move from sea to land.

The rhythms of the tides were then and continue to be a major environmental feature for marine organisms. The daily predictable changes in water movement establish both a physical and temporal framework onto which life has adapted. In addition, the cycle of moonlight is something that is used by both predator and prey. Lunar nocturnal light, absent at New Moon, favors invisibility. In contrast, the brightness of the Full Moon allows for visual navigation. Both are features that guide the migration of fish. One famous example is the California grunion, which uses both New and Full Moon as guides for mating events on the beach. The tides are highest at New and Full Moon, and eggs laid at one of these events will remain buried until the tide once again reaches them two weeks later.

The idea of life latching onto the natural rhythms of the environment, like those of the Moon, may explain why the human female menstruation cycle, which averages twenty-eight to twenty-nine days, is essentially the same as the lunar cycle. It should be mentioned that there are several lunar cycles. Measuring the Moon relative to a star (the sidereal cycle) is a cycle of 27.3 days and measuring relative to the Sun is one of 29.5 days. This is a very close match, and yet resistance to acknowledging this link is intense and there are plenty of studies that are cited to discredit any linkage. It does appear that those who argue against a human response to the Moon are looking for a precise correlation—that is, more women menstruate at Full Moon or New Moon. But this may not be the case at all. The correlation is probably more likely to be found in individual resonances with the cycle, and it's one that can change over time. For example, a woman's cycle may follow the Moon when it is at a specific point, for example in the sign Aries for several months. Then a shift occurs, perhaps due to stress or changing life circumstances, and the entrainment fails and the timing becomes more chaotic for a few months, but then later re-engages with the Moon when it is in the sign Taurus. Any scientific study seeking a simple correlation between menstrual cycles and the Moon will not see this.

From stabilizing the axis to being a regular pulse on which life can build and regularize its many processes, the Moon has been absolutely critical to Earth and its inhabitants. Earth without our Moon would probably be a hostile place with climate extremes, not an easy world for higher life forms to develop. Without the Moon it would be less likely that humans would have evolved, and the dominant form of life might have been bacterial, which implies that the atmosphere would be poisonous to life as we know it today. There would be no regular rhythms of gravity to drive tides and no light that life could use to live at night or to regulate its internal functions and behaviors. Earth, while it may have taken a big hit early on, has been very lucky to have such a Moon as ours.

References

Angier, Natalie. "The Moon Comes Around Again." *The New York Times*. September 7, 2014. https://www.nytimes.com/2014/09/09 /science/revisiting-the-moon.html.

Hazen, Robert M. *The Story of Earth: The First 4.5 Billion Years, from Stardust to Living Planet*. New York: Penguin Books, 2013.

Jakobsen, Hanne. "What Would We do Without the Moon?" ScienceNordic. January 12, 2012. http://sciencenordic.com/what -would-we-do-without-moon.

Shaw, Justine M. *White Roads of the Yucatán: Changing Social Landscapes of the Yucatec Maya*. Tucson, AZ: University of Arizona Press, 2008.

Lunar Conspiracy Theories

by Michelle Perrin, Astrology Detective

*To you we say we have only completed a beginning. We leave you much
that is undone. There are great ideas undiscovered, breakthroughs
available to those who can remove one of the truth's protective layers.*
—Neil Armstrong, 1994.

The lunar missions of the 1960s are probably the first time in
man's history when people risked life and limb to explore
new areas—at considerable public expense—and never go back.
If we managed to get to the Moon relatively easily and safely, in
eight short years using 1960s technology, why has no one both-
ered to reproduce this feat? Constructing the first lunar base, no
matter how basic, would be a major geopolitical and scientific
advantage for any nation.

There is no doubt that the Apollo missions were beautifully carried out and photographed. Images of the astronauts frolicking and running about carelessly on the Moon's surface, when a single rip in their space suit would cause immediate death, have become a fundamental part of the American mythos, which has always been defined by a childlike vibrancy mixed with the manly ability to face all risks without breaking a sweat. From Apollo 11's first flawless mission to the dramatic emergency of Apollo 13 to the denouement and resolution, defined by establishing a détente with Russia and establishing a joint space mission in the name of world peace, the Apollo program followed an almost perfect narrative arc.

Could it have all been faked? Nothing stated here is given as fact but simply as a reportage on several conspiracy theory alternatives to the official narrative of the Moon landing.

Background: The Cold War and the Space Race

At the time of the Moon landing program, the West was in a Cold War with the Soviet Union, with the looming, ever-present threat of nuclear attack hanging over the entire world. It must be stressed, therefore, that the program was never conceived of as a scientific endeavor; it was always primarily considered a wartime mission. Likewise, the astronauts were not scientists; they were all military pilots, descended from military families. They were trained to accomplish their mission in a time of war, with precision and secrecy.

When Kennedy made his famous September 1962 speech to the country announcing US plans to land man on the Moon by the end of the decade, it was just months after the Bay of Pigs disaster, a failed attempt by CIA-backed forces to invade and overthrow the communist Cuban government. It came also on the heels of the successful mission by Soviet cosmonaut Yuri Gagarin, making him the first human to enter outer space. The US and Soviets had been in a race to put humans in space during the '50s, and this was a major blow to American power. After consulting with NASA officials, Kennedy was informed that placing man on the Moon by the end of the decade was a possibility, leading to his famous declaration.

In a way, the space race led to a thaw in the Cold War, culminating in the détente of 1972, when Nixon and the Soviets agreed to work together on space projects, culminating with the symbolic Apollo-Soyuz mission, where separate US and Soviet crafts docked together in space. At this point, Apollo seemed to accomplish its mission, and future Apollo Moon flights were scrapped. Conspiracy theorists believe this détente was a win/win for both countries, allowing them to end costly programs that they knew could never reach the Moon due to technological limitations.

The Imagery: Kubrick's *2001*, Almost-Miraculous Photography, and an Artist's Confessional

The prevailing opinion of Moon landing conspiracy theorists is that the photos and video footage were faked. One major theory, developed by Jay Weidner, is that the director Stanley Kubrick was recruited to help NASA stage the Moon landings due to his work on his previous film *Dr. Strangelove* and that *2001: A Space Odyssey* was a research project for the final, faked footage. Later, he supposedly confessed his involvement through a wealth of alleged visual clues in another of his works: *The Shining*.

Firstly, it must be noted that the development and production of *2001* perfectly coincided with the establishment and development of the Apollo missions, with both projects starting in 1964. In a 1966 letter from Thomas Turner, president of the National Space Club, there is talk of NASA clearance for the movie's script.

For *2001*, Kubrick employed a rarely used effect known as front-screen projection (a precursor to today's green screen), which creates seemingly vast, infinite, realistic landscapes in extremely small studios. This is the same technology that supposedly made

the Moon landing footage possible. The film was released in 1968, while the first Moon landing followed in 1969. Kubrick worked closely with NASA advisors Frederick Ordway and Harry Lange, who served as on-set consultants. He also received visits from the director of NASA's Manned Spacecraft Center, George Mueller, and astronaut Donald K. Slayton, as well as consulted with Julian Scheer, NASA's Administrator for Public Affairs. There were so many links between Kubrick and the space agency that the UK set jokingly became referred to as "NASA East."

Conspiracy theorists also raise questions about the Apollo photos and video footage. For the still photos taken on the lunar surface, the Apollo mission used standard, commercial Ektachrome film, modified only to allow for more pictures per roll, in customized Hasselblad cameras, which were mounted to the astronauts' chests. The cameras had only minor additions to mitigate the Moon's extreme temperatures and protect from the radioactive rays of outer space, which should have damaged the quality of the

film. Additionally, the cameras had no viewfinder and required manual adjustment of the exposure setting for each shot, as was common before the age of auto-focus cameras. All this had to be done while wearing the equivalent of air-inflated gardening gloves. Yet, shot after shot shows flawlessly framed, pristine photos, such as the one where Buzz Aldrin is looking head on at the camera with the American flag, lunar module, his own shadow, and the photographer, Neil Armstrong, reflected in his visor. Getting one snap like this by chance would be a professional photographer's jackpot, but obtaining an entire roll of such shots while not using a viewfinder is a virtual miracle.

Perhaps even more telling, the astronauts were not able to bend completely at the waist in their pressurized suits, yet there are perfectly framed shots of footprints that could only be taken by having the lens pointing directly down. This would not be possible as the camera was strapped to the astronauts' chests.

After Kubrick supposedly masterminded the video footage for NASA, many believe Weidner's theory that *The Shining* represents his psychological horror from helping fake the Apollo landing and maintaining his part in its secret.

Weidner has found a myriad of visual clues in *The Shining* that serve as Kubrick's confessional, such as the protagonist's son, Danny, dressed in an Apollo 11 sweater, who keeps seeing apparitions of twins, which represent NASA's Gemini space program. In Stephen King's original work, there was only a single child. The hotel is snowed in, denoting the Cold War, and the film uses an abundance of bear imagery, the symbol of the Soviet Union. Moreover, Wendy discovers that instead of writing his novel, Jack is merely writing one phrase over and over: "All work and no play makes Jack a dull boy." The typewriter's font makes the word "All" appear as the letter "A" followed by the number eleven. In other words, Apollo 11.

Also interesting to note is that in the original Stephen King book, pivotal scenes took place in Room 217, but Kubrick changed it to 237 for the movie. At that time, many books stated that 237,000 miles is the mean distance from Earth to the Moon, a number that has since been revised.

Houston, We've Lost the Originals and the Question of the Moon Rocks

The Moon landings were broadcast live on TV. In order to be broadcast into people's homes, the original live feed, which produced an extremely sharp image, had to be converted to standard TV format, producing a very degraded, ghostly picture. The original tapes also contained crucial telemetry data that included the astronaut's vital signs at every moment of their trip—information that could be used to prove, without doubt, the veracity of the Moon landing.

There is just one problem. The original tapes were lost. What we view now in retrospect are the original TV broadcasts, not the original direct feed from the lunar surface. NASA says they don't know what happened to them but speculate that they were probably thrown away or taped over. While that may make sense for a network TV show from the era, this was the most important human achievement in the history of mankind. Why was greater care not taken to store and preserve them?

The Moon rocks have also been called into question. Recent testing of a lunar rock gifted to the Netherlands after the Apollo 11 mission has shown it to be a piece of petrified wood. Likewise, a recent Chinese rover sent back data on collected Moon rocks, showing them to be extremely different from those collected by Apollo and the Soviets in the 1960s. Scientists theorize this is because the Moon's surface is more geologically diverse than previously thought, but the differences are still startling to conspiracy theorists.

Moon rocks that came to the Earth as meteorites have only been found in a few places, including Antarctica. The first Antarctic Moon rocks were discovered by Japanese researchers in 1969. Curiously, however, one of NASA's leading engineers, Wernher von Braun, carried out an expedition to Antarctica in late '66 and early '67 with other top NASA management. Americans have had bases in Antarctica since the 1950s. Is it possible they discovered Moon rocks there prior to the Japanese and kept it top secret? Rocks they later passed off as coming from the Apollo missions or used them to create reproductions in a lab?

Making an Example Out of Whistleblowers

The Apollo Mission can be divided into two distinct time periods: pre- and post-1967. Before 1967, the Apollo project was in shambles, and nothing was going right. One of NASA's top astronauts Gus Grissom was growing upset with how disorganized the mission was and did not believe it could get to the Moon. He started acting out publicly by hanging a lemon on the door of the simulator and, worse, making on-the-record statements to the press. During a routine preflight test inside the command module in early 1967, Grissom is heard saying, "How are we going to get to the moon if we can't talk between two or three buildings?" These were his last words. A spark caused a fire in the 100 percent oxygen environment, instantly burning up Grissom and his two fellow astronauts.

Around the same time, Thomas Ronald Baron, a safety inspector for one of NASA's subcontractors, reported, "Does NASA know or realize that every spec that we have is inadequate for the task being done?...Are they fully aware of the compromising position that NAA [North American Aviation] has put the program in?" He, too, started talking to the press and testifying before Congress. Just days after appearing before the House, in April 1967, he was killed, along with his wife and daughter, when his car was struck by a train. His five-hundred-page expanded report was nowhere to be found.

Conspiracy theorists believe the deaths of these whistleblowers and their family and colleagues served as an example, and explains why astronauts and NASA workers never spoke out if the Apollo Mission were, indeed, a hoax.

Will We Ever Remove "One of the Truth's Protective Layers"?

When writing an article on conspiracy theories, you can't help but start searching for clues in every corner, and I stumbled across my own piece of the puzzle that I hadn't seen mentioned on any of the conspiracy sites. I will finish by leaving my own contribution to the Moon landing mystery.

In Armstrong's 2011 interview with CPA Australia, he was asked what he thought of all the people who claimed the Moon landing was a fake. Armstrong smiled and answered, "I know one day, somebody is going to go fly back up there and pick up that camera I left." Armstrong and Aldrin left many things on the surface of the Moon, including an American flag, a commemorative plaque, and the Lunar Module's descent stage (which was used as a launch pad when it was time to leave), but he specifically mentioned a camera.

Within a year, Armstrong passed away while undergoing surgery. His wife found a bag in the closet that she had never seen before, a treasure trove of items Armstrong had secretly stowed away on his return trip from the Moon. Allan Needell, the Space History Department curator of the Air and Space Museum, clarified, "As far as we know, Neil has never discussed the existence of these items and no one else has seen them in the 45 years since he returned from the Moon." What was in the bag? The camera that filmed Armstrong's first steps on the Moon. The same camera that Armstrong supposedly left on its surface when he returned to Earth over fifty years ago.

References

ACS Staff. "Photographing Apollo 11." American Cinematographer. American Society of Cinematographers. July 16, 2019. https://ascmag.com/articles/flashback-photographing-apollo-11.

Allen, Nick. "Neil Armstrong's Widow Discovers Moon Camera in Cupboard." *The Telegraph*. February 9, 2015. https://www.telegraph.co.uk/news/worldnews/northamerica/usa/11401781/Neil-Armstrongs-widow-discovers-moon-camera-in-cupboard.html.

"Apollo's Lunar Leftovers." Edited by Jeanne Ryba. NASA. Updated November 22, 2007. https://www.nasa.gov/missions/solarsystem/f_leftovers.html.

Aulis. *What Happened on the Moon? An Investigation into Apollo Parts 1-3*. Aulis Film Publications. Documentary, 2000.

"Baron Report (1965-1966)." NASA Historical Reference Collection, NASA History Office, NASA Headquarters, Washington, DC. Updated February 3, 2003. https://history.nasa.gov/Apollo204/barron.html.

BEC Crew. "China's Rover Has Discovered a New Type of Moon Rock." ScienceAlert. December 23, 2015. https://www.sciencealert.com/china-s-rover-just-discovered-a-new-type-of-moon-rock.

Biography.com Editors. "Michael Collins." Biography.com. A&E Television Networks. Updated July 25, 2019. https://www.biography.com/astronaut/michael-collins.

Brooks, Courtney G., James M. Grimwood, and Loyd S. Swenson Jr. *Chariots for Apollo: The NASA History of Manned Lunar Spacecraft to 1969*. Mineola, New York: Dover Publications, 2009.

Gaia Staff. "The Apollo 1 Conspiracy; Did NASA Cover Up Gus Grissom's Death?" Gaia. November 3, 2017. https://www.gaia.com/article/the-apollo-1-conspiracy-did-nasa-covered-up-gus-grissoms-death.

History.com Editors. "Buzz Aldrin." History. A&E Television Networks, LLC. Updated July 21, 2019. https://www.history.com/topics/space-exploration/buzz-aldrin.

Hollingham, Richard. "The Fire that May Have Saved the Apollo Programe." BBC Future. BBC. November 11, 2019. https://www.bbc.com/future/article/20170125-the-fire-may-have-saved-the-apollo-programme.

Howell, Elizabeth. "Apollo 1: The Fatal Fire." Space. Future US Inc. November 16, 2017. https://www.space.com/17338-apollo-1.html.

Howell, Elizabeth. "Neil Armstrong: First Man on the Moon." Space. Future US Inc. Updated January 17, 2020. https://www.space.com/15519-neil-armstrong-man-moon.html.

Leopold, George. *Calculated Risk: The Supersonic Life and Times of Gus Grissom*. West Lafayette, IN: Purdue University Press, 2016.

Mazzucco, Massimo, dir. *American Moon*. Italy. Documentary, 2017.

Needell, Allan. "The Armstrong Purse: Flown Apollo 11 Lunar Artifacts." Smithsonian National Air and Space Museum. Smithsonian Institution. February 6, 2015. https://airandspace.si.edu/stories/editorial/armstrong-purse-flown-apollo-11-lunar-artifacts.

Office of Antarctic Programs, National Science Foundation, and U.S. Naval Support Force, Antarctica, Department of Defense. "NASA Officials Visit Antarctica." *Antarctic Journal of the United States*, 2, no. 2 (March-April 1967): 52-3. https://books.google.com/books?id=i-C2DMzBv10C&newbks=1&newbks_redir=0&dq="NASA+officials+visit+Antarctica,"+Antarctic+Journal+of+the+United+States&source=gbs_navlinks_s.

Rubie, G. *The British Celestial Atlas: Being a Complete Guide to the Attainment of a Practical Knowledge of the Heavenly Bodies [...]*. London: Baldwin & Cradock, 1830.

Scott, David Meerman, and Richard Jurek. *Marketing the Moon: The Selling of the Apollo Lunar Program*. Cambridge, MA: The MIT Press. 2014.

Siegel, Robert. "Neil Armstrong Opens Up in Rare Interview." *All Things Considered*. NPR. Podcast. May 25, 2012. https://www.npr.org/2012/05/25/153723307/neil-armstrong-opens-up-in-rare-interview.

Sibrel, Bart, dir. *A Funny Thing Happened on the Way to the Moon*. USA. Documentary, 2001.

Sterling, Toby. "'Moon Rock' in Museum is Just Petrified Wood." Space on NBC News. NBC News. Updated August 27, 2009. http://www.nbcnews.com/id/32581790/ns/technology_and_science-space/t/moon-rock-museum-just-petrified-wood/#.XiCc7S2ZNBw.

"The Apollo-Soyuz Mission." NASA. Updated August 7, 2017. https://www.nasa.gov/mission_pages/apollo-soyuz/astp_mission.html.

"The Apollo 11 Telemetry Data Recordings: A Final Report." NASA. Accessed February 3, 2019. https://history.nasa.gov/alsj/a11/Apollo_11_TV_Tapes_Report.pdf.

Wadhwa, Meenakshi. "Exploring the Solar System from the Ends of the Earth." Slate. The Slate Group, LLC. https://slate.com/technology/2013/09/the-best-meteorites-are-found-in-antarctica.html.

Webb, James E., and Robert McNamara. "NASA Memo Exploring the Moon." Smithsonian National Air and Space Museum. Smithsonian Institute. Accessed February 3, 2020. https://airandspace.si.edu/multimedia-gallery/5086hjpg?id=5086.

Weidner, Jay, dir. *Kubrick's Odyssey: Secrets Hidden in the Films of Stanley Kubrick; Part One: Kubrick and Apollo*. USA: Cubed Brick Productions. Documentary, 2011.

Wisnewski, Gerhard. *One Small Step? The Great Moon Hoax and the Race to Dominate Earth from Space*. Translated by Johanna Collis. Hillside House, UK: Clairview Books, 2007.

"25th Apollo Anniversary Commemoration." C-SPAN. National Cable Satellite Corporation. July 20, 1994. Video, 24:01. https://www.c-span.org/video/?58831-1/25th-apollo-anniversary-commemoration.

About the Contributors

Mireille Blacke, MA, LADC, RD, CD-N, is a registered dietitian, certified dietitian-nutritionist, and addiction specialist residing in Connecticut. Mireille is the bariatric program coordinator for Trinity Health of New England at Saint Francis Hospital in Hartford, with years of experience as a bariatric dietitian, educator, and counselor. As an adjunct professor at the University of Saint Joseph in West Hartford, Mireille teaches graduate-level courses in nutrition and media. She has been published in Llewellyn's *Moon Sign Book*, *Herbal Almanac*, and *Magical Almanac*; *Today's Dietitian*; and *OKRA Magazine*. Mireille worked in rock radio for two decades before shifting her career focus to psychology, nutrition, and addiction counseling. She is obsessed with the city of New Orleans, the various works of Joss Whedon, and her beloved (if psychotic) Bengal cats.

Pam Ciampi was a professional astrologer from 1975 until her passing in 2019. She served as president of the San Diego Astrological Society and was President Emeritus of the San Diego Chapter of NCGR. Pam was the author of the Weekly Forecasts for Llewellyn's best-selling *Daily Planetary Guide* since 2007. Her latest contribution was an astrological gardening guide titled *Gardening by the Light of the Moon*. In its fourth printed edition, it is now available in a calendar format.

Sally Cragin is an award-winning journalist whose arts, writing, and theater reviews appeared regularly in the *Boston Phoenix*, *Boston Herald*, and most recently, the *Boston Globe*. She has won two Penney-Missouri Journalism awards for feature writing.

From 1999 to 2001, she was the chief drama critic for the St. Louis *Riverfront Times*. She has also taught critical writing at Harvard Extension School, Webster University (St. Louis), and Fitchburg

State University. From 1997 to 2013, she wrote "Moon Signs" for many newspapers nationwide, including the Boston *Phoenix* chain. She is the author of *The Astrological Elements* and *Astrology on the Cusp* (Llewellyn Worldwide), which have been translated and sold in a number of countries, including India, Russia, Canada, the British Virgin Islands, the Czech Republic, and Estonia. From 1999 to 2001, she provided weekly astrological audio forecasts for Audible.com. She has provided the new and full moon forecasts for Llewellyn Worldwide for many years and written calendars with astrological forecasts for numerous companies. Call or text 978-320-1335; visit "Sally Cragin Astrology and Tarot" on Facebook; or email sallycragin@verizon.net.

Shelby Deering is a lifestyle writer living in Madison, Wisconsin. After receiving her master's degree in journalism and working as an editor at a national magazine, she went on to pursue freelance writing full-time. She's contributed décor articles, home tours, wellness features, and writings on mental health and organic beauty to national publications including *Good Housekeeping*, *Better Homes & Gardens*, *Domino*, *Country Living*, *Healthline*, *Prevention*, and more. She is a mental health advocate, often writing about her own experiences with anxiety, panic attacks, and seasonal depression. And she frequently writes about one of her greatest loves—vintage décor. You can learn more about Shelby at www.shelbydeering.com.

Alice DeVille is known internationally as an astrologer, consultant, and writer. She also held credentials as a Realtor (22 years) in the Commonwealth of Virginia, earned real estate appraisal credentials, and certifications in diverse real estate specialties. Her knowledge of Feng Shui led to development of numerous workshops and seminars including those that provided Realtors with tips to enhance selling homes and working with buyers. Alice specializes in relationships of all types that call for solid problem-solving advice to get to the core of issues and give clients options for meeting critical needs. Clients seek solutions in business practices, career and change management, real estate, relationships, and training. Numerous websites and publications such as The Star IQ, Astral Hearts, Llewellyn, Meta Arts, Inner Self, Share-ItLiveIt, and Twitter feature her articles. Quotes from her work on relationships appear in books, publications, training materials, calendars, planners, audio tapes, and on World-Famous Quotes. Alice's Llewellyn material on relationships appeared in Sarah Ban Breathnach's *Something More*, Oprah's website, and in *Through God's Eyes* by Phil Bolsta. She is available for writing books and articles for publishers, newspapers, or magazines; conducting workshops; and doing radio or TV interviews. Contact Alice at DeVilleAA@aol.com or alice.deville27@gmail.com.

Penny Kelly is a writer, teacher, author, publisher, consultant, and naturopathic physician. After purchasing Lily Hill Farm in southwest Michigan in 1987, she raised grapes for Welch Foods for a dozen years and established Lily Hill Learning Center, where she teaches courses such as Developing Intuition and the Gift of Consciousness, Getting Well Again Naturally, and Organic Gardening. She is the mother of four children, has cowritten or edited twenty-three books with others, and has written seven books of her own. Penny lives, gardens, and writes in Lawton, Michigan.

Robin Ivy Payton is a yoga teacher and intuitive astrologer living in Portland, Maine. A lifelong student and practitioner of intuitive arts, Robin began writing and broadcasting her astrology forecast, Robin's Zodiac Zone, in 1999, and has been contributing to Llewellyn publications since 2003. She trains yoga teachers and tarot readers in southern Maine and offers weekly classes and workshops, including Vinyasa Flow, Yin, Restorative, Gentle

Yoga, and Yoga Nidra. Find Robin's forecasts and schedule at www.robinszodiaczone.com.

Michelle Perrin, aka Astrology Detective, has built a reputation as one of the world's most trusted and sought-after astrologers for more than ten years. Her work has appeared in some of the most influential titles online and in print, making her one of the few astrologers who has garnered respect from both a mass audience and the astrological community. Her horoscopes have appeared on the websites for Canada's W Dish and Slice TV Networks, Tarot.com's "Daily Horoscope" page, and *Dell Horoscope* magazine, among others. Her writings have also been featured in *The Mountain Astrologer*, the leading trade journal for the astrological community, and astrology.com.

Kris Brandt Riske is the executive director and a professional member of the American Federation of Astrologers (AFA), the oldest US astrological organization, founded in 1938; and a member of the National Council for Geocosmic Research (NCGR). She has a master's degree in journalism and a certificate of achievement in weather forecasting from Penn State. Kris is the author of several books, including *Llewellyn's Complete Book of Astrology: The Easy Way to Learn Astrology*, *Mapping Your Money*, and *Mapping Your Future*. She is also the coauthor of *Mapping Your Travels and Relocation* and *Astrometeorology: Planetary Powers in Weather Forecasting*. Her newest book is *Llewellyn's Complete Book of Predictive Astrology*. She writes for astrology publications and contributes to the annual weather forecast for *Llewellyn's Moon Sign Book*. In addition to astrometeorology, she specializes in predictive astrology. Kris is an avid NASCAR fan, although she'd rather be a driver than a spectator. In 2011, she fulfilled her dream when she drove a stock car for twelve fast laps. She posts a weather forecast for each of the thirty-six race weekends (qualifying and race day) for NASCAR drivers and fans. Visit her at astroweathervane .com. Kris also enjoys gardening, reading, jazz, and her cat.

Kim Rogers-Gallagher has been a professional astrologer, writer, and lecturer for over twenty years. Based in Florida, Kim is the author of *Astrology for the Light Side of the Brain* and *Astrology for the Light Side of the Future*. Her monthly, weekly, and daily columns appear in *Dell Horoscope* and other astrological websites. She served on the board and edited the quarterly journal for the International Society for Astrological Research and was a Steering Committee Member of AFAN (Association for Astrological Networking).

Bruce Scofield, PhD, is an author of books and articles and has taught evolution at the University of Massachusetts and astronomy and astrology for Kepler College. For many years, he maintained an international astrological consulting practice. His interest in Mesoamerican astrology, mythology, and astronomy has a web presence at www.onereed.com.

Christeen Skinner is a director of Cityscopes London Ltd, a future-casting company. She holds a diploma from the Faculty of Astrological Studies, where she taught for some years, has been chair of the Astrological Association of Great Britain, is presently chair of the Advisory Board of the National Council for Geocosmic Research, and is a director of the Alexandria iBase Project. Through www.financialuniverse.co.uk, her company offers services to investors and entrepreneurs who value the timing and trend services provided. She also writes regularly for www.horoscopes.co.uk and for www. cityscopes.com. Christeen is author of several books: *Exploring the Financial Universe* (2016), *The Beginner's Guide to the Financial Universe* (2017), and *Navigating the Financial Universe* (2019). She can be reached via office@cityscopes.com.

Charlie Rainbow Wolf is happiest when she is creating something, especially if it can be made from items that others have cast aside. Pottery, writing, knitting, astrology, herbs, and tarot are her deepest interests, but she happily confesses that she's easily distracted, because life offers so many wonderful things to explore. She is an advocate of organic gardening and cooking, and she lives in the Midwest with her husband and special-needs Great Danes. Follow her at www.charlierainbow.com.

Moon Sign Book Resources

Weekly Tips provided by Penny Kelly, Shelby Deering, and Mireille Blacke

"The Methods of the *Moon Sign Book*" by Penny Kelly

"Gardening by the Moon" by Pam Ciampi

Notes

Notes

Notes